THE
ETHICAL
BEING

A Catholic Guide
to Contemporary Issues

Scott Kline

NOVALIS

For Megan and Kieran

© 2013 Novalis Publishing Inc.

Cover: Blair Turner
Layout: Audrey Wells

Published by Novalis

Publishing Office
10 Lower Spadina Avenue, Suite 400
Toronto, Ontario, Canada
M5V 2Z2

Head Office
4475 Frontenac Street
Montréal, Québec, Canada
H2H 2S2

www.novalis.ca

Library and Archives Canada Cataloguing in Publication

Kline, Scott Travis, 1966-   The ethical being : a Catholic guide to contemporary issues / Scott Kline.
Issued also in an electronic format. ISBN 978-2-89646-324-4
          1. Christian ethics--Catholic authors. 2. Christian life-- Catholic authors.
I. Title.

BJ1249.K55 2013   241'.042   C2012-906687-7

Printed in Canada.

Scriptural citations are from *The New Oxford Annotated Bible,* Third edition (New Revised Standard Bible) published by Oxford University Press, 2001.

We acknowledge the financial support of the Government of Canada through the Canada Book Fund for business development activities.

5 4 3 2 1   17 16 15 14 13

Acknowledgements

The idea for this book took shape while I was on a sabbatical leave in early 2009. After nearly ten years of full-time teaching, including two years as a doctoral student, I felt as though I finally had the time and space for a creative thought or two. I am grateful for that time and space, because I know it comes at a cost. The slowdown in the global economy has had a trickle-down effect on universities as governments have implemented cutbacks in education funding, which in turn has resulted in universities cutting back on non-revenue generating ventures, including sabbatical leaves. Fortunately, the Board of Governors, the senior administration, and the faculty at St. Jerome's University (SJU) in the University of Waterloo, where I have had the privilege to work for the past decade, understand that sabbaticals help create a climate of intellectual vitality, which ultimately serves students, the community, and society. I want to thank St. Jerome's University for this leave.

I'm happy to acknowledge that I used funds from a Canadian Social Sciences and Humanities Research Council (SSHRC) general research grant I received with the Mennonite theologian Jim Reimer. We lost Jim to cancer in 2010, just as I was turning my attention to this book.

Many people supported me while I put this book together. My colleagues in the religious studies department at SJU, David Seljak, Myroslaw Tataryn, and Cristina Vanin, and at the University of Waterloo, form the basis of a nurturing academic community, one with the right blend of intellectual curiosity and large doses of self-effacing humour.

The library staff at SJU responded, without question or criticism, to my requests, even when I made extraordinary demands of them while working abroad. My teaching assistants Nick Shrubsole, David Feltmate, and Margie Patrick helped clarify a number of lectures that I incorporated into this book—cockeyed looks from my teaching assistants during a lecture usually meant, "Did you really just say that?"

Joseph Sinasac, the publishing director at Novalis, enthusiastically accepted the idea for the book not long after I presented it to him. Michael O'Hearn and Anne Louise Mahoney, my editors with Novalis, cleaned up my messes. Andrew Atkinson offered constructive feedback at a crucial point in this book's development. Students in my graduate seminars on sexual ethics and Christian ethics read early drafts of these chapters and offered useful criticism. The book has directly benefited from conversations I've had with Stephanie Shore, Mike McKay, Erin Riley, Erin Runions, Steven Bednarski, Joe Gunn, John Siebert, Renée Soulodre La France, and Barbara Budd. The enthusiasm and encouragement of John and Pauline Shore were true blessings. I am especially grateful to Gregory Baum, whose mentorship, friendship, and commitment to social justice have made an indelible mark on my character and way of "being." Thanks to all of you.

Although they are absent by name in this book, my parents, Fritz Kline and Pam Kline, play a leading role in it. If ethical being is about character formation, and character formation begins with the family and community, then what I've done in this book is merely give words to the morality and values I first learned from them. My brother, Brent, and my sister, Natalie, are always happy to put me back in line when I miss the mark.

I could not have completed this book without the love and support of my wife, Megan Shore. Not only is she my most fervent fan, she is also my staunchest critic. She willingly carried the load around the house while I was holed up writing. That load increased dramatically on September 29, 2011, with the birth of our lovely little boy, Kieran Kline Shore. I'm thrilled that I can dedicate this book to them.

Contents

Introduction

One of the undergraduate courses I regularly teach is an introduction to Christian ethics. At the beginning of each term, the first question I pose is "What is ethics?" Immediately, a sizeable number of students quickly raise their hands and respond enthusiastically with variations on the following:

"Ethics means following a moral code."

"It's doing good."

"Ethics means doing what your religion or culture tells you."

"It's following the law."

"Ethics means being true to yourself."

I then complicate matters by asking, "What is Christian ethics?" Fewer hands go up this time, and I see more puzzled looks on the faces of my students. Those courageous enough to answer typically respond along these lines:

"Christian ethics is following the Ten Commandments and the teachings of Jesus."

"Christian ethics means doing what the Bible tells us to."

"Christian ethics means following the teachings of the Church."

I then ask them, "So is there a difference between ethics and Christian ethics? Or is 'Christian ethics' merely a sub-set of 'ethics' generally?" More often than not, no hands go up when I pose this question, and

I imagine that it is at this moment that students first say to themselves, "This is going to be a long term."

My reason for starting with this series of questions is to make a point: in spite of the widespread usage of the term "ethics" in our everyday language, we actually do not operate with a widely shared understanding of what we mean by "ethics." Drawing from the examples provided by my students, if ethics means following a moral code, then we should ask, "Which moral code? Will any moral code do?" Or if ethics means "doing good," then we should demand to know, "How do you define 'good'?" In pluralistic societies, surely we're going to disagree. Even the term "Christian ethics," the topic of my course, is complicated by the fact that "Christian" includes a vast array of theological, doctrinal, and ritual differences. In short, "ethics" is one of those words we use that may mean something quite specific to an individual or a particular group, but in practice, the term is so flexible that any of my students' definitions could easily serve as one's understanding of "ethics."

The Dismantling of Ethics and Morality

Has the term "ethics" always been so flexible? According to the philosopher Alasdair MacIntyre, the answer is "No." In his book *After Virtue*, MacIntyre attempts to identify the reasons for the lack of shared meaning in our contemporary moral language. MacIntyre argues that, in the Western tradition, there was a common moral language until around the time of the Enlightenment in the eighteenth century. During this pivotal century, philosophers largely abandoned the notion that ethics had to be rooted in a culture's history and aimed toward a good end. This shift in ethics coincided with major shifts in the political and social landscape of Europe. The feudal order was on the verge of collapse and Christendom had all but crumbled as citizens revolted in favour of secular political institutions. These disruptions to the old order spurred on the moral imaginations of Enlightenment thinkers—people like Voltaire, Jean-Jacques Rousseau, David Hume, and Immanuel Kant. Revolutions taking place outside their windows were proof that society had jettisoned the idea that providence and a divinely ordered creation determined one's place in life. As Enlightenment thought spread throughout Europe and North America, some people began to conclude that individuals had no predetermined end or purpose—they began to believe they could be free from social, political, economic, and religious structures that determined where they worked, whom they married, and where they lived. They increasingly rejected the old-order idea that humans were created to be farmers, miners, fishers, peasants, servants, monarchs, or anything other than a human person with individual rights and freedoms. They grew suspicious of the old-order belief that the Christian Church was the guardian of truth, especially moral truth, and that all human activity ought to be oriented to please (a distant and sometimes angry) God, who may or may not exist. Also liberated from predetermined ends were society, nature, and history. Simply put, by the beginning of the nineteenth century, the old moral framework was in ruins, and in its place moral philosophers attempted to construct rational, secular accounts of a morality that transcended history and rejected parochial claims of the good.

But according to MacIntyre, these attempts to develop a rational, secular morality have failed. Instead of cohesion, there is only confusion, with modern philosophical approaches such as empiricism, idealism, utilitarianism, and pragmatism all vying to fill the space created by the Enlightenment. According to MacIntyre, these modern philosophies have left behind nothing but fragments of a moral framework that structured Western morality from Athens in the fourth century BC to Enlightenment Paris in the eighteenth century. With a great deal of lament, MacIntyre concludes that, after three centuries of trying to find alternatives, we now find ourselves unable to reconstruct the moral framework that once provided the Western tradition with a sense of purpose in history and a concept of the good. So today, with ethics stripped of historical context and untethered from all good ends, all that remains is a vocabulary list with few shared definitions and no common concept of the good.

A primary objective of ethics, then, must be to retrieve the ethical theory that, MacIntyre believes, will provide the much-needed clarity. To do that, MacIntyre asserts, we need to return to the classical Greek philosophers Plato (423–347 BC) and Aristotle (384–322 BC) and their attempts to develop a system of ethics.[1]

In the *Republic*, for example, Plato set out to answer one overriding question: Is it always better to be just than unjust? For Plato, the question is not easily answered. To begin, there is the problem of defining "justice" and why it is that many people believe justice to be a valuable part of a good human life. In one memorable exchange in the *Republic*, Plato depicts a conversation between Socrates and a bombastic philosopher called Thrasymachus, who mounts a spirited defence in favour of injustice. According to Thrasymachus, "justice is nothing other than the advantage of the stronger."[2] In political terms, justice is simply a convention established by the strong to keep the weak powerless and incapable of disrupting the political order. As a result, political regimes will always make laws in the interest of the ruling party, but they will "declare what they have made—what is to their own advantage—to be just for their subjects."[3] Moreover, the brash philosopher asserts, "injustice, if it is on a large enough scale, is stronger, freer, and more masterly than justice."[4] Bluntly put, Thrasymachus is convinced that most of us would be far better off in life if we ignored the limits imposed on us by abstract notions of justice and simply pursued our own self-interest. However, Socrates rebuts the fiery philosopher by getting him to admit that rulers, like doctors and musicians, do their crafts well because they ultimately serve a good greater than themselves. Doctors pursue the good of health, musicians pursue the good of artistic beauty, and rulers pursue the good of justice. A defeated man, Thrasymachus realizes that mere self-interest and political strength are actually insufficient to define and enforce "justice." Thus Socrates concludes that a real ruler should happily serve weaker subjects not because it could lead to further election victories or more political power, but because the ruler is serving a greater good—namely, the virtue of doing justice.

For Plato, justice is the most fundamental element of ethics and an essential component of a well-run state. Individually, we should pursue wisdom and the virtue of justice on our own. However, if we discover that we're incapable of pursuing wisdom and justice on our own, then we should follow the wisest guides we can find, which for Plato means engaging in a study of philosophy under a recognized master.

But mentorship is only one piece of the puzzle, Plato's critics charged, and it's not the most important piece—we also need a social and political culture rooted in justice, since culture guides both teachers and students, or so thought Aristotle, one of Plato's former students and later one of Plato's biggest critics.

In his *Nicomachean Ethics*, Aristotle describes a relationship between politics and ethics in which both work together for the purpose of serving the common good. On the one hand, politics is the overarching framework that governs the administrative aspects of the city, including the military and public policy. On the other hand, we engage in ethics to improve our lives and to consider the nature of human well-being. Like Plato, Aristotle regards the ethical virtue of justice as a complex rational, emotional, and social skill. But Aristotle disagrees with Plato's idea that studying philosophy or training under a philosopher is a necessary requirement for a full understanding of the good. For Aristotle, Plato was wrong to insist that ethics must be the pursuit of a true form that exists beyond the day-to-day life of this world—in other words, we don't need to seek a transcendent notion of justice or any other virtue. Instead, what we need to live well is a proper appreciation of the way in which goods such as friendship, pleasure, virtue, honour, and wealth fit together as a whole in human relationships. Aristotle's understanding of ethics, then, means that we must acquire, through proper upbringing and habits, the ability to see in each situation which course of action is best supported by "reason." Aristotle refers to this ability to determine the best course of action as "practical wisdom" or "prudence." We acquire practical wisdom not just by learning general rules or by studying philosophy but also through practice, which requires us to use our deliberative, emotional, and social skills. Aristotle assumes that the forum in which we develop our practical wisdom is the community, which has been established for the sake of some good.

Today, though, we are a long way from the social and political contexts of the classical Greek philosophers. Their city-states functioned as relatively cohesive communities, while our cities are sprawling metropolises composed of residents who, to a great extent, have become alienated from the political process. The Greeks lived in communities that shared a common moral vision and a common moral language, while we live in societies that are multicultural, each with our own set of moral values. Their world was relatively small, while our world, because of modern technology, is increasingly global. They assumed that politics and ethics served the same end—namely, justice and human flourishing—while we often assume that politics and ethics are fundamentally at odds with each other. They understood ethics as a matter relating to the public arena, while we, at our peril, tend to think of ethics mainly as a private matter.

We are also a long way from the social, political, and economic contexts of St. Augustine, St. Thomas Aquinas, and the other Christian thinkers of the Middle Ages who helped develop the moral and ethical teachings of the Christian Church. As alluring as it may be to some, there's no going back to the old order. We're not going to recreate Christendom, the Church isn't going to be at the centre of a new Christian society, and political leaders aren't going to snap into line with the Vatican when they fall out of step with the teachings of the Magisterium. In Canada, for example, the Quebec Quiet Revolution in the 1960s effectively disestablished the Church's role in providing the province's education and health care.

Besides, many elements of the old order weren't *that* good after all, especially if we recall that women weren't treated as equals, slavery was accepted by the Church and political leaders as naturally ordered, wars were justified by the Church and political leaders on the basis that they were stamping out religious heresies, and Christian leaders, both in the Church and in politics, abused power in ways that would likely make today's worst despot gush with admiration. I can't imagine that we want to bring back *those* "good ol' days."

And yet MacIntyre's analysis points to a profound tension today's Catholics face as we seek to enter into a discussion of contemporary ethical issues. On the one hand, we Catholics have inherited a relatively cohesive moral vocabulary and a tradition of ethics that grew out of *and* in fact sustained the old order. On the other hand, we Catholics are attempting to use the Church's language of moral theology and a Catholic ethical framework to engage in meaningful discussions about issues in the modern world, a world that has basically rejected the social, political, economic, religious, and philosophical foundations that grounded the moral reasoning of Augustine, Thomas Aquinas, and other Catholic thinkers up until the nineteenth century.

Perhaps the most difficult problem we Catholics face, then, is this: How do we use the moral teachings of the Church and the Catholic ethical tradition to address contemporary issues without making the (implicit) argument that we merely want to reinstate the old order? To some Catholics, this may seem like an overly dramatic question. However, to many modern ears, a return to the old order is precisely what the Catholic Church seems to be advocating when, for instance, bishops threaten politicians and public officials with excommunication for not adhering to official Church teaching—or, to be more precise, Church teaching usually related to abortion, contraception, and same-sex relationships.

Catholic Ethics and the Modern World

To help us address this challenge of making traditional Catholic moral reasoning applicable in the modern world, we can turn to the example provided by the bishops at the Second Vatican Council (1962–1965), who understood that the Church needed renewal to respond to the demands of the modern world. In the Vatican II document *Gaudium et spes* (Pastoral Constitution on the Church in the Modern World, 1965), the Council says that the Church has an obligation to speak in a "language intelligible to each generation," so it "can respond to the perennial questions which men ask about this present life and the life to come, and about the relationship of the one to the other." But first, the bishops concluded, we must "recognize and understand the world in which we live, its explanations, its longings, and its often dramatic characteristics." At the Council, the bishops spoke of the Church's newly conceived relationship with the world in terms of discerning the "signs of the times."[5] Their inspiration for this conceptual language was Pope John XXIII, who in the early 1960s had become convinced, after hearing stories of gross human rights violations from Holocaust survivors, that the Universal Declaration of Human Rights, adopted by the United Nations in 1948, was consistent with the Church's teaching regarding the dignity of the human person. In his encyclical *Pacem in terris* (Peace in the World, 1963), he concluded:

> Any well-regulated and productive association of men in society demands the acceptance of one fundamental principle: that

each individual man is truly a person. His is a nature, that is, endowed with intelligence and free will. As such he has rights and duties, which together flow as a direct consequence from his nature. These rights and duties are universal and inviolable, and therefore altogether inalienable. (PT, no. 9)

It's important to note that the pope's conclusion was in fact a departure from received Church teaching. For instance, Pope Pius IX, in the *Syllabus of Errors* (1864), condemned the notion that religion should be "left to the freedom of each individual to embrace and profess that religion which by the guidance of the light of reason he deems to be the true one" (no. 15). Similarly, Pope Leo XIII stated that religious freedom must be denied to those practising false religions—that is, religions other than Catholicism—since the state would, in effect, be giving "every one ... unbounded license to think whatever he chooses and to publish abroad whatever he thinks" (*Immortale Dei*, On the Christian Constitution of States, 1855, no. 26). The popes feared that personal freedoms would undermine the worldview, norms, and values that provided the foundations of society and ensured social cohesion and well-being. Their primary argument was that religious freedom allowed states to sanction religious error by allowing religions other than Catholicism to receive state support. Nevertheless, in dialoguing with the world and discerning the signs of the times, Pope John and the bishops at Vatican II boldly concluded that the social teachings of the Church must include the protection of human rights, including the right to practise a religion other than Catholicism.

The Second Vatican Council's project of *aggiornamento* (Italian for "bringing up to date" or "renewal") is important to Catholic ethics because it marks a shift in how we *do* ethics. Prior to the Second Vatican Council, Catholic moral theology followed what scholars call a *classicist* or a *traditionalist* approach. It's an approach that stems from classic Greek philosophers such as Plato and Aristotle and was passed down in the Church through Augustine and, particularly, Thomas Aquinas. Stated briefly, the classicist approach understands the world as fixed and unchanging. This is also true of morality—moral principles are fixed in nature, universal, unchanging, *and* eternal. Since these principles are stable and ordered to be in harmony with all that exists, a moral theologian or philosopher need only look at nature to achieve a high level of certainty that moral principles deduced from the natural order are right and good, and they are forever right and good. Moral living thus requires that we learn to live in conformity with that order. More specifically, Catholic moral theology from its inception in the early Christian tradition through Vatican II entailed answering moral questions primarily by applying universal moral rules or laws to any given context. Indeed, the context mattered little, since it was the context that had to conform to the established natural order, and not vice versa. With this approach, the moral theologian's chief task was to serve the Church by mastering the laws and rules of the natural moral order and applying them to questions raised by Catholics or to situations in which Catholics strayed from the Church's moral teachings.[6]

However, Vatican II recognized the need for a *historically conscious* approach to Catholic moral theology. In contrast to the classicist moral theology, a historical approach understands the human person as one who both changes and is changed by history. According to a historically conscious moral theology, the world is always in a state of development. The same is true of the human person—we are always in a state of "becoming." Our social, economic, political, and religious positions in life aren't fixed. Moreover, knowledge isn't fixed, but instead is conditioned to varying degrees by culture, socio-economic class, and other factors such as gender, race, and political status. Truth still exists, but it must be reinterpreted and translated for new contexts and audiences. Also, a historically conscious moral theology is one informed by human experiences. A good example of this historically conscious approach in the teachings of the Church is the obligation we have to do ethics with a preferential option for the poor, which we will discuss in greater detail in chapter six. Following a historical approach to moral theology, the task of the moral theologian is to serve the Church by listening to people's experiences, reinterpreting and translating the teachings of the Church for new audiences, and engaging in public discussions on today's central ethical issues.

But let's be clear: there remains an unresolved tension in the Church's official teaching between the classicist (or traditionalist) approach and the historically conscious approach, which has sometimes been called a "revisionist" approach. I have no doubt that the appearance of these two approaches in the official teachings of the Church has contributed to some of the confusion and frustration that many Catholics feel when they appeal to the Catholic tradition to make sense of contemporary ethical issues. As will become evident when you read chapters four and five, this tension between the classicist and historically conscious approaches is most profoundly manifested when we turn to issues regarding sexuality, life, and death. Unfortunately, because these issues have become so politically charged, some people in the Church and the media have been quick to label those who tend to follow the classicist approach "conservative" or "right wing." Similarly, some have also been quick to label those who tend to follow the historical approach "liberal" or "left wing." In my view, people who think of Catholic theology and ethics only in terms of conservative versus liberal, right wing versus left wing, have overly politicized Catholic thought. But what is even more problematic is that I don't find these labels all that useful or descriptive of the Catholic tradition. In fact, they're confusing. Am I conservative because I maintain that morality and ethics are rooted in the natural law precept "do good and avoid evil"? Or am I a liberal because I contend that our understanding of morality and ethics must be informed by human experience and our first act of ethics should be to listen to people describe their experiences? Put in these terms, I would say "yes" to both—and so, too, would the social teachings of the Catholic Church. So perhaps *Catholic* is the best label, even when we disagree with each other.

The Goal of this Book

I have written this book with one overarching goal: to introduce Catholics to a way of thinking about and acting on contemporary ethical issues, and doing so as Catholics. It arises from my deeply held belief that Catholics—and I'm speaking primarily to Catholic laity—have something valuable to contribute in public debates over today's most pressing ethical issues, particularly those related to sexuality, life and death, the global economy, war and peacemaking, and the environment. But to engage in those debates, we likely need some guidance, since so few of us are trained in philosophy, theology, political theory, medicine, law, or any of the other fields that routinely address complicated ethical problems.

To help provide this guidance, I have focused on meeting three objectives. First, I want to provide readers with a *basic vocabulary* used in the language of ethics. I realize many of us have experienced ethical debates as little more than jargon-filled exercises in frustration and futility. I have to be honest. I'm sure this is what my students think only a few moments into our first class, just as I make my point that we actually don't know what we mean when we use the term "ethics." Second, I want to construct a basic *framework* that will allow us to engage in a critical and "systematic reflection on morality, values, and character."[7] And third, I want to situate issues within a *historical context*, including a brief history of the issues before us, the Church's official teaching regarding those issues, and the responses of contemporary Catholic ethicists.

The book is divided into two parts. Part I, "A Framework for Ethical Reflection," mainly addresses my first two objectives: developing the vocabulary of ethics and constructing an interpretative framework. Chapter one defines our terms—for instance, what ethics is, what ethics isn't, who the ethical actors are, and what the difference is between ethics and morality. Chapter two identifies the two general tasks of ethics and what we call the "six factors" in doing ethics. These factors focus on (1) who we are as persons, (2) how we view the world around us, (3) what norms and values we hold, (4) what groups we're loyal to, (5) what experiences have influenced our moral judgments, and (6) how we make ethical decisions. Chapter three is an introduction to the four sources of Catholic ethics: scripture, tradition, reason, and experience. Part II, "Contemporary Issues," consists of five chapters, each one containing brief discussions of specific issues related to sexuality (chapter four), life and death issues (chapter five), the economy (chapter six), war and peacemaking (chapter seven), and the environment (chapter eight).

Finally, I'd like to say a quick word about "the ethical being," the title of this book. As we will see at various points in upcoming chapters, the idea of "ethical being" is linked to a Catholic tradition of virtue ethics. In chapter one, I make the case that ethics traditionally asks two general questions: "How shall I/we live?" and "Who do I/we wish to become?" Historically, the first question has been important to ethical theories that emphasize *action*, while the second has focused on *being* (or becoming). In this book, I tend to treat them as complementary questions. That is, in response to the question "How shall we live?" we respond with "Act so that it is consistent with who I wish to become as a person and who we wish to become in our communities, institutions, and societies." My underlying assumption in this book is that we can really only answer the question of who we wish to become if we're in engaging in ethical reflection on our morality, values, and character.

Part I

A Framework for Ethical Reflection

CHAPTER 1

Ethics: How Shall We Live?
Who Do We Hope to Become?

M ohamed Bouazizi is a hero. In 2011, *The Times* of the United Kingdom named him "Man of the Year." Also in 2011 he received the Sakharov Prize, which is given annually to individuals or organizations devoted to the defence of human rights and freedom of thought. Named after the Soviet scientist and dissident Andrei Sakharov, the prize's first recipient, in 1988, was Nelson Mandela, the anti-apartheid activist and later the first Black person to be elected president of South Africa. Other notable recipients include Aung San Suu Kyi, the Burmese opposition leader who spent nearly fifteen years as a political prisoner, and the Mothers of the Plaza de Mayo, a group of Argentinian mothers whose children disappeared during Argentina's Dirty War (1976–1983).

Bouazizi received these honours because of his unwitting role in sparking the demonstrations that eventually led to the Tunisian Revolution, the ouster of then-president Zine El Abidine Ben Ali, who had ruled for 23 years, and the uprisings that became the Arab Spring. Bouazizi was not a political leader, an academic, or a public figure. To the contrary, he was a street vendor who sold fruit to passersby. He earned less than $75 per week. On December 17, 2010, he set himself on fire to protest the confiscation of his scales, the destruction of his fruit, and the harassment and humiliation that he reported were inflicted on him by a municipal official and her aides. His act became symbolic of the frustration many Tunisians felt toward the heavy-handed, anti-democratic government of the Tunisian dictator Ben Ali. Recalling Bouazizi's actions, *The Times* remarked, "The humble fruit merchant whose struggle for justice has made history."[1]

The story of Mohamed Bouazizi reminds us that the pursuit of justice does not begin with definitions of ethics and morality; rather, the pursuit of justice stems from the experiences of those suffering from injustices such as racism, economic marginalization, torture, sexism, political imprisonment, forced displacement from one's homeland, and starvation. Bertolt Brecht, the German dramatist and social critic, made a similar observation in his famous musical *The Threepenny Opera*. Through the character Mackie the Knife, Brecht declares, "First comes the grub, then comes the ethics."[2] Brecht's line stands as an indictment against anyone trying to do ethics merely as an abstract, intellectual exercise. The social teachings of the Catholic Church make this same point when they conclude that love, justice, and other moral virtues must begin with and be judged against the experiences of the poor and marginalized. As the United States Conference of Catholic Bishops wrote in its letter *Economic Justice for All* (1986), "The obligation to provide justice for all means that the poor have the single most urgent economic claim on the conscience of the nation."[3]

And yet ethics requires a level of abstraction and critical distance. Without some abstraction and critical distance, there could be no language of ethics (language is always abstract and symbolic), no framework to help us understand and assess the problems presented to us when people cry out that the good is *not* being done, and no distance that would enable us to consider how our responses have contributed to or diminished human flourishing.

The aim of this chapter is to present a basic definition of ethics. We begin by stating what ethics is *not*. We then offer a definition of "ethics" that includes the purpose of ethics, the "stuff" of ethics (namely, morality, values, and character), and the actors who can engage in ethical reflection.

What Ethics Is Not

To help clear up some of this historical confusion and to pave a way toward a definition of ethics, let's agree at the outset on what ethics is *not*.

First, ethics is not solely a personal, private matter. Our modern way of thinking typically divides our social realities into the public and private realms. In the public realm, we engage in business and politics. In the private realm, we live in our homes, love our families, and practise our religion. On the whole, modern societies operate on the principle that entities in the public realm, such as parliament or congress, should not interfere with private interactions, such as attending church or engaging in sexual relationships. Likewise, modern societies can become quite anxious when private entities, such as religious organizations, attempt to intervene in public interactions, such as policymaking or the economy. In the United States, the dichotomy between public and private realms is enshrined in the legal doctrine of "separation of church and state." While Canada has no similar legal doctrine, the public-private dichotomy remains firmly entrenched in the socio-political imagination of many Canadians.

For instance, in the wake of the devastating earthquake that struck Haiti in 2010, a number of Canadians were upset to learn that for years the Canadian government had been funding faith-based humanitarian aid organizations not only in Haiti but also in other developing countries around the world. In the case of Haiti, Canada did not have the capacity to deliver humanitarian assistance to Haitians. Instead, the Canadian government, through the Canadian International Development Agency (CIDA), relied heavily on networks of faith-based organizations that maintained a presence in Haiti to distribute the needed aid. Among these organizations was Development and Peace, the international development organization of the Canadian Catholic Church, which has a long track record of partnering with CIDA on development projects around the globe. While a few may want to debate whether federal tax dollars should be sent to faith-based development organizations, the reality is that, in many countries facing humanitarian crises, it is the faith-based organizations that have the necessary logistical infrastructure, such as warehouses and trucks, to receive and deliver food, medicine, and building supplies, as well as people already on the ground to oversee such projects.

In theory, a strict separation between public politics and private religious ethics might work if we were living in a post-Enlightenment philosopher's ideal of a liberal, secularized society. But in our practical reality of everyday life, the public–private dichotomy routinely breaks down. The personal choices we make, such as the clothes we wear, have moral and political repercussions. The shirt you're wearing, if you purchased it at Banana Republic, the GAP, or any retail store, was likely made in Cambodia, Bangladesh, or China, where cheap labour, carried out in often unthinkable working conditions, enables consumers in economically developed countries to buy their clothes at a fraction of the cost were these produced domestically. For many of us, the experience of buying and wearing clothes is a personal one, and perhaps one that does not involve moral reasoning. But our personal actions can, and often do, affect the lives of people we will never meet. In short, our private actions have public consequences.

Second, ethics is not reducible to following a list of laws, rules, or a code of conduct. All societies attempt to regulate social behaviour by enacting laws and meting out punishment for those who break those laws. For instance, one of the oldest and most basic laws is "an eye for an eye." Although at times brutal and bloody, the "eye for an eye" law of reciprocity serves both as a way to prevent excessive punishment at the hands of an avenger or the state and as a way to regulate behaviour by making the punishment of unjust actions predictable. In Latin, this type of law is referred to as *lex talionis*, or "law of retaliation." This principle of *lex talionis* appears in the Bible, including in the well-known passage in Exodus 21:24-25: "If any harm follows, then you shall give life for life, eye for eye, tooth for tooth, hand for hand, foot for foot, burn for burn, wound for wound, stripe for stripe." In response to this crude law of retaliation, Jesus declared in the Sermon on the Mount: "You have heard that it was said, 'An eye for an eye and a tooth for a tooth.' But I say to you, 'Do not resist an evildoer. But if anyone strikes you on the right cheek, turn the other also'" (Matthew 5:38-39).

The Bible is home to another ancient law, the Decalogue (also known as the Ten Commandments). Found in Exodus 20:2-17 and

Deuteronomy 5:6-21, the Decalogue consists of demands placed on the children of Israel as they wandered in the desert in search of the land God had promised after their flight from Egypt. In the Christian tradition, the Decalogue has traditionally served as the foundational statement on moral behaviour, beginning with the first commandment, "I am the Lord your God, who brought you up out of the land of Egypt, out of the house of slavery; you shall have no other gods before me" (Deuteronomy 5:6-7). The list of shalls covers keeping the Sabbath holy and honouring parents, while the list of shall nots extends to prohibitions against idol worship, taking the Lord's name in vain, murder, committing adultery, stealing, lying, and coveting your neighbour's possessions, including your neighbour's wife.

But is adhering to the commandments in the Decalogue the same as doing ethics? In a word, "No." Walter Brueggemann, a renowned biblical scholar, maintains that "biblical morality is not found in the Ten Commandments or in any part of them, but in the action of the Holy Spirit."[4] Brueggemann's provocative statement is intended to avert a slide toward legalism, which is what happens when Christians mistakenly believe that adhering to the letter of the law is the primary, if not sole, requirement for authentic moral action. In the United States, some Christian leaders adopt a legalistic understanding of ethics when they argue that the Decalogue should remain in schoolrooms, courtrooms, and other public spaces. For these Christians, the social and political problems facing Americans are moral problems, which no public policy or legal decision can adequately address. As Rev. Robert Schenck stated in an interview with ABC News, "We need a moral code to address [social problems]. There is no better educational and moral code than the Ten Commandments."[5]

In general, the problem with reducing ethics to laws or moral codes is that so much of everyday life is about negotiating fuzzy moral boundaries. Moreover, if we're intellectually honest, we must recognize that laws themselves are, to varying degrees, indeterminate. Simply put, laws, rules, and moral codes require interpretation. The fifth commandment, "You shall not kill," provides us with a good example of the ambiguity of moral rules. Is the prohibition against killing limited only to other human beings, or does it extend, as some Christian vegans argue, to all sentient beings? Does this commandment mean that the taking of human life is categorically wrong? If so, then all killing is prohibited, including killing another person while defending one's family, neighbour, or country. But if the commandment means, "You shall not murder," then we should expect to see arguments about what constitutes murder, what constitutes a just killing, what conditions must be met before a state can declare war or invoke the death penalty, and other such contentious matters. Indeed, in the Christian tradition, we see precisely these arguments in debates over the moral use of force, capital punishment, euthanasia, stem-cell research, and abortion. At the core of these debates, including the ones that play out in the public arena, are appeals to individual conscience, the common good, the nature of a human subject, moral responsibility, human rights, and conceptions of justice. In other words, the law requires ethical reflection. *Interpreting* moral laws, rules, and codes means we inevitably engage in a process of *evaluating* our morality and making moral judgments.

Third, ethics is not synonymous with crisis decision-making. Malcolm Gladwell, in his widely read book *Blink*, argues on the basis of examples from scientific research, advertising, sales, and medicine that we human beings apparently have an ability to gauge what is really important through "the blink of an eye."[6] He calls this ability to make determinations quickly "thin-slicing." Gladwell thinks that spontaneous decisions, made on the basis of thin-slicing, are often as good as, or even better than, carefully planned and considered ones. Thin-slicing is an especially valuable asset to possess in the fast-paced world of business and technology, where ideas and decisions must be presented quickly, concisely, and with confidence. As the old adage goes, time is money. With ethics becoming an increasingly important part of business, the process of doing ethics has sped up to the point where ethical decisions must be made in a limited time frame and with little deliberation.

Business and technology are not the only entities that have adopted crisis decision-making as ethics. Hospitals, where life-and-death issues occur with regularity, and research universities, where delays in ethics approval mean lost hours on time-sensitive research projects, are just a couple of publicly funded institutions that require ethics committees to act with alacrity. This can make deliberative ethics almost impossible.

For example, a few years ago, while sitting on my university's research ethics committee, my fellow committee members and I received a research proposal that involved a series of tests conducted by my colleagues in optometry on the effectiveness of a new contact lens. As usual, a week before the committee was scheduled to meet, I received my package of cases for consideration. As I thumbed through the thick package, I came across this contact lens research project and its supporting documents, which included pages of medical jargon, technical manuals for proper installation, and diagrams of dissected eyeballs. I began to panic. I longed for the contemplative environment that enabled Aristotle to cultivate practical wisdom. In the time frame I had been given, I simply didn't have the technical expertise required to make a fully informed decision. Frustrated, I wondered somewhat cynically, "What would Jesus do?" I couldn't imagine Jesus spending hours trying to cipher through dense medical jargon and making sense of dissected eyeballs. But I could imagine him taking some dirt, spitting in it, and then rubbing the mud in the eyes of the person with afflicted eyesight (John 9:6). Certain that the ethics committee would reject my offer to do the same, and not convinced myself that it would work, I realized that the crisis-oriented question "What would Jesus do?" was not a particularly helpful guide for me in doing my job on this ethics committee. Reduced to nothing more than a wordsmith who possessed the vocabulary of ethics, I ended up providing suggestions on how to improve the full-disclosure wording in the invitation letter, which noted the research project had cleared the university's research ethics committee.

At best, a crisis decision-making approach to ethics can be a part of an institution's larger system of risk management, one that includes adequate training for decision-makers and researchers, clear ethical guidelines to help in the decision-making process, and trained staff who ensure compliance with the guidelines. In fact, the vast majority of hospitals, universities, and other institutions with functioning ethics committees operate in this fashion. At worst, however, this crisis decision-making approach provides businesses and publicly funded institutions with only a thin veneer of ethics. In either case, deliberative approaches to ethics are not well suited to organizational cultures, whether corporate or publicly funded, in which thin-slicing decision-making is more valuable than deliberate moral reasoning. Culturally, we may value instant access to knowledge, real-time global communication, and even fast food. But we should not accept the idea that "thinly sliced" ethics *alone* is good for society, the Church, our public institutions, government, the environment, or, in the long run, business. We need to carve out time and space in our schedules and institutional processes to allow for deliberative moral reasoning to take place.

Constructing a Definition of Ethics

Now that we've hopefully put to rest the common misconceptions that ethics is essentially a personal-private matter, obedience to a list of rules, or synonymous with crisis decision-making, let's agree on a positive definition of ethics: *Ethics is systematic reflection on morality, values, and character that is worked out through individuals, communities, institutions, and society as a whole.* Admittedly, our definition is not particularly elegant. However, it should be useful because it highlights key elements typically involved in the process of doing ethics. First, it defines the central purpose of ethics: systematic reflection. Second, it identifies the "stuff" that ethics reflects upon: morality, values, and character. And third, it names the actors who have morality, values, and character: individuals, communities, institutions, and societies. Let's take a few moments to discuss these key elements in our definition.

Systematic Reflection

One of the primary markers that distinguishes ethics from preference or from merely having an opinion is that ethics requires a systematic framework of analysis. All of us can think of social behaviours, political decisions, and economic arrangements we don't like. Moreover, we can probably recall conversations with friends, family, and colleagues where we voiced our opinions on today's pressing issues: the state of the economy, universal health care, publicly funded education, immigration reform, tax rates, organized labour, global warming, and what to do about global terrorism. If your experiences are like mine, very little is systematic about these conversation or our analyses. The sources we cite can range from something we read in last week's *Economist* to something we heard on CBC Radio. When the debate turns to matters involving the U.S., someone inevitably trundles out news stories they heard on Fox News and National Public Radio as authorities. And when the argument gets white-hot, we have a tendency to recite a provocative quote from the Bible or make vague references to the magisterial teachings of the Church.

As an ethicist, I am encouraged by these exchanges, since they can be important precursors to a more nuanced discussion we would expect from sustained ethical reflection. Nevertheless, the unstructured, undisciplined manner in which these conversations take place is an insufficient basis for a systematic approach to ethics. So if we are going to engage in ethics, we will need to step back from the melee, find some critical distance, and begin to analyze foundational elements in our individual and collective arguments and social interactions. In doing so, we should become more self-aware of the sources of our morality, including a number of sources that were likely hidden behind habits that we've unconsciously developed over time. We should be better able to recognize and assess our values. And we should be able to examine the social, political, and theological forces that went into the development of our character. In the next chapter, we will develop a framework that will enable us to engage in critical, systematic reflection.

Morality

In the simplest terms, morality is customary action. Morality is not simply an abstract notion of right and wrong, but a lived experience that each of us learns through practice and social affirmation. Moreover, morality is an inevitable part of being human. Every action we perform contributes to our moral formation and our development as persons. Our families, schools, religious communities, social organizations, and societies provide standards of behaviour that help in our moral maturity. They help us in our quest to be what we ought to be. With a few exceptions, it is virtually impossible to be "amoral," that is, "without morality."[7] However, it is possible to be "immoral."

But what does it mean to be immoral? On the one hand, immorality means that we do not live up to the moral standards of communities, institutions, and societies. Statements such as "sweatshop labour is immoral" and "blood diamonds are immoral" convey the sense that goods obtained through unjust working conditions violate our moral standards. On the other hand, immorality also means the improper shaping of human persons. This is a more fundamental conception of immorality and one that often causes a significant amount of social and political tension because it often demands a radical reassessment, if not transformation, of our morality, values, and character.

For example, assume that we live in a country with a revered military tradition and that our country is engaged in a protracted war. This country budgets more for military spending than it does for education. It celebrates soldiers and those who support the war, while it demeans conscientious objectors and criminalizes anti-war protests. The leader of the country is admired by the vast majority of citizens for his willingness to fight enemies abroad before they come ashore. Now assume that we are convinced that this country's priorities are fundamentally out of order. We have grave concerns that this country's political leadership is preying on its citizens' strong sense of national pride to garner support for the war. In short, we believe that we're living in a culture of violence that is dehumanizing soldiers, foreign "enemies," and even, to some degree, its own citizens. What can we do to free ourselves from this culture of violence and deceit? How do we transform this society?

In the 1970s, young people with concerns similar to these took to the streets in the United States to protest the Vietnam War. With chants such as "Make love, not war," anti-war protestors offended the moral sensibilities of many Americans. Daniel Ellsberg, a Pentagon insider who had access to secret files indicating that U.S. leaders had been lying to the public about the war in Vietnam, took the courageous step to release the documents that became known as the Pentagon Papers. At a public conference in January 1971, just weeks before the release of the Pentagon Papers, Ellsberg questioned National Security Advisor Henry Kissinger about the morality of the war and the role that the Nixon administration had played in constructing a morality that dehumanized populations in Laos, Cambodia, and Vietnam:

> You said that the White House is not a place for moral philosophizing. But in fact the White House does educate people by everything that it does and everything it says and does not say. Specifically, tonight you *are* expressing moral values when you tell us the war is trending down, and then in that connection you mention only U.S. troop presence and U.S. casualties. By your

omission, you are telling the American people that they need not and ought not to care about our impact on the Indochinese people. So I have one question for you. What is your best estimate of the number of Indochinese that we will kill, pursuing your policy, in the next twelve months?[8]

Many Americans deemed Ellsberg's actions to be immoral because he opposed the social morality that supported the war. Many also considered his actions criminal, if not treasonous. President Nixon stated publicly, "I think it is time in this country to quit making national heroes out of those who steal secrets and publish them in the newspaper."[9] Believing that the publication of the Pentagon Papers constituted a serious national security risk, Kissinger called Ellsberg the most dangerous man in America and ordered him stopped at any cost. It was, however, too late. Ellsberg's "immoral" and potentially criminal actions—he was never convicted—ended up exposing the injustice, the immorality, of the Vietnam War and contributed to the growing anti-war movement in the U.S. As the case of Daniel Ellsberg illustrates, identifying and transforming immoral actions, which are rooted in immoral structures that prohibit us from realizing our humanity, can be highly conflictual and a source of tremendous social and political tension.

One reason why questioning morality can be so upsetting is that it is so deeply ingrained in us—it is part of our self-identity. Morality is so much a part of us that we often have a difficult time determining the foundations of our sense of right and wrong. As part of our systematic reflection on morality, the general question we need to ask is this: Where did that sense of right and wrong come from?

Our morality is also habit forming. As with any habit, moral actions often do not require conscious forethought. When we engage in moral action, the line between *what we ought to do* and *what we want to become* can become virtually indistinguishable. We tell the truth because we are honest. We pay our debts because we are trustworthy. We maintain our homes because we are hospitable. And we care for our family because we are loving and responsible. All of us know stories of people who, without a single moment of hesitation, risked their own lives by running into a burning home or diving into a raging river to save another's life. We rightly call these people who risk their lives for others "heroes." But their actions are not superhuman. In fact, we can call these people "heroes" because, when the time came, they unflinchingly acted in accordance with the morality instilled in them by their families, friends, and communities.

■ ■ ■

You may have noticed that, with our definition of morality as customary action, we are making a distinction between the terms "ethics" and "morality." While many philosophers and theologians do not maintain this distinction, it should be preserved because it highlights the critical difference between patterns of behaviour (morality) and the systematic study of morality (ethics).

To help us better understand the distinction between ethics and morality, let's consider the customary act of shaking hands. In North America, when we are introduced to someone for the first time in a business setting or in a formal situation, we commonly extend our right hand and place it firmly in our acquaintance's right hand. We then do two or three quick pumps while verbally introducing ourselves. It is an act that many of us perform routinely, without the slightest feeling of discomfort and without much, if any, conscious effort. Now imagine that someone broke our cultural protocol and tried to greet you by extending his or her left hand. At the very least, we would find this act awkward. Immediately, we would likely have to make a conscious decision either to extend our left hand or, if we are convinced that a proper handshake ought to be done with the right hand, leave our right hand extended, hoping that our acquaintance picks up on our cue. Also, we would likely expect an explanation from our acquaintance to clarify why his or her right hand is unavailable—perhaps arthritis or another medical condition. But if no explanation were offered, we would likely conclude that there is something a bit odd about that person.

We could make the argument that shaking hands is not a good example of moral action since its seriousness doesn't rise to the magnitude involved in issues we will discuss later, such as stem-cell research, euthanasia, military force and peacebuilding, and ecological sustainability. We might suggest that shaking hands is more properly a matter of etiquette. However, such an argument would miss the moral reasoning underlying the act of shaking hands. So if we are to engage in ethics, we should ask this basic question: Why do we shake with our right hand? Indeed, to help my students begin to think of ethics as "systematic reflection," I ask them precisely this question. Over the years, their answers have coalesced around these themes:

"Historically, the right hand was used for doing battle—it was the sword hand."

"The left hand is 'unclean,' since it is used for wiping—it's the poo hand."

"In some parts of the world, the left hand is the 'Devil's Hand.'"

"The majority of us are right-handed."

Remarkably, in spite of having had no formal education on historical meanings of the left and right hand, my students' answers are consistent with the findings of historians.

There is, however, one compelling answer that my students tend to leave out. It concerns the Latin terms for "right" and "left." In Latin, *dexter* is the word meaning "right." In contemporary English, we find this Latin root in the word "dexterity," which means skillfulness, agility, or flexibility. We are dexterous if we perform a skill well or move with ease. Conversely, the Latin word for "left" is *sinistra*. We find this root in the English word "sinister," which means evil, devious, or ominous. Morally, it is good to be dexterous and bad to be sinister. Until quite recently, in the Western tradition the moral meanings of *dexter* and *sinistra* were linked to the body. If we have family roots in Europe, we can likely recount family stories of how a left-handed parent or a grandparent was disciplined by family members, schoolteachers, or religious figures to use the right hand. Continued use of the left hand was a sign of suspicious moral character and had to be corrected.

Now consider the term we use for a person who is able to use both the left and right hand equally well: "ambidextrous." Notice that nowhere in that word do we find the word *sinistra*. But we do find the word dexter. The term "ambidextrous" literally means "both right" or "both right hands." While there is much more to this history, it is safe to say that the moral disgust of many of our forbearers toward *sinistra* was so deep-seated that it was virtually inconceivable for them to place any "good," whether physical or moral, in actions that stemmed from the left hand.[10] Over time, the customary action of using the right hand to greet each other became so entrenched that questioning why became pointless. To some degree, then, our custom of shaking right hands is a vestige of a morality that ascribed notions of good and bad to parts of the human body.

My purpose in this benign example is not to raise questions about whether we should continue shaking hands in the way we do, although we could raise objections based on public health concerns; rather, it is to illustrate the difference between ethics as "systematic reflection" and morality as "customary action." In short, we move from the morality of handshaking to ethics once we begin to examine a moral act and uncover its underlying structures, leaving us in the critical position to question whether we ought to continue with the practice.

Values

The next element in our definition of ethics is values. When ethicists use the term "values," they are normally referring to the moral "goods" that we seek to foster both individually and collectively. Values that we desire may include freedom, democracy, trust, transparency, compassion, hope, human dignity, responsibility, forgiveness, reconciliation, social justice, peace, love, solidarity, and cooperation, to name a few. Values are moral ideals that serve as signposts in a well-lived life. They are the bedrock of our morality. The Catholic ethicist Daniel Maguire writes, "Moral values are more basic than all other values, because moral values touch, not just on what we do or experience or have, but on what we 'are.'"[11] Maguire is making an important distinction between moral values and material values, such as beauty, health, wealth, and security. Material values are contingent values, while moral values have the capacity to be absolute. Also, material values are often linked to complementary moral values, whether directly, as the basis for an action, or indirectly, as the result of an action. For instance, we may value our health because we are narcissistic and, consequently, spend exorbitant amounts of money on Botox injections, special diets, and spa treatments. Or we may eat a balanced diet, get regular exercise, and maintain a healthy weight because we believe that God wants us to respect and care for our bodies, given that they are temples of the Holy Spirit (1 Corinthians 6:19)—the indirect result of which, if performed on a large scale, reduces health care costs. My reason for raising this issue is not to open up a discussion of the health care system or the beauty industry, but only to note that, as we begin to examine contemporary ethical challenges in upcoming chapters, it will be important for us to keep in mind that underlying any material good and any moral action is a set of moral values.

With the inclusion of "values" in our definition of ethics, we must acknowledge that "values language" has proliferated over the past few years. Values language has become good business for everyone from the self-help industry to oil companies, and from school boards to corporate boardrooms. Everyone seems to have values. The yoga clothing retailer Lululemon, for example, proudly displays its values in its Workplace Code of Conduct: "At lululemon athletica, our core values are: Quality, Product, Integrity, Balance, Entrepreneurship, Fun and Greatness. When choosing manufacturers and vendors, we will work with people who have common values and operate using responsible business practices."[12] As consumers, we're not just buying high-end yoga gear, we're buying Lululemon's values, which presumably are also our values

Any cynicism aside, clothing manufacturers targeting socially conscious consumers must declare that their goods are not made in sweatshops. Oil companies must state they're "green." Even universities must list their values on their recruitment literature. Why? It's because we're living in an age where values language has currency. As a result, the ubiquity of values language has led some critical thinkers to con-clude that the term "values" is a weasel word invoked primarily to mask morally suspect practices. This conclusion should serve as a reminder to Catholics that the gospel values of love, truth, and justice must never be invoked to mask bigotry, error, or injustice.

Character

Character is the third element in our definition of ethics. The term is derived from the Greek word *charakter* and originally referred to the impression left on a coin. Moral character is a status we acquire over time as we seek to live a moral life. To be of good character means that we consistently act in accordance with our individual and collective moral-ity and values, while to be of suspect character means that we routinely

34

contravene the morality and values of the communities, institutions, and societies to which we belong. Plato, Aristotle, and many of the early Greek philosophers thought that character was an essential part of moral reasoning. For the Greeks, a well-lived life, or "well-being," is the general goal for all moral beings. To reach this goal, we rationally choose to live a virtuous life. But we do not make this choice without support. Developing good moral character requires communities, institutions, and societies to be of good character.

Character is relationally oriented. We draw conclusions about another's character by observing how that person relates to others based on our shared morality and values. Because of its highly interpretive nature, judging character can be a staggeringly complex matter. Consider the meaning of eye contact in interpersonal relations. In North America, we have a tendency to be suspicious of people who do not meet our eyes in conversations or when we are first introduced to them. We regard them as shifty, untrustworthy types. We believe that people who avoid eye contact lack leadership skills, are poor communicators, and perhaps have something to hide. To overcome lingering suspicions about Russian President Vladimir Putin, who was a former KGB agent and director of Russian state security, U.S. President George W. Bush stated shortly after meeting him for the first time in June 2001, "I looked the man in the eye. I found him to be very straight forward and trustworthy and we had a very good dialogue." Bush added, "I was able to get a sense of his soul."[13]

Cross-cultural character judgments can be especially precarious since so much of our conduct is culturally conditioned. Contrast George W. Bush's penchant for looking world leaders squarely in the eye and judging their souls with Barack Obama's practice of greeting leaders from Saudi Arabia and Japan by avoiding eye contact and bowing. (Maybe President Obama was trying to determine their character by looking at their soles?) For many Americans, particularly on the political right, Obama's genuflecting before Saudi King Abdullah and Emperor Akihito is indicative of certain character flaws: untrustworthiness, weak leadership, and unbelief in American exceptionalism. Obama's critics believe that, by avoiding eye contact and bowing, he is kowtowing to foreign leaders and demeaning the authority of the United States. Others regard Obama's greetings as gestures of cross-cultural recognition and respect.

Individuals

St. Thomas Aquinas (1225–1274), the great philosopher of the late Middle Ages, defined the individual as a being undivided in itself but separated from other beings.[14] For Thomas, the individual is a unity and yet separate. Drawing on the thought of Aristotle, Thomas believed that there is a form, or an unconditioned basis, of the "individual" that provides the conceptual unity required for us to distinguish between different corporeal beings. In other words, following Thomas, we have to have a common, abstract idea of the "individual" to recognize others around us as distinct individual beings. However, as the Canadian philosopher Charles Taylor noted in his little book *The Malaise of Modernity*, the Enlightenment radically transformed the pre-modern understanding of the individual.[15] One of the primary reasons for this transformation was because Enlightenment thinkers had concluded that matter, including human beings, had no purpose, no end, and no intentionality. After the Enlightenment, God and God's divine order no longer determined the value and purpose of things—humans did. Enlightened human beings, equipped with the newly discovered tools of science, found themselves needing to attribute scientific, technical meaning to everything from the stars to the land they lived on. In a very crude way, the turn toward science and technological reason contributed to the birth of the modern individual and individualism. Unlike Aristotle and Thomas, Enlightenment thinkers severed the individual from the conceptual ideal that had enabled pre-moderns to make determinations about what an individual is and ought to be. For Enlightenment thinkers, the formation of a self-conscious subject not only enabled people to become individuals but also created a new sense of freedom. Having freed themselves from the externally imposed standards of the Church and the medieval social structure, modern individuals turned inward, toward their own reason, to construct their identities.

Today, we find evidence of a radical individualism with roots in the Enlightenment in the work of the objectivist philosopher and author of *Atlas Shrugged* Ayn Rand (1905–1982). Rand believed that we are essentially self-interested individuals and, as such, each of us must live solely for ourselves, neither sacrificing ourselves to others nor sacrificing others to help us. In her book *The Virtue of Selfishness*, she sums up her radically individualistic ethic in these terms: "To live for his own sake means that the achievement of his own happiness is man's highest moral purpose."[16] We can also find radical individualism in the writings of the Austrian economist Friedrich von Hayek (1882–1992), who stated in his influential book, *The Road to Serfdom*, "The guiding principle that a policy of freedom for the individual is the only truly progressive policy remains as true today as it was in the nineteenth century."[17] The individualism represented by Rand and Hayek is neither value free nor politically neutral. Both Rand and Hayek are revered by defenders of free-market capitalism, anti-government libertarians, and those who align themselves with the Tea Party movement, which rose to political prominence in the United States in response to President Barack Obama's health care plan.

Many of us, however, are probably not as ideologically committed to radical individual freedom and self-interest as Rand, Hayek, or their dedicated followers. Instead, many of us have simply acquired our understanding of the individual and developed our individual identity over time spent with our families, friends, peers, teachers, and influential media personalities. As with our moral formation, we have likely been unaware of the process of individualization—it just happened. As we grew older, we probably thought more specifically about our own individual identity, including what kind of persons we wanted to be, what we wanted to do in life, what we wished to study, where we wanted to worship, where we hoped to live, and with whom we would like to spend our lives. As Taylor indicated, this sense of being detached from an external determining order is a modern dilemma, which began to appear in the nineteenth century, and remains with us in the 21st century. In North America, in particular, we have come to believe that we can become whatever we want to be and that, if we just strive hard enough and persevere long enough, we will largely determine our own futures.

As a matter of ethics, then, it is inevitable that we identify individuals as actors who have morality, values, and character. Indeed, because we've inherited an Enlightenment understanding of the individual, many us believe that we, as individuals, are the authors of our own morality, values, and character. Many of my students who answer the question "What is ethics?" with the response "Ethics means being true to yourself" certainly believe this to be the case. However, the belief that we create our own individual morality, values, and character on our own does not square with the reality that all of us, including even the most ardent radical individualist, belong to communities, are associated with various institutions, and live in societies. And while we may define ourselves primarily as individuals, we actually develop our morality, values, and character in our communities, within institutions, and in societies.

Community

The Catholic theologian Bernard Lonergan defined community not in terms of a geographical space, but as an "achievement of common meaning."[18] For Lonergan, it is only within communities that we are conceived, born, and reared. The community must have both a common field of experience and complementary ways of understanding. In the community, there is a common language, a commonly understood way of transmitting knowledge and social patterns, and a common network for the diffusion of information. Above all, there is a common will to maintain the community, which is continually reaffirmed by individual interactions and through the community's institutions. As Lonergan rightly observes, this process has a variety of names. For educators, it is education. For the sociologist, it is socialization. And for the cultural anthropologist, it is acculturation. But for the individual seeking self-understanding, it is his or her becoming a mature ethical being.

Communities are crucial in the development of moral actions. We need community since it is there that moral imperatives, the do's and don'ts that we live by, have a context and meaning. As Walter Brueggemann said, morality is much more than just meeting obligations and adhering to a set of rules. Instead, morality is a way of being developed through a process of moral formation that comes from sharing in a community's stories and values.

Religious congregations, urban neighourhoods, and rural villages are just a few examples of communities that provide shared meaning and cultivate moral behaviour. As people living in modern societies, we can belong to a number of communities at the same time. I, for example, grew up in a small town in Missouri, which is still very much "home." I currently live in a small town in southern Ontario with my wife and young son. As a Catholic, I participate in a local parish community and a universal worshipping community. Moreover, my morality, values, and character have been shaped by the Church's teachings on the sanctity of life, the dignity of the human person, the importance of family, the common good, social justice, the dignity of work, and solidarity with the poor.

Institutions

Social institutions, the next actor in our definition of ethics, play an integral role in our moral formation. In general, social institutions serve to promote a society's "goods," such as freedom, order, justice, knowledge, health, and economic exchange. They are social forms that endure over generations. Some of our oldest human institutions include marriage and the family. Social institutions can be organizations or systems of organization. For instance, capitalism is an institution that has social consequences. It is a system of organization that consists of entities such as multinational corporations, banks, and stock markets. Institutions can also be organizations that organize other organizations—these are called meta-institutions. Government is a good example of a meta-institution. A government typically regulates and coordinates educational institutions, police and military organizations, health care systems, economic institutions such as banks, and the legal system, to name just a few.

As citizens associated with these institutions, we share in their morality, values, and character. For instance, a student who decides to attend a Catholic university instead of a secular university should expect a quality education that orients students to serve the gospel values of love, truth, justice, and the common good. As an institution, the Catholic university, like a secular university, serves society at large by educating citizens. One signficant difference between the two is that, within the Catholic university, students should find more opportunities to put their education to use in the pursuit of a more just and peaceable world. Moreover, they should expect to work with faculty, staff, and administration who actively promote Catholic values and character. When Catholic universities fail to provide these opportunities and when they do not meet these expectations, they become nominally Catholic institutions that are virtually indistinguishable from secular institutions.

Society

The final actor in our definition of ethics is society. We can speak of two general conceptions of society. First, a society is a group of people who share a culture, institutions, and structures of interaction. This group of people is often defined by geographical boundaries. We can talk about Canadian society, European society, and American society. Canadians who have backpacked in Europe know, even if intuitively, that societies based on geographical boundaries have different moralities, values, and characters. For decades, young Canadians travelling abroad have sewn Canadian flags on their backpacks to distinguish themselves from Americans. Ask a Canadian what it means to be Canadian and you'll likely get answers such as "Canadians believe in peacekeeping," "Canadians value multiculturalism," and, when all else fails, "Canadians know they're not Americans."

Second, we can conceive of society as a structure that brings coherence to interpersonal, community, and institutional relationships. As sociologist Anthony Giddens states, a society is only a "form, and that form only has effects on people, insofar as structure is produced and reproduced in what people do."[19] By conceiving of society as a structure that affects people's behaviours and is reinforced by their actions, we can talk of pre-modern societies, industrial societies, modern societies, postmodern societies, liberal societies, and conservative societies. For instance, the nineteenth-century German sociologist Ferdinand Toennies, in his famous book *Community and Society*, published in 1887, observed that pre-modern communities were characterized by a prioritization of the collective "we" over the individual "I." Pre-moderns believed that they were born into an organic community and into an order that could be traced all the way back to creation. In keeping with the medieval political structures, monarchs ruled based on inheritance. However, in industrial, modern societies, individuals prioritized the "I" over the "we." They believed that societies were human creations and individuals should be free to climb socio-economic ladders. And they believed that political leadership should be chosen through democratic elections. As Giddens has argued, in pre-modern social arrangements, individual actions did not require extensive thought because available choices were already predetermined by the customs and traditions of the community in which they lived. The authoritative perspective for pre-moderns was backward looking, for it was the past that oriented people in the social order and provided the foundations for their self-identity. By contrast, in modern social arrangements, individual actions require forward, strategic thinking. Modern individuals, if they are to be successful, must plan for the future. And modern self-identity depends less on family ties and community roots than on an individual's creative capacity, intellectual ability, and perseverance to construct an identity of one's own making. Yet, in spite of the increasing individualization of modern society, we still tend to identify with a large network of social relations we call a society, whether it's Canadian, Quebec, Western, American, Midwestern, Southern, Latino, Caribbean, British, or European, to name just a few.

■ ■ ■

Before we leave our definition of ethics, we need to highlight an important reality: as individuals who live in modern societies, we may find ourselves disagreeing with the morality, values, and character of our communities, institutions, and societies. Unlike our pre-modern ancestors, who were beholden to custom, tradition, and authoritative leadership, we moderns tend to believe that we have a responsibility to improve not only our lives but also the communities, institutions, and societies to which we belong.[20] To put this in stronger terms, many of us believe that we have a moral obligation not only to challenge but also to transform our churches, civil society organizations, schools, health care providers, and governments when they fail to live up to our individual and collective standards for morality, values, and character. As the case of Daniel Ellsberg demonstrates, when we raise challenging questions about the morality, values, and character of our communities, institutions, and societies, the likelihood of unsettling social, political, and moral tension is high. How we negotiate that tension is a matter of ethics, for it gets at the core of what ethics is about—that is, answering in both word and deed the two basic questions of ethics: "How shall we live?" and "Who do we hope to become?"

CHAPTER 2

The Examined Moral Life

The cadre of men wearing their neatly tailored uniforms and buttoned-up collars belied the fact that Thursday, July 20, 1944, was an especially warm day in the forest outside Rastenburg, Germany, a small town near the Russian border and just a short drive from the Baltic Sea. These men, high-ranking officials in Adolf Hitler's National Socialist government, had assembled in a heavily wooded compound called *Wolfsschanze*, the Wolf's Lair, to discuss military plans for victory on the Eastern Front. Among those scheduled to attend this meeting was Colonel Claus Schenk Graf von Stauffenberg, a Catholic, an aristocrat, a German nationalist, a decorated soldier, and Chief of Staff to General Friedrich Fromm, the head of the German Replacement Army. Stauffenberg was in attendance serving two roles: officially, he was there to participate in a military briefing; unofficially, he was there to kill Adolf Hitler.

Since the early 1940s, and after seeing German soldiers and police torture Russian citizens, Stauffenberg had been associated with the German Resistance movement, which was planning to overthrow the Nazi regime—codename Operation Valkyrie. Arriving late to the meeting, with a leather briefcase in hand, Stauffenberg took his seat at a table surrounded by some of the Fatherland's most senior military leaders. Shortly after noon, he excused himself to use the washroom. It was in fact an excuse to activate a detonator and place it in the bomb hidden away in his briefcase. Returning quickly to the meeting, he put the briefcase under the table and sat down. As planned, a few minutes later Stauffenberg received a phone call and once again asked to be excused. But this time he left his briefcase behind. Unbeknownst to him, an officer sitting next to him nudged the briefcase further under the thick wood table, propping it up against a table leg. Within minutes the bomb went off, destroying the conference room. Amidst the chaos, Stauffenberg managed to escape the compound and catch a planned flight back to Berlin. Upon his arrival in the German capital, he noticed that plans seemed to be unravelling—Hitler's forces were still in control. By early evening Stauffenberg heard the devastating news that Hitler had survived the bomb blast. The table leg ended up shielding Hitler from a direct hit and the lack of buttressed walls in the conference room dissipated the force of the explosion. Undeterred, Stauffenberg pressed for the coup d'état to go ahead as planned. To his way of thinking, if Germany were ever to negotiate a truce with Allied forces, Hitler and his brutal regime had to be removed. However, with Hitler still in control, Operation Valkyrie was doomed to failure. Shortly after dark, General Fromm had Stauffenberg arrested and held for an impromptu court marshalling, conducted solely by Fromm. Found guilty of treason against the German state, Stauffenberg was sentenced to death. Just after midnight on July 21, 1944, Stauffenberg, along with a number of his co-conspirators in the German Armed Forces, was executed in the courtyard outside the Bendlerblock, the large building that housed the German Armed Forces.

The case of Stauffenberg and the German Resistance movement provides us with a classic ethical problem: At what point do we move from recognizing unjust behaviours and social structures to undertaking practical actions that attempt to foster justice and promote the common good? For many thinkers, the line between "knowing what is" and "doing what we ought" can be quite fuzzy. Plato insisted that to know the good is to do the good. Yet St. Thomas Aquinas, following Aristotle, believed that we do what we ought primarily as a result of virtuous practice. For Thomas, we may know what we ought to do; but if we lack courage (or fortitude), our moral actions will fall short of their natural ends. In Stauffenberg's case, the ethical decision, that Hitler and his mad regime had to be resisted, flew in the face of political power; and it cost Stauffenberg his life.

Most of us will never find ourselves engaging in personal ethical reflection on matters that will change the course of history. Still, we face difficult moral problems and we strive to act in ways that are consistent with our morality, values, and character. The purpose of this chapter is to provide an interpretive framework that will enable us to engage in a process of "systematic reflection" and to act on the bases of ethically informed decisions.

The Two General Tasks of Ethics

Ethics consists of two general tasks: (1) the descriptive task of identifying integral elements associated with the moral problem we are addressing, and (2) the prescriptive task of determining what we ought to do.

The descriptive task of ethics is important because it provides an inventory of personal and collective behaviours. It uses the language of *is*. It asks, "What *is* the matter?" To perform this task well, we can appeal to the resources of the academy, particularly the works of historians, sociologists, economists, philosophers, legal theorists, and literary scholars, who take an active role in describing and critiquing the various textures of culture and society. When we turn to issues relating to bioethics or the environment, we call on the work of scientists to provide us with the necessary expertise to help us make informed ethical decisions. When we engage in the descriptive task of ethics, we are, to use one of Plato's analogies, diagnosing a body that is unwell. Like the doctor, those of us engaged in ethics must rely on solid diagnostic training and research to ensure that the illness and underlying causes are properly identified. Also like the doctor, we cannot just diagnose a problem—we are obligated to act. Once a critical mass of information has been gathered, we have to prescribe a practical course of action to treat the problem.

This prescriptive (or normative) task of ethics requires evaluation. It judges actions against moral norms and values, while at the same time asking whether those norms and values are adequate. The prescriptive task uses the language of *ought*. It prescribes a course of action based on our morality, values, and character. It raises often-uncomfortable questions about our firmly held convictions and the normal course of life. Consequently, individuals, communities, institutions, and societies can experience the prescriptive task of ethics as a disruptive act.

Consider this example. In North America, we believe that men and women are equal under the law and should not be disadvantaged because of our gender. However, in both Canada and the United States there exists a noticeable gender wage gap. Women typically earn less than men. According to OECD (Organisation for Economic Cooperation and Development) statistics from 2008, women earned roughly 79 cents for every dollar earned by men in Canada and the United States.[1] Is that a pay gap that indicates fairness? Are women unjustly suffering from systematic discrimination? How can we explain this discrepancy?

To answer these types of questions, we must first do the descriptive work of examining our social behaviours and our socio-economic structures. If we had the time and space here to review the research into the pay gap, we would find that the inequity *is* caused by many factors, including family responsibilities, loss of seniority, educational levels, career choices, less unionization among female workers, and, in an estimated 10 to 15 percent of cases, blatant discrimination. Prescriptively, what *ought* we to do?

Since the 1960s, women's rights groups have advocated for equal pay for comparable work. Unions have bargained for affirmative action measures in hiring processes. And governments have enacted laws that establish pay equity guidelines. Recently, a number of churches have addressed the pay gap in theological terms. For instance, in 2008 the Presbyterian Church (USA) published *God's Work in Women's Hands: Pay Equity and Just Compensation*.[2] It presents theological and ethical arguments that attempt to interpret historical teachings in light of the recognition that women, in particular, appear to be disadvantaged when it comes to compensation and promotion. Furthermore, it proposes steps to redress pay discrepancies. Among these proposals is the development of public policies that provide for generous financial support for stay-at-home mothers. It is worth noting that, even before the economic crisis in 2008, the United States joined Swaziland and Papua New Guinea as the only countries that clearly offered no federally funded paid parental leave program.[3] Nevertheless, many critics in the U.S. contend that such proposals, if enacted, would disrupt the U.S. economic system and be the first step onto a slippery slope toward big government and state socialism.

As this example helps demonstrate, when we move from the descriptive *is* to the prescriptive *ought*, we need to recognize that this movement is neither linear nor terminal. Or to put it another way, in the process of doing ethics we do not start at point A (the point where we first encountered a moral problem—say, the gender pay gap) and then move step by step through the process until we reach a solution or prescription, the terminal point Z (providing generous financial support to stay-at-home mothers). This conception of ethics can give us the false impression that, once we have prescribed an *ought*, the problem has been solved.

In the Catholic tradition, however, there is a history of moral reasoning that is linear-terminal. From roughly the sixteenth century to the middle of the twentieth century, Catholics answered moral questions with the use of manuals of moral theology. These manuals were used to train seminarians for their roles as confessors. Based primarily on the distilled teachings of Thomas Aquinas, and coupled with carefully selected cases to demonstrate the truthfulness of the teachings, these manuals were the Church's authoritative sources of moral behaviour until the Second Vatican Council (1962–1965). Given that the intended purpose of these manuals was to help seminarians provide clear instructions to penitents on how to avoid sinful behaviour, the movement from the *is* (sin) to the *ought* (moral behaviour) had a terminal quality. To avoid sin (immorality), the penitent needed to act according to the prescribed behaviour in the manuals. With no room to quibble about sin or to question the prescribed action, penitents could walk away from confession confident that they were meeting the minimal requirements to receive the sacraments. Moral behaviour was thus reduced to compliance with the manual's prescriptions.

Just prior to the Second Vatican Council, however, some Catholic theologians began to identify fundamental problems with the manualist approach to moral theology. First, it was an approach developed to address a pastoral concern, namely, the lack of educated clergy to act as judges in the sacrament of penance. Consequently, it was an approach that didn't invite intellectual dialogue or renewal. Second, because it established only the minimal requirements to live a moral Christian life, it didn't lead to discussions about the fullness of the moral life or the nature of the human being. Love was subordinated to legal commandments. Third, it adopted a moral theology that was separated from scripture. The Church's law (canon law) regarding who was eligible for the sacraments became the primary source of moral authority. Fourth, it narrowly defined morality in terms of individual actions relating to legal norms spelled out in canon law. There was no room to consider what it meant to lead a virtuous moral life apart from adhering to specific moral laws spelled out in the manuals. And fifth, the manualist approach lost a prior Aristotelian and Thomistic understanding of moral reasoning (ethics) as a process of discovery, that is, one that acknowledges ambiguity in the development of practical reason and the virtuous life.

Since the Second Vatican Council, many Catholic ethicists have joined a great number of Protestant ethicists in understanding the process of doing ethics as a constant movement between the *is* and the *ought*. Think of this process as a critical feedback loop. Once we have described what the moral issue *is*, and we have proposed (and perhaps enacted) an *ought*, we have created a new moral situation—a new *is*. The next task of ethics, then, is to evaluate this new *is*. Did our prescription adequately address the moral problem? What new problems were created? How did the prescription affect those most directly involved in the problem? Once a critical mass of descriptive work has been reached, we then move again to the prescriptive *ought*. And so the process of ethics continues.

Obviously, a number of moral problems have been settled in the Christians tradition and, for this reason, there is no ongoing need to question the foundational moral arguments that led to the settled *ought*. For example, Christians no longer consider the institution of slavery morally legitimate. It is unequivocally immoral. Susan Neiman, a philosopher and author of *Moral Clarity*, says that the "distinction between *is* and *ought* is the most important one we ever draw."[4] She's right. When we engage in ethics—systematic reflection on our morality, values, and character—we need facts. We need to be able to determine whether a claim is true, whether an outcome has had an adverse effect on human well-being. We need to examine the practical elements of our ethical reflection.

The perspective we're developing here is that the ethical being is one motivated by a sense of the good to reflect systematically on those consequences and to engage in the ethical process of moving back and forth between the *is* and the *ought*. At the heart of this process is this overriding question: What kind of moral character do we wish to develop as individuals, communities, institutions, and societies?

Let's now turn our attention toward developing an interpretive framework that will help us reflect on and inform our actions.

The Six Factors

The formation of our morality, values, and character is a complex process that entails both rational and non-rational aspects. Who we are today as ethical beings depends on a wide range of variables: the place of our birth, the communities and institutions that nurtured us, beliefs instilled in us as children, choices we've made and didn't make as adults, friendships we've forged and lost, intimate relationships, our emotional responses to perceived acts of justice and injustice, and we're just getting started. Identifying everything that has influenced us is simply impossible. Nevertheless, certain factors are foundational in the process of doing ethics. Generally, these concern (1) who we are as persons, (2) how we view the world around us, (3) what norms and values we hold, (4) what groups we're loyal to, (5) what experiences have significantly influenced our moral judgments, and (6) how we make ethical decisions.

Anthropology

In June 2006, a small group of U.S. religious leaders, which included the evangelical pastor Rick Warren, Nobel laureate Elie Wiesel, and Cardinal Theodore E. McCarrick of Washington, signed a provocative statement, "Torture Is a Moral Issue." They were responding to public reports about the U.S. government using torture techniques, including water boarding, on so-called enemy combatants and others held in detentions centres in Afghanistan, Iraq, and Guantanamo Bay. They demanded that the U.S. cease all torture practices. In words that allowed for little equivocation, they declared: "Torture violates the basic dignity of the human person that all religions hold dear. It degrades everyone involved—policy-makers, perpetrators and victims. It contradicts our nation's most cherished ideals. Any policies that permit torture and inhumane treatment are shocking and morally intolerable."[5] At the core of their argument is an appeal to a shared understanding of the human person. In more technical terms, they are making their argument based on a shared anthropology: humans have a basic dignity.

When ethicists use the term "anthropology," they are usually not referring to the academic discipline that studies human beings, their cultures, their languages, and their artifacts; rather, they are referring to a philosophical or a theological anthropology. In general, they are interested in abstract notions of what it means to be a human being. They ask those big existential questions: "Who am I? Why am I here? Where am I going?" Answers to these questions provide ethicists with insight into how we understand ourselves, our relationship to others, and our place in the world.

Consider how the different anthropologies in these questions might affect how we engage in ethics: Are we, as Buddhists and Hindus believe, beings caught up in a cycle of birth and rebirth (reincarnation), in which good actions will lead toward a better next life and take us one step closer to enlightenment (nirvana)? Are we, as Gandhi believed, born basically good but then corrupted by dehumanizing human social structures? Are we merely biological beings that exist in this present form for some 80 years, die, and then disintegrate into other forms of matter? Or are we beings created by God, part of a divine plan, and longing to spend eternity with our Creator? The questions and answers can be endless. Still, each offers a perspective on human nature, the human condition, human flourishing, and the purpose of human relationships.

Three of the most important modern political philosophers— Thomas Hobbes, Karl Marx, and Immanuel Kant—based their philosophies on strong anthropological foundations. In the seventeenth century the English philosopher Thomas Hobbes concluded in his book *Leviathan* that life is "nasty, brutish, and short." According to Hobbes, human beings are self-interested individuals who seek power and personal glory. If we're left to our own devices, we will inevitably destroy each other in a war of all against all. Hobbes's pessimistic understanding of human nature provides the basis for a hypothetical condition called the "state of nature." This state of nature was a state of lawlessness. With no legal authority to regulate human behaviour, our ancestors—the wild hordes—fought continuous battles against one another. With no common authority to resolve disputes, the "state of nature" could be nothing but a perpetual "state of war," with the highest level of conflict being a "war of all against all." And yet, we somehow survived. The question is how? To Hobbes's way of thinking, we survived because we freely gave all our power to a sovereign, the Leviathan, who has the authority to impose order on bloody madness and to prevent an all-out war. This is the basis of Hobbes's social contract theory—namely, to overcome our fear of death, we (implicitly) agreed to cede power to a powerful leader who can keep us from killing ourselves.

In sharp contrast to Hobbes's view that all human beings are essentially greedy thugs who have just enough rationality to hand power over to an absolute sovereign, Karl Marx claimed that human beings are, to a large extent, capable of making or shaping their own nature. Marx rejected the idea that we have an essential human nature that can be categorized in terms like "greedy," "selfish," "sinful," or even "virtuous." These are, Marx contends, external attributes imposed on individuals to socialize them into the dominant social and economic patterns. This imposition comes from two sources: powerful individuals in society who consciously invoke these categories to maintain class distinctions and divisions of labour, and the structure of society itself, which continually reaffirms a projected human nature by stressing the need for business managers to oversee an employee's work, authoritarian leaders to ensure compliance with the law, and clergy to help people overcome their spiritual and moral deficiencies. Marx was especially critical of ideologies that portrayed human beings as essentially selfish, greedy, sinful, and in need of divine salvation and a political overlord. He believed that such assertions were merely social constructions that reaffirmed a capitalist social structure. Moreover, he thought that by continually telling the poor masses (the proletariat) that they were, by nature, savages, and by instilling in them the idea that they were essentially damnable beings without God's love and mercy, the bourgeoisie (those who control the means of production) could exploit the labour of the poor without objection. In effect, in the capitalist system the poor functioned as cogs in the industrialist's machine. A reliable ally in this system of injustice was, Marx concluded, religion.

Marx famously declared: "Religion is the sigh of the oppressed creature, the heart of a heartless world, and the soul of soulless conditions. It is the opium of the people."[6] Religion, like opium, promises happiness, but in fact it only destroys human beings. To gain authentic freedom and happiness, Marx said, people should abandon the illusion of religion and the happiness it purports to offer. Marx's reasoning here is that once the masses reject the religiously inspired illusions about their condition (which is, they're worthless sinners without God) they will reject the socio-political condition that requires illusions (the condition being capitalism). In other words, if the masses want authentic freedom and happiness, individuals need to band together in solidarity to mount a social and political revolution against those persons and institutions that support capitalism.

In the waning days of the German Enlightenment (1720–1790), the philosopher Immanuel Kant argued that the defining feature of human beings is our rational autonomy, that is, our capacity to be "self-legislating" when it comes to determining just moral actions. We deny our human dignity, Kant believed, when we act solely on the basis of appetite and desire or when we allow others to determine for us how we ought to live. This ability to decide for ourselves how we ought to live is what identifies us as human subjects instead of objects. In his famous essay "What Is Enlightenment?" Kant wrote, "Enlightenment is man's release from his self-incurred tutelage. Tutelage is man's inability to make use of his understanding without direction from another. Self-incurred is this tutelage when its cause lies not in lack of reason but in lack of resolution and courage to use it without direction from another. *Sapere aude*! 'Have courage to use your own reason!' That is the motto of enlightenment."[7] Kant is more complicated than he may seem here because of his idea of the "categorical imperative," by which he asserts that all actions must be able to be undertaken by all members of the human species. It isn't just that the individuals can use reason to determine their own course; it is that this reason must be universalizable, checked against the entire species. We will develop this more fully in the next chapter.

Of course, human dignity and freedom are not just topics for modern philosophers such as Kant. Christian theologians also speak of human dignity and freedom as integral to the human person. However, modern philosophers and Christian theologians do not always agree on what those terms mean. In the Christian tradition, human dignity commonly refers to the anthropological claim that every human person has been created in the likeness of God. The basis for this claim is Genesis 1:26-27:

> Then God said, "Let us make humankind in our image, according to our likeness; and let them have dominion over the fish of the sea, and over the birds of the air, and over the cattle, and over all the wild animals of the earth, and over every creeping thing that creeps upon the earth." So God created humankind in his image, in the image of God he created them; male and female he created them.

Theologians have long puzzled over the meaning of the "image of God" (*imago Dei*). The trickiness lies in the fact that, in the Christian tradition, God is not a corporeal being, except for that brief period of time in which Jesus lives on earth as a man. God is essentially spirit.

So if the *imago Dei* doesn't refer to the likeness of a material body, then what possible interpretations are there? In general, theologians have developed three lines of interpretation. First, the *imago Dei* means that human beings fulfill a functional role like the one that God plays. Just as God has dominion over us, human beings have dominion over animals. Second, the *imago Dei* refers to our ability to establish and maintain complex relationships that make us like God. The primary example is the relationship between the man and the woman. Together, they're intended to forge spiritual as well as physical unions (Genesis 5:1-2). And third, the *imago Dei* means that human beings have been created with a substantial characteristic of God. Given the premise that God has no body, any substantial likeness has to be in the composition of the human person's non-physical attributes. For this reason, some theologians maintain that there is an essential spiritual commonality with God, one that directly relates us to God. Another possibility is that *imago Dei* refers to our ability to exercise free will and reason.

Broadly speaking, theologians will typically emphasize one of these three interpretations, but may adopt aspects of each in developing their theological anthropology. The *Catechism of the Catholic Church*, for example, tends to emphasize the substantive aspects of the *imago Dei*, but with elements of the relational interpretation:

> Being in the image of God the human individual possesses the dignity of a person, who is not just something, but someone. He is capable of self-knowledge, of self-possession and of freely giving himself and entering into communion with other persons. And he is called by grace to a covenant with his Creator, to offer him a response of faith and love that no other creature can give in his stead.[8]

In other words, because God has created human beings in God's own likeness, each person has the freedom and the capacity to enter into relationships with others. The moral principle underlying this anthropology is that we have an obligation to love others as we love God since each human person is an expression of God. We are to preserve the human dignity of the other by acting in ways that promote human flourishing and foster community. Or at least that is what we ought to do.

In the Christian tradition, there is an anthropological argument that provides the reasons for why we often fail to live up to the *ought* implied in the *imago Dei*. It is called "sin." According to a traditional, Augustinian interpretation of "the Fall," found in Genesis 3, these punishments all point to ruptured relationships. We human beings are now out of harmony with nature. We have an estranged relationship with God. And we are alienated from ourselves, leading to anxiety, conflict with others, and even murder (Genesis 4). So not only have we inherited the punishment meted out by God for the original man and woman's transgressions, but we have also inherited a nature that is tainted with sin. We are, in short, born with an element of sin in our nature. And it is only through the sacrifice of Christ's death that God and humans are reconciled. The Eastern Christian tradition, however, holds that Jesus's death and resurrection effectively restored the original goodness of creation.

One of the major theological debates in the Christian tradition concerns the extent to which the "original sin" of the man and the woman has affected the *imago Dei*. Have human beings actually lost every shred of God's likeness (often called "total depravity"), including the freedom to choose and the ability to rely on reason—and is it only with Christ's death and resurrection that God's likeness appears in the human person? Or has the element of sin only clouded the likeness of God in human beings, which has remained essentially unchanged? Indeed, Catholic, Orthodox, and Protestant theologians have historically argued about the degree to which humanity can "reason" effectively without the grace of God.

If we were to sum up a Catholic anthropology, it would go something like this: God has created human beings in the image of God. This *imago Dei* remains in all human beings—Christians and non-Christians—at all times, and regardless of their actions. For this reason, human beings retain dignity even when their actions are destructive to the human community and to themselves. In this sense, human beings are equal—each has an unassailable dignity, regardless of whether they are feeding the poor in the streets of São Paulo, Brazil, or sitting on death row in the Louisiana State Penitentiary. Moreover, God has given us human beings the freedom to make ethical decisions, without coercion or force. Or as the Vatican II document *Gaudium et spes* (Pastoral Constitution on the Church in the Modern World, 1965) put it:

> Human dignity demands that each person act according to a knowing and free choice that is personally motivated and prompted from within, not under blind internal impulse nor by mere external pressure. Since humanity's freedom has been damaged by sin, only by the aid of God's grace can one bring such a relationship with God into full flower. Before the judgment seat of God each individual must render an account of one's own life, whether one has done good or evil. (GS, no. 17)

From a Catholic perspective, then, our understanding of the human person is integrally linked to our moral actions. As bearers of God's image, we possess a dignity that enables us to make ethical decisions that contribute to human flourishing and the fostering of human community.

Worldview

Think of a worldview as an interpretive lens. Each of us, over time, acquires a particular way of looking at reality. It is as though we've been equipped with a set of glasses that defines the world around us. Switch those glasses, and all of sudden the world can look quite different. We see things we've never seen before. Like the first time we put on a pair of 3-D glasses and watched a movie in an IMAX theatre, a shift in worldview can be dizzying as our minds try to comprehend apparently new realities. Our entire outlook on life and our relation to the world around us can change. In the midst of a worldview change, individuals can become anxious, fearful of new experiences, and uncertain of the future. What we thought made sense no longer does. When a society experiences a worldview change, there can be social panic, calls for a return to the old way, and social revolutions.

Today, we speak of many different worldviews. For example, we sometimes hear people say they have a Christian worldview, which usually means that they believe in God, believe the Bible is a source of truth and moral authority, and associate with a particular Christian denomination. More broadly, we sometimes hear of people laying claims to Eastern, Buddhist, Hindu, Arab, Islamic, African, and Indigenous worldviews. Since the advent of modern science and medicine, we also hear people talk about scientific and medical worldviews. In the nineteenth century, the West moved from a pre-modern to a modern worldview, which included a new anthropology, social order, and economic system. Also, we might encounter moral claims made by people who proclaim that they're operating out of a feminist, Black, post-colonial, or marginalized people's worldview. The important point here is that, by identifying with a particular worldview, we are claiming that perspective matters to moral reasoning.

Many of us, though, don't think about our worldviews. The frameworks we use to interpret the world around us are often hidden from us. We likely assume that our view of reality is universal—everyone experiences life as we do. But of course, this isn't the case. Mang Juan, a Filipino peasant, tried to explain these differences a number of years ago. "You must realize that we live in two different worlds," Juan said. "It is as if you live in the world of the birds of the air, and we in that of the fishes of the sea." The birds flying above the ocean have a vastly different view than the fishes swimming in the ocean. While both the birds and the fishes might be looking at the same ocean, if they could talk, they would undoubtedly tell quite different stories about what they're seeing and what the ocean means to them. Birds fly fast and high, fish swim slow and deep. But it sometimes happens, Juan said, that "some birds want to do good for us from the height in which they fly. Condescendingly, they say, 'Mr. Fish, progress! Move like I do—this way and that way—so you could come faster!'" But, Juan concluded, "fish of course cannot follow because we have to move in this ocean of usury, and tenancy and other unjust relations."[9]

So what's my point? In the process of doing ethics, it is important to recognize our worldview and the worldviews of those with whom we are in conversation. If we fail to account for our different worldviews, we will likely not only misdiagnose the moral problem before us, but we will also likely engage in ethical actions that are unhelpful, unwarranted, and perhaps unjust. When we scrutinize our own worldviews, we are asking fundamental questions about our anthropological assumptions and the kind of people we hope to be. This requires the critical reflection between the *is* and the *ought*. When we engage others in ethical discourse, one of our guiding principles is mutual respect. In that way, ethicists seek to learn from one another, to gain enhanced perspectives on the world. This conclusion might be unsettling to a few people in the Christian tradition. But as the Catholic ethicist Gregory Baum argues in his book *Amazing Church*, for the past 50 years the Catholic Church has been embarked on a renewal process that has enabled it to respond to the demands of the modern world. This renewal process is not a slide toward moral relativism, as some critics claim, but an evolution of its official positions on theological and ethical issues. It is a period in the history of the Church marked "by a new ethical horizon," namely, a Church "willing to reread its Scriptures and traditional teaching to respond critically and creatively to the new historical situation."[10]

Norms and Values

In the previous chapter, we defined "values" as the moral goods we seek to foster both individually and collectively. These values might include freedom, democracy, trust, transparency, compassion, hope, human dignity, responsibility, forgiveness, reconciliation, social justice, peace, love, solidarity, and cooperation. Norms are the standards or rules by which we judge our moral actions. In contrast to the way social scientists sometimes use the term, ethicists usually do not think of "norms" as normal patterns of behaviour. For instance, they're not looking to derive moral norms from consumer buying patterns, the way men and women interact with each other in the workplace, or the choices we make in eating organic food. In these cases, the term "norms" points to prior actions and are indicators of moral habits. Instead, ethicists tend to use the term "norms" to refer to the benchmarks that guide future actions and serve as evaluative standards for past actions.

Loyalties

When ethicists speak of loyalties, they are referring to individuals and groups of people with whom we wish to identify. These people help us develop our character. They typically share our anthropological assumptions, our worldview, and our norms and values. They are the individuals, communities, institutions, and societies we look to for moral guidance. They are the ones who affirm our *oughts*. And it is in relationships with these people that we primarily develop the emotional aspects of our morality, including love, friendship, affection, faithfulness, admiration, and respect. Many of us don't even realize how many groups we belong to because we move seamlessly between them. However, there are times when our loyalty groups collide and we're faced with having to decide which group takes priority. To help us work through those times, we have likely developed a hierarchy of loyalties, perhaps starting with our families and followed by our church communities, employers, friends, and so on. For many of us, this hierarchy of loyalties is not something we developed consciously, in advance of any conflict between our loyalty groups. Instead, it likely emerged out of necessity.

Consider again the case of Colonel Claus von Stauffenberg, a man who found himself trying to come to terms with which loyalties should prevail in his ethical decision-making. Should he remain loyal to Adolf Hitler, to whom he pledged an oath to serve? As Stauffenberg's biographer has noted, Stauffenberg believed that oaths are, in principle, sacred.[11] Should he remain loyal to a Prussian military tradition that placed the utmost importance on honour, discipline, order, and following the chain of command? Should he remain loyal to his family? If the assassination attempt failed, he would not only be unable to provide for them, but he would also be placing them at risk of retribution by forces loyal to Hitler. Should he be loyal to Germany, whose citizens might well consider his actions traitorous? Or should he be loyal to a group of conspirators who shared the conviction that Hitler's Germany was inhumane, self-destructive, and ultimately a force for evil in the world? Stauffenberg, like many other Christians living under Hitler's Nazi regime—including notable figures such as the Catholic pacifist Franz Jägerstätter and the Lutheran pastor Dietrich Bonhoeffer—would end up dead because they denied any loyalty to National Socialism.

You might be wondering if it is possible to be "loyal to God." The easy answer would be "Yes." But the answer is more complex than this. To begin, what does the phrase "loyalty to a church" mean? Adherence to a doctrine or to our preferred interpretation of scripture? Or perhaps obedience to God? Let's consider the classic case of Abraham being obedient to God's command to sacrifice his son Isaac. Now put this story in today's context. If a man were to tell me that he had been instructed by God to sacrifice his son, in the same way Abraham had been instructed by God, I would not hesitate to stop this man, call the authorities, and do everything in my power to prevent a murder. Why would I do this? Quite simply, there is no moral justification for murdering a child (or any other human being, for that matter). It is an act that fundamentally denies a person their human dignity and their right to life. No Christian today could morally justify their actions on the basis of "obedience to God," simply because we understand that the God of justice would not command an unjust act. But if we're going to use the phrase "loyal to God" in ethics, I believe we must agree on at least two cautionary principles. First, in making the claim that we're "loyal to God," we must ensure that our loyalty to God extends beyond mere subjective whim. In other words, we should want others to question our loyalty to God and all actions that proceed from that loyalty. Second, we must ensure that actions undertaken in the name of "loyalty to God" are the result of systematic reflection on morality, values, and character, and not simply a way to avoid ethical debates by claiming God's authority.

As ethical beings, we need to critically examine all of our loyalties and subordinate them to the demands of human dignity, love, and justice. Because of our emotional attachments to our loyalties, we can become blind to their influences. Without ethical reflection, we can easily become entrenched in our loyalties and blind to potential injustices. We can easily absolutize their claims on us. When this happens, we end up with brazenly cavalier statements such as "America, right or wrong," "What's good for General Motors is good for the country," and "What's good for Wall Street is good for Main Street." We find ourselves either unwilling or unable to see the darker side of our group's actions. Ethical reflection on our loyalties thus requires us to gain a measure of critical distance, some independence, so we can see how our loyalties are affecting our moral actions. For instance, if our loyalties are primarily to wealthy individuals and groups committed to small government, unregulated markets, and the accumulation of capital, it will likely be difficult to support public policies advocated by those who work in community development and with the poor. As one of my ethics professors once said to me, "If possible, Scott, you should choose your loyalties according to the type of person you want to be."

Prejudices

When we hear the term "prejudice," we normally associate it with something morally bad. This term has become synonymous with bigotry, intolerance, injustice, and racism. However, this is only one meaning of "prejudice." The German philosopher Hans-Georg Gadamer talked about prejudices as "fore-structures" of understanding.[12] Basically, what Gadamer means is this: When we encounter new ideas and things around us, we typically do not try to understand these new ideas and things from scratch. Instead, we appeal to structures of understanding that we have at our disposal. We engage in a process of interpretation, a kind of back-and-forth between what we already know (prejudged knowledge) and what we're encountering. The process of interpreting and understanding is a little bit like putting together a difficult puzzle. We usually start by finding the corner pieces and then the long edges—we start here because we recognize the basic outline of the problem before us. Once those defining pieces are together, we search for pieces that have similar colours or seem to be the basis for an object in the puzzle. Getting the full, coherent picture to come together then becomes a process of trial and error. Similarly for Gadamer, then, all interpretation is necessarily prejudgmental because our attempt to interpret phenomena always orients matters to our present concerns and interests. In other words, our understanding of ideas and things depends on prejudgments about how we might possibly use the knowledge and why it could be important to us. Knowledge, therefore, is not just a matter of clarification and explanation, but also a matter of practical *application*—or, as Aristotle and Thomas Aquinas called it, "practical wisdom." It is knowledge rooted in a particular context. It is also knowledge situated within our larger worldview.

In making a case for a positive understanding of prejudices in ethics, we must remember that some prejudices can lead to injustice and stifle human flourishing. For this reason, we need to make sure we regularly find the critical distance necessary to evaluate our prejudices. In basic terms, we need to ask ourselves: What do we take for granted in our moral actions? Do we assume that everyone is like us, sees the world as we do, and has the same social and economic standing as we do? Do we prejudge the morality, values, and character of strangers as static and fixed in the human person, which effectively denies the possibility that our prejudgments might fail to hold up under ethical scrutiny? These kinds of questions are important since, without their critical perspective, our prejudgments can distort interpretations and contribute to poor ethical decision-making.

Approaches to Ethical Decision-Making

In the Western intellectual tradition, there are three general approaches to ethical decision-making: (1) deontological, (2) teleological, and (3) virtue ethics approaches. We will discuss each of these in greater detail in the next chapter. But for now, let's briefly highlight their primary features.

Derived from the Greek words *deon* (which means "duty," "rule," or "law") and *logos* (which means "study" or "science"), *deontological* approaches to ethics are based on the premise that moral behaviour entails following a set of rules or laws. These laws may be codified religious laws, such as Jewish law or the Ten Commandments, or they may be universal moral rules, such as the famous Golden Rule, "Do unto others as you would have them do unto you." Strict deontologists are not concerned with the consequences of following the law. It may well be that following a law or a rule may result in some pain for the individual or a group of people; and in some cases it might create far more happiness for the individual or a group if a law or rule were disobeyed. However, our obligation to obey the law and follow moral rules takes priority over consequences. In a word, the strict deontologist believes that the law determines right moral action.

Derived from the Greek word *telos* (meaning "end" or "goal"), *teleological* approaches posit some end as a good to be achieved in an action. With that good as our goal, we can know that actions are right insofar as they move us closer to achieving that good. Conversely, we can know that actions are wrong if they move us away from that good. In teleological ethics, then, the good (that is, the desired end) determines the "rightness" of an action. A teleological approach focuses on the end or purpose of an action. Sometimes called "utilitarian ethics" or "consequentialist ethics," the teleological approach defines an end, a consequence, or a "good" that our actions ought to realize. Following this approach, we can judge actions to be "right" if they achieve the desired outcome. The aphorism "the ends justify the means" is one popular expression of a teleological approach to ethics.

In comparison to deontological and teleological approaches to ethics, which are often portrayed in introductions to ethics as discrete ethical systems (which they're really not), *virtue ethics* is less concerned with the decision-making process than with the development of an actor's moral character. While it tends to be teleological in orientation, virtue ethics ultimately holds that immediate ends and duties are secondary concerns. The primary concern for virtue ethics is the place of the moral actor, or moral agent, within a community and that community's story. Rooted in the work of Aristotle and Thomas Aquinas, virtue ethicists think that our moral actions are developed in relation to our community's values. Moreover, we understand ourselves in relation to a narrative that inspires us to act in unity with those values. Alasdair MacIntyre, in his book *After Virtue*, describes virtue ethics as a narrative quest on the part of moral agents to determine what path will make the best sense for their lives. MacIntyre writes, "I can only answer the question 'What am I to do?' if I can answer the prior question 'Of what story or stories do I find myself a part?'"[13] In virtue ethics, then, ethical decision-making is more about interpreting our community's values and our life stories than about achieving some well-defined end or acting in compliance with a law. Or to put it another way, the guiding question of virtue ethics is not "What should I do?" but instead "Who should I become?"

The approach to decision-making emphasized in following chapters will most closely resemble virtue ethics. As we will see in more detail in the next chapter, I think virtue ethics enables us to maintain certain universal principles while at the same time recognizing that much of our moral action is conditioned by social convention and history. By emphasizing a virtue ethics approach, I am not suggesting we avoid discussions of each and every individual action. Indeed, as I stated earlier in this chapter, I agree with Susan Neiman that the distinction between the *is* and the *ought* is one of the more important that we make as ethical beings. Relying primarily on virtue ethics, I want to situate our decision-making in our moral communities and in our stories. At the same time, I would like us to consider how communities of character can inform our ethical decisions. In short, this is an invitation to contemplate what kind of beings we hope to become and what kind of communities, institutions, and societies we should foster to help us in our quest to live a life of ethical being.

CHAPTER 3

The Sources of Christian Ethics

On the evening of September 12, 1960, then-Democratic presidential nominee John F. Kennedy entered the ballroom at Rice Hotel in Houston, Texas, to deliver the most important speech yet in his political career. He was there to address the Greater Houston Ministerial Association as well as the many who would hear his speech on the radio and see it on television. Kennedy's goal was to allay the fears of many Protestant Christians who believed that a Catholic president would be beholden to the Vatican and would attempt to impose Catholic doctrine on public policy.

With a presidential election hanging in the balance, Senator Kennedy opened his speech by identifying what he considered to be the real issues of the campaign: the spread of Communism, the loss of respect for the presidency, hunger, poverty, inadequate housing, education, and space exploration. "These are the real issues," Kennedy said, "which should decide this campaign. And they are not religious issues—for war and hunger and ignorance and despair know no religious barriers. But because I am a Catholic, and no Catholic has ever been elected president, the real issues in this campaign have been obscured—perhaps deliberately, in some quarters less responsible than this. So it is apparently necessary for me to state once again not what kind of church I believe in—for that should be important only to me—but what kind of America I believe in." Referencing the pastoral letter from the U.S. Catholic Bishops entitled *The Christian in Action*, published in 1948,[1] Kennedy stated three beliefs. First, he said he believed "in an America where the separation of church and state is absolute—where no Catholic prelate would tell the President (should he be Catholic) how to act, and no Protestant minister would tell his parishioners for whom to vote—where no church or church school is granted any public funds or political preference—and where no man is denied public office merely because his religion differs from the President who might appoint him or the people who might elect him." Second, he believed in a secular state; that is, a state with no official religion and "where no public official either requests or accepts instructions on public policy from the Pope, the National Council of Churches or any other ecclesiastical source—where no religious body seeks to impose its will directly or indirectly upon the general populace or the public acts of its officials—and where religious liberty is so indivisible that an act against one church is treated as an act against all." And third, Kennedy professed a belief in an America that practised religious tolerance, which didn't discriminate between Catholics and anti-Catholics, and didn't splinter off into religiously identified voting blocs.

On the key issue of decision-making, Kennedy said, "Whatever issue may come before me as president—on birth control, divorce, censorship, gambling, or any other subject—I will make my decision in accordance with these views, in accordance with what my conscience tells me to be the national interest, and without regard to outside religious pressures or dictates. And no power or threat of punishment could cause me to decide otherwise."[2]

As a political response, Kennedy's assurance that he would not be controlled by Rome or by any bishop was an attempt to sway the large number of moderate mainline Christians (Lutherans, Presbyterians, Methodists, and Episcopalians) to vote for a Catholic. In the end, it worked. He was elected in one of the closest presidential races in U.S. history. As an ethical response, however, Kennedy's appeal to conscience as his basis for decision-making raised far more questions than it answered. How would he apply conscience to issues of national interest? Should all religious moral reasoning be excluded in his decision-making?

Should government be neutral on issues relating to morality? Following a general cultural trend that was beginning to appear in the late 1950s and early 1960s, Kennedy (and Nixon, we should note) thought religious morality should not be brought to bear on political matters.

At the core of Kennedy's "Catholic problem" is this question: What sources guide moral reasoning? Or to put it another way, what sources provide authoritative guidelines when we find ourselves having to make morally relevant decisions? Kennedy's critics believed the Catholic Church would dictate decisions on moral matters such as abortion, divorce, gambling, the public funding of parochial schools, and the use of force. To his critics, the Church hierarchy (or, more precisely, the Magisterium) was the sole source of moral authority.

Since the Second Vatican Council (1962–1965), Catholic ethicists generally appeal to four primary sources: scripture, tradition, reason, and experience. We sometimes think of these four sources as elements in a "hermeneutical circle."[3] The term "hermeneutical" comes from the Greek word *Hermes*, the figure in Greek mythology who was the messenger of the gods. The term "hermeneutics" has long been used in biblical scholarship to mean the art and science of interpreting sacred scripture. Philosophers use the term more generally—for them, it's the way in which we understand, interpret, and communicate meaning. For Christian ethicists, the term "hermeneutical circle" refers to the ways we understand things (by "things," think of the six factors in doing ethics, described in the previous chapter), interpret and prioritize them, and engage in ethically informed action. Or to put this matter in the form of a question, how does our reading of scripture, the Church's traditional teachings, the use of reason, and our experience provide guidance for our lives? This question is the focus of this chapter.

Scripture

On the whole, Christians believe that the Bible has, or should have, an integral role in the formation of our morality, values, and character. Historically, ethicists in the Protestant tradition have tended to be far more insistent on the centrality of the Bible than Catholic ethicists. This is due in large part to the Reformation principle of *sola scriptura*, "by scripture alone." Following Martin Luther (1483–1546) and other

Reformers, Protestants believe that the Bible is the only source of divinely revealed knowledge. For that reason, in the Protestant tradition the Bible is the foundation for all doctrine and moral action. All doctrine and moral action must be subordinate to biblical teachings.

In the Catholic moral tradition, however, the use of scripture has not always been a priority. Before the Second Vatican Council, Catholic moral theology was based primarily on a narrow reading of the natural law tradition, which we will address later in this chapter. Because the natural law derives principles from nature and reason, theologians treated scripture mainly as a repository of proof texts that could be accessed when needed to add weight to a position arrived at through other means. This approach to scripture had its clearest expression in the moral manual tradition, which was predominant in the Church from the sixteenth to the middle of the twentieth century. As we noted in the previous chapter, these manuals were drafted to help clergy determine whether a person was legally authorized to partake in the sacraments. Their moral basis was not scripture but the seven deadly sins (pride, greed, lust, anger, gluttony, envy, and sloth).

Just prior to Vatican II, theologians such as Fritz Tillman, Josef Fuchs, and Bernard Häring had begun to argue that the manual tradition should be jettisoned in order to rediscover a Christian ethical tradition that drew broadly from the other sources of moral knowledge. These theologians called for a re-examination of the teachings of Thomas Aquinas and a re-engagement with scripture. In scripture, they argued, we find that human beings have a relationship with the divine. In the New Testament, this relationship takes shape in the incarnation of Christ and in the Christian community, not in following a law or responding to a set of theological dictates. The bishops at the Second Vatican Council largely agreed with this renewed emphasis on scripture. The conciliar document *Optatam totius* (Decree on Priestly Training, 1965) declared: "Special care must be given to the perfecting of moral theology. Its scientific exposition, nourished more on the teaching of the Bible, should shed light on the loftiness of the calling of the faithful in Christ and the obligation that is theirs of bearing fruit in charity for the life of the world" (OT, no. 16). The Vatican II document *Dei verbum* (Dogmatic Constitution of Divine Revelation, 1965) went beyond calling for scriptural emphasis. It provided an introduction to how to understand the Old and New Testaments, how to discover God's revelation in both, how to interpret scripture, and how to use scripture to bring life to the Church.

The Four Tasks of Scriptural Engagement

To help guide Catholic ethicists as they seek to integrate ethics and scripture, the Franciscan moral theologian Kenneth Himes has highlighted four tasks of scriptural engagement: exegetical, hermeneutical, methodological, and theological.[4]

The *exegetical* task entails a study of a text to determine what the author likely intended to communicate and what the original audience likely understood. Because many ethicists are not trained in biblical studies, they must rely on the work of biblical scholars. Himes notes that, while ethicists tend to be more interested in the *now* than in the *then*, the exegetical task remains important because it requires ethicists to pay attention to a text's history through source, redaction, and historical criticism. This in turn helps deter ethicists from appropriating scripture as nothing more than rhetorical support.

The second task is *hermeneutics*. The aim of hermeneutics is not to focus solely on what the text meant to an author or an audience but to ask what the text means for us. For example, how should we interpret Paul's injunction for women to cover their heads (1 Corinthians 11:4-14)? Is it a universal instruction requiring all Christian women to wear veils at all times? Is it a universal requirement for women to veil their heads in a Christian church? Or is Paul merely instructing the Corinthian church to abide by local custom? The majority of Christian churches have decided that Paul's instruction regarding veiling was, in spite of his appeal to nature, a culturally specific custom and therefore not required of Christian women beyond Corinth.

The *methodological* task is next. The methods we use to interpret the Bible are never purely objective; they contain presuppositions about what it means to be human (anthropology), how we view reality (worldview), what moral standards and goods we should embrace (norms and values), what groups of people we identify with (loyalties), what kinds of experiences have gone into our initial judgments (prejudices), and how we make ethical decisions (mode of decision-making). Himes suggests that one way in which ethicists can utilize scripture is to see it as "informing but not determining our particular judgments," illuminating but not prescribing specific actions. We can and should learn from the *then* meaning of a text to help us live better *now*. Himes writes, "The Bible helps us to know a God who acts in history and thus informs moral reflection by supplying a framework that allows the individual to recognize divine action." As a general principle, we should look for this framework in the entirety of scripture, not in a specific book. Moreover, we should consider predominant biblical themes in our attempt to relate ethics and scripture: divine creation; human sin; justice; the life, death, and resurrection of Jesus; love; preferential option for the poor; and the reign of God to name just a few.

The fourth task is *theological*. For Himes, this means embedding our engagement with scripture in the wider church community. As a Catholic theologian, Himes understands scripture as one source of authority, but not the sole source of authority. He writes, "To say that the Bible is authoritative is, of course, not the same as understanding its function in an authoritarian manner. To acknowledge the scriptures as authoritative does not mean that we are coerced into accepting certain beliefs; rather it is only to say that the believer views the Bible as an essential guide for faithful discipleship." First and foremost, the Bible provides the church community with stories of God's interaction with the people of faith. Through those stories, we have guidelines for the development of a community of character.

Dangers to Be Avoided in Our Appeal to Scripture

In our appeal to scripture as a source for ethics, we must avoid a few dangers. First, there is the danger of *biblical literalism*. The literalist approach to scripture requires interpreters to believe that the Bible is inerrant in every respect. For instance, a literalist approach holds that there were six 24-hour days of creation. Adam and Eve were the first two human beings. And there is a place somewhere on earth that was once the Garden of Eden and inhabited by Adam and Eve. Biblical literalism began to emerge in the late nineteenth century as a response to modern theology, which had begun to adopt aspects of post-Enlightenment philosophy and sociology. The danger with literalism, though, is that the literalist's object of faith is actually an interpretation of the Bible and not God. Moreover, when a supposed "literal fact" in the Bible turns out to be false—for instance, life has been on earth far longer than the account in Genesis—there is an immediate crisis of faith for the literalist, since the scriptural error of "literal fact" would effectively mean that God is fallible.

The Catholic tradition, by contrast, holds that scripture comes to us in two different senses: the literal and the spiritual. The literal sense is the explicit meaning of scripture, which is discovered by exegesis following the rules of sound interpretation. The spiritual sense of scripture speaks to the unity of God's plan not only in the text, but also in the realities and events about which the text speaks through spiritual signs. The spiritual sense is communicated in three additional senses. The allegorical sense of scripture provides "a more profound understanding of events by recognizing their significance in Christ." For example, the Israelites crossing the Red Sea (Exodus 13:17–14:29) is a sign or type of Christ's victory and also of Christian baptism. The moral sense calls for us to read scripture in light of the universal obligation to engage in just moral action. And in the anagogical sense, from the Greek word *anagoge*, meaning "leading," we read scripture for its eternal significance. For instance, the Church on earth is a sign of the heavenly Jerusalem, the faithful's true and eventual homeland.

Another danger is *proof texting*. This happens when we look for passages in the Bible that support a predetermined position on doctrine or moral action. For instance, one classic case of proof texting is the story of Onan "spilling his seed" (Genesis 38:6-10). As we will discuss in more detail in chapter four, this story has been used in the Christian tradition to prohibit male masturbation. But biblical scholars today recognize that the "sin of Onan" had nothing to do with masturbation—the issue was a violation of tribal custom, which obligated Onan to marry and impregnate his brother's widow. To overcome any inclination toward proof texting, readers of scripture must place passages in context and recognize that sometimes other passages can challenge evidently clear passages. As one of my former professors liked to remind his students, "A text without a context is a pretext for a proof text." Ultimately, proof texting can undermine good reasons for holding a particular doctrine or advocating certain moral actions.

"*Hippy-dippy-bumper-sticker morality*" is one of the most common dangers we ethicists face, and it should be avoided. In a word, hippy-dippy-bumper-sticker morality is a tendency for some Christians to reduce the moral attributes of God, Jesus, the Bible, and the Christian ethical tradition to shallow slogans. You've likely seen these stickers. They declare: "God is love." "You've got a friend in Jesus." And "Jesus is the missing peace." I've often heard people say, "Jesus preached unconditional love" and "Jesus would never condone violence." But of course, nowhere in scripture does Jesus preach unconditional love. Instead, we actually find Jesus putting conditions on love: "If you wish to be perfect, go, sell your possessions, and give the money to the poor, and you will have treasure in heaven; then come, follow me" (Matthew 19:21). Nor do we find Jesus preaching a gospel of absolute pacifism: "Do you think that I have come to establish peace on the earth? No, I tell you, but rather division!" (Luke 12:51). The danger is that amidst the feel-good bumper-sticker morality, we miss the radical first-century Jewish prophet who challenged religious authorities, disrupted the political status quo, spoke harshly against the wealthy, and befriended the outcast. Without a scriptural understanding of Jesus, the cost of discipleship, and the prophetic demands for social justice, the message of Christianity can too easily become a therapeutic gospel of personal self-fulfillment.

Tradition

Tradition is a vital part of a living faith community. While scripture was written at a particular point in time and for a particular audience, tradition is what keeps the narrative in scripture alive and meaningful to believers. Tradition is the retelling, reliving, and reinterpreting of those stories for believers. When Christian ethicists look to tradition as a source of authority, we find ourselves entering into a historical conversation with the universal Church, both past and present.

Take the use of nuclear weapons as an example. Scripture says nothing about nuclear weapons. Yet the Catholic Church rejects nuclear weapons. As we will read in more detail in chapter seven, Pope John XXIII declared, "Nuclear weapons must be banned" (*Pacem in terris*, Peace on Earth, 1963, no. 112). The Church bases its rejection not primarily on scripture, but on an appeal to medieval thinkers who pondered the possibility of a just war. For these medieval thinkers, the use of the longbow and crossbow in war were unjustified because they violated principles of proportionality (they dramatically increased the number of casualities) and discrimination (their range and crude aiming mechanisms meant that discriminating between civilians and soldiers was virtually impossible). In response to the use of nuclear weapons, the Church has made the same argument: nuclear weapons violate principles of proportionality and discrimination. In effect, our appeal to tradition means that we do not have to tackle contemporary problems in isolation; rather, we can learn from the ways Christians thought about and acted on similar moral challenges in their day. In this way, tradition is continually evolving, living, and learning. It is responding to the signs of the times and the movement of the Holy Spirit.

"Tradition"—the Magisterium and Theologians

Many contemporary Catholic ethicists make a distinction between the two senses of tradition as an authority for ethical reflection. The first sense is Tradition with a capital "T," and it is the process or means of handing on the teachings of the Church. The second sense is tradition with a lowercase "t." This second sense of tradition is the content, that is, the specific teachings that have been handed down over time. Let's briefly examine both senses.

For many Catholics, this sense of Tradition refers primarily to the teaching authority of the Catholic Church, commonly called "the Magisterium" (from the Latin *magister*, meaning "teacher" or "master"). The Magisterium consists of bishops, archbishops, and the pope, who is himself the bishop of Rome and who exercises authority over the other bishops. Vatican II affirmed both the role of the Magisterium and its hierarchical authority in two of its documents. In its document *Lumen gentium* (Dogmatic Constitution the Church, 1964), the Council refers to the bishops as the Church's "authentic teachers, that is, teachers endowed with the authority of Christ" (LG, no. 25). In *Dei verbum* (Dogmatic Constitution on Divine Revelation, 1965), the Council declares that "the task of authentically interpreting the word of God, whether written or handed on, has been entrusted exclusively to the living teaching office of the Church, whose authority is exercised in the name of Jesus Christ" (DV, no. 10).[5]

As the authoritative teaching body of the Church, the Magisterium performs its teaching role in two ways: one that is "extraordinary" (or "solemn") and one that is "ordinary." An extraordinary exercise of teaching authority happens when a doctrine is specifically defined either (a) by the bishops gathered by and with the pope in an ecumenical council—such as the Council of Trent, the First Vatican Council, or the Second Vatican Council—and in unison on a particular teaching, or (b) by a pope speaking *ex cathedra*, that is, "from the chair," which means the pope is exercising his formal teaching authority in a special way. When the Magisterium or the pope exercises extraordinary teaching authority, the teaching is promoted as infallible. To designate a teaching as infallible means that the teaching is irreformable and requires the faithful's religious assent.

A lot is made about the "infallibility" of the pope. But this mode of speaking has been evoked only twice: Pope Pius IX's teaching regarding Mary's immaculate conception (1854) and Pope Pius XII's teaching concerning her assumption into heaven (1950). All teachings of the Magisterium on moral issues are at this point non-infallible. In other words, the moral teachings of the Church are open to faithful, and yet critical, re-evaluation and reform. Here theologians and knowledgeable laity play a particularly vital role as we seek truth and understanding.

Vatican II brought about a change in the way Catholics understand Church governing and teaching authority. Instead of a pyramidal concept of religious authority and moral knowledge, which had the Magisterium at the top of the pyramid and the laity at the bottom, Vatican II introduced a communion (*communio*) model. This communion model is based on the premise that the Church is composed of the "people of God" (the *communio*), including the Magisterium, theologians, and the laity, who work collectively to move the Church through history and toward a fuller relationship with God. In this model, moral knowledge is discerned by the entire *communio*. Guided by the Holy Spirit, and in light of scripture, reason, and experience, the Magisterium, theologians, and laity find themselves in conversations regarding moral questions. As Gregory Baum has observed in his book *Amazing Church*, the *communio* model has led the Church to change its teaching regarding human rights, God's redemptive presence in history, the preferential option for the poor, the culture of peace, and the Church's openness to religious pluralism.[6]

The "tradition"—the Content

While the Church has responded to social, political, and economic issues for centuries, Pope Leo XIII's encyclical *Rerum novarum* (On Capital and Labour, 1891) serves as a turning point in the Catholic ethical tradition because it focused exclusively on the pressing social problem of the time, namely, "the misery and wretchedness pressing so unjustly on the majority of the working class" (RN, no. 3). Pope Leo's bold work was precedent setting. Since then, nearly every pope has published at least one encyclical to address a contemporary social, political, or economic issue. A number of popes, especially John Paul II and Benedict XVI, have made it a point to address these issues in numerous letters, speeches, and public statements. Individual bishops and conferences of bishops have also been taking positions on large issues, such as the use of military force and poverty, as well as issues that directly impact their congregations, including issues as specific as undocumented worker rights, inadequate housing for the poor, polluted drinking water, and access to essential services. Moreover, theologians, ethicists, and other experts continue to raise the Church's awareness of these issues of social justice. On the whole, the Catholic tradition has produced a robust body of ethical literature on nearly every major social, political, and economic issue: labour, capitalism, communism, globalization, economic and social development, poverty, the role of women in society, racism, military spending, non-conventional weapons, peacebuilding, and access to natural resources, to name only a few. Collectively, this body of teaching is known as Catholic Social Teaching (CST). Although there is no official list, Catholic ethicists can identify at least ten common themes or ethical values in CST. Below is that list of ten. Because we will address many of these themes in our following chapters, I will highlight only a few of the texts and statements that have been integral to the development of CST.

1. **The Dignity of the Human Person:** The U.S. Conference of Catholic Bishops stated in their pastoral letter *The Challenge of Peace* (1983), "At the center of all Catholic social teaching are the transcendence of God and the dignity of the human person. The human person

is the clearest reflection of God's presence in the world; all of the Church's work in pursuit of both justice and peace is designed to protect and promote the dignity of every person. For each person not only reflects God, but is the expression of God's creative work and the meaning of Christ's redemptive ministry."[7] Consequently, actions that deny the dignity of the human person are dehumanizing and unjust. Human beings must be treated as "ends" in themselves and not as "tools" or "instruments" used toward some end.

2. **Family, Community, and the Common Good:** From the family and our community we learn that we are not simply self-interested individuals, but interconnected beings who have broad social commitments, or a share in the "common good"; thus, as *Gaudium et spes* (Pastoral Constitution on the Church in the Modern World, 1965) concludes, "It is imperative that no one ... would indulge in a merely individualistic morality" (GS, no. 30).

3. **Participation in Economic, Political, and Cultural Life:** The Second Vatican Council spoke to this concern in relation to international and economic development: "Economic development must remain under the people's control; it is not to be left to the judgment of a few individuals or groups possessing too much economic power, nor to the political community alone, nor to a few powerful nations. It is proper, on the contrary, that at every level the largest number of people have an active share in directing that development" (GS, no. 65).

4. **Rights and Responsibilities:** Pope John XXIII's encyclical *Pacem in terris* (Peace on Earth, 1963) endorses the project of human rights, including the right to life, to bodily integrity, and to the means that are suitable for the proper development of life; namely, food, clothing, shelter, rest, medical care, and access to necessary social services (no. 11). They also include the right to employment, free association, free speech, family life, and the pursuit of art, to name just some of the rights articulated in CST. These rights have corresponding obligations or duties. For instance, the right to employment requires us to work to the best of our abilities for our employer. In turn, the employer has a right to conduct business and an obligation to provide working conditions that are safe and just.

5. **Subsidiarity:** The principle of subsidiarity holds that the functions of government and social institutions should be performed at the lowest level possible, as long as they can be performed adequately. If these functions cannot be performed adequately, the next highest level that can perform these functions has an obligation to act. The U.S. Bishops write in their pastoral letter *Economic Justice for All* (1986): "[The principle of subsidiarity] states that, in order to protect basic justice, government should undertake only those initiatives which exceed the capacities of individuals or private groups acting independently. Government should not replace or destroy smaller communities and individual initiative. Rather it should help them contribute more effectively to social well-being and supplement their activity when the demands of justice exceed their capacities."[8]

6. **Economic Justice:** According to CST, the economy is subservient to human flourishing. The economy is fundamentally a relationship between human beings and does not exist apart from human interaction. Moreover, the economy should not be regarded as a sphere in which anarchy prevails and moral values to guide human actions are absent. As Pope Leo argued in *Rerum novarum*, all workers have a right to productive work, to a living wage, and to safe working conditions. Workers also have a right to organize and join unions. People have a right to economic initiative and private property. However, these rights have limits. Catholic teaching holds that nobody is allowed to amass excessive wealth when others lack the basic necessities of life.

7. **The Option for the Poor and the Vulnerable:** CST holds that the moral test of a society is the way it treats its most vulnerable members. Instead of focusing on indicators like the Dow Jones Index, the Toronto Stock Market (the S&P/TSX) or a country's gross domestic product (GDP), society needs to base its economic, social, and political policies on how its vulnerable members will be affected by such policies. The U.S. bishops write in *Economic Justice for All*: "The obligation to evaluate social and economic activity from the viewpoint of the poor and the powerless arises from the radical command to love one's neighbor as one's self. Those who are marginalized and whose rights are denied have privileged claims if

society is to provide justice for all."[9] This privileged claim is called the "preferential option for the poor."

8. **Global Solidarity and Development:** In his encyclical *Sollicitudo rei socialis* (On Social Concerns, 1987), Pope John Paul II says that solidarity "is not a feeling of vague compassion or shallow distress at the misfortune of so many people, both near and far. On the contrary, it is a firm and persevering determination to commit oneself to the common good; that is to say to the good of all and of each individual, because we are all really responsible for all" (no. 38). More than just feeling connected to others, solidarity is a virtue that compels us to act for the good of others.

9. **Promotion of Peace and Disarmament:** Pope John XXIII's encyclical *Pacem in terris* inaugurated a movement in the Catholic tradition toward peace and disarmament. Echoing the prophetic work of *Pacem in terris*, Pope John Paul II linked peace and justice: "Peace is not just the absence of war. It involves mutual respect and confidence between peoples and nations. It involves collaboration and binding agreements."[10]

10. **Ecological Justice:** In his World Day of Prayer for Peace Message, 1990, Pope John Paul II stated, "Today the ecological crisis has assumed such proportions as to be the responsibility of everyone ... its various aspects demonstrate the need for concerted efforts aimed at establishing the duties and obligations that belong to individuals, peoples, States and the international community."[11] According to Pope John Paul, an adequate response to the ecological crisis should be rooted in the common good and in solidarity with those who are being most adversely affected by ecological devastation.

Reason

The relationship between faith and reason is an age-old problem in the Christian tradition. Tertullian (160–230), one of the most important leaders in the early Church, presented the problem in the form of a question: "What has Athens to do with Jerusalem?" In his question, Athens represents reason, rationality, and philosophical truth, while Jerusalem represents faith and religious truth. Tertullian believed that Athens had very little, if anything, to do with Jerusalem. But he recognized certain influences on the emerging Christian tradition. St. Anselm of Canterbury (1033–1109), in stark contrast to Tertullian, thought faith and reason share a complementary relationship. According to Anselm, we can best understand theology as "faith seeking understanding" (*fides quaerens intellectum*). The foundation of theology is always faith, he argued; but faith need not be and should not be uninformed or irrational. Because we are created with an intellect and the ability to reason, human beings can and should ask intelligent, reasoned questions of faith. In the Catholic tradition, Anselm's argument has largely prevailed.

In the field of Christian ethics, reason is necessary to explain or justify a moral argument. We appeal to reason when we prescribe a course of action or an *ought*. Indeed, ethics requires reason because without it, the prescriptive task of ethics can be reduced to nothing more than feeling, taste, or whim (what ethicists call "emotivism"), a trend or contextual differences ("relativism"), self-interest ("egoism"), claims of intuition or instinct ("intuitionism") or mere opinion masquerading as faith. Moreover, without the rigour of reason, ethics cannot be a *systematic* reflection on morality, values, and character. In sum, ethics requires reason to develop a method of decision-making.

As we briefly noted in the previous chapter, in the Christian ethical tradition, there are three general approaches to ethical decision-making. Deontological approaches focus on laws and obligations, teleological approaches focus on the consequences or the ends of an action, and virtue ethics focuses on the kind of human beings we wish to become. Let's examine these approaches in a bit more depth.

Deontological Approaches

Deontological approaches to ethics are rule-, law-, or duty-based ethics. The rightness or wrongness of an act is determined by judging our actions against a moral code or obligation. Jesus invoked one of the most basic forms of deontological ethics, the so-called Golden Rule, when he said: "In everything do to others as you would have them do to you; for this is the law and the prophets" (Matthew 7:12). Although Christianity has largely resisted impulses to become a religion of laws, deontological approaches have found their way into Christian ethics.

Divine command ethics is one of the ways in which deontological ethics has been a part of the Christian ethical tradition. According to a divine command approach, we know an action is right if God has commanded the action. But how do we know what God commands of us? First, we would look to scripture. There we have the Ten Commandments, Jesus's teaching regarding faithful discipleship, and divinely sanctioned rules for both personal conduct and the conduct of the Church. Second, we have Christian leadership interpreting the will of God for the Church. And third, we have individuals who believe God has commanded them to engage in a particular activity.

Many Christian ethicists today dismiss the divine command approach for a host of reasons. First, in the case of appealing solely to scriptural commandments, the divine command approach reduces ethics to an uncritical form of legalism. In principle, it doesn't ask about motives or reasons. It demands only obedience. But as we noted in chapter one, in our discussion of why ethics cannot be reduced to following a code or a set of rules, attempts to turn ethics into following a law inevitably require interpretation, debate, an appeal to conscience, and a sense of the common good—in sum, they require critical reflection. Second, when groups or individuals claim that God speaks only and unequivocally through them, they are claiming the sole authority to determine religious, political, and moral actions. This type of "God-talk" is non-rational because the one claiming to be God's sole authorized agent cannot be rationally challenged. The claim is intended to stifle critical reflection and debate. In many cases, a claim of sole authority is either asserted along with a threat (such as expulsion from a group) or it is unquestioned by loyal followers. At this point in the Christian tradition, ethicists reject these claims because they are nothing more than attempts to impose theocratic rule or to provide divine legitimacy on actions that might otherwise be regarded as morally illicit. Third, the divine command approach poses a number of moral dilemmas. For example, can God command an action that is immoral? As we recall from the brief discussion in the previous chapter, scripture contains a number of stories in which God commands people to engage in activities that, today, we would regard not only as moral failures, but as crimes against humanity, such as the genocide God commanded in Deuteronomy 7. Here is another example: What if scripture has no law for a contemporary problem like stem-cell research, in vitro fertilization, organ transplants, cloning, or nuclear weapons, to name just a few? In these cases, there are no clear divine commands in scripture. Thus while we may find vestiges of divine command ethics in scripture and at certain points in the history of Christianity, many contemporary Christian ethicists, both Protestant and Catholic, have a very low regard for such an approach in today's world.

Immanuel Kant's categorical imperative is a deontological approach to ethics that has influenced the Christian ethical tradition. Kant believed that just moral action must be just for everyone, everywhere, and at all times. Justice cannot be contingent on factors beyond our control, such as historical circumstances, coincidence, or fortune (what we might call "luck"). Moreover, Kant insisted, because a consequence or an end of an action cannot be good "in and of itself," due to the fact that consequences rely on contingent factors, ethics must be rooted in the only thing that we can declare good "in and of itself," namely, the autonomous person's free will. Based on our ability to reason as "self-legislating" persons, we can establish rules that all other reasonable persons would recognize as morally just. Kant called this approach to ethics "the categorical imperative." This approach is "categorical" because it applies unconditionally to everyone, everywhere, and at all times; and it is "imperative" because we have a moral duty to follow categorical rules, since in following them, we respect the dignity of others and ourselves.

Kant's categorical imperative has two basic forms. The first form is the principle of universalization. Kant's formulation goes like this: "Act only in accordance with that maxim through which you can at the same time will that it become a universal law."[12] Or to put it another way, an action is morally right if we can reasonably will that everyone would act the same way in the same situation. Suppose we choose to cheat on our taxes. While we might have more money in our pockets, government social programs, schools, hospitals, police and fire departments, and other essential services would likely disappear if everyone were to cheat. Cheating on taxes, then, isn't merely a minor exception you make for yourself; rather, it's a threat to the foundations of society and communal trust.

The second form of the categorical imperative is the principle of human reciprocity. Kant put it this way: "Act in such a way that you treat human beings, whether in your own person or in the person of any other, never merely as a means to an end, but always at the same time as an end."[13] For Kant, just actions must acknowledge and maintain the subjectivity of others. If we treat others as means toward some end, we are essentially turning them into tools to use to achieve our objective.

While no Christian ethicist has ever suggested Kant's ethical method should become the only way we do Christian ethics, a number of them have incorporated various aspects of Kant's method into discussions regarding racism, gender relations, pay equity, human rights, patients' rights, universal health care, same-sex relationships, sexual violence, the treatment of refugees and displaced persons, economic globalization, and consumerism, to name just a few.

Teleological Approaches

Teleological approaches to ethics focus on the ends or outcomes of actions. Generally speaking, teleological ethics has become synonymous with utilitarian (sometimes called "consequentialist") ethics. Utilitarian ethics is not typically associated with Christianity or any other religious tradition. It is the product of modern European political and social philosophers attempting to devise a system of decision-making that covered not just private moral issues but also public issues, such as economic policy, social services, prison reform, and taxation schemes.

Utilitarian ethics judges the rightness or wrongness of acts solely on what produces the greatest amount of happiness for the greatest number of people. Undoubtedly, you've heard the utilitarian-inspired phrase "The greatest good for the greatest number." The first self-professed utilitarian was Jeremy Bentham (1748–1832), a British legal theorist, philosopher, animal rights activist, and social reformer. In his book *An Introduction to the Principles of Morals and Legislation*, published in 1789, Bentham argued that, when trying to figure out the proper course of action in a given situation, we should begin by assigning pleasure units to whatever increases happiness, and pain units to whatever decreases happiness. We should then add up the total number of pleasure units in one column and the total number of pain units in another column, and then take an account of the number of people affected by the decision. After adding up all of the pleasure and pain units, and then determining how many people are affected by the proposed courses of action, we are then able to calculate what action will lead to the greatest good for the greatest number. Having generated thousands of tables based on this pleasure-pain calculation, Bentham thought that the utilitarian principle could guide individuals in their decision-making and even function as an organizing principle for society. In fact, Bentham was convinced that the rightness or wrongness of every act could be determined by going through this pleasure-pain calculation. For this reason, Bentham's utilitarianism is sometimes called "act utilitarianism" or "strict utilitarianism."

One major problem with the strict utilitarian approach is that pleasure and pain are not easily quantifiable. John Stuart Mill (1806–1873), a British political philosopher and politician, recognized the impracticality of Bentham's strict utilitarianism. Instead of calculating every act, he said we could think of utilitarianism in terms of general principles or, to use a colloquial phrase, as a "rule of thumb." Mill's approach is often referred to as "rule utilitarianism." It is based on the premise that we basically know what is right and wrong, what actions lead to pain and what actions lead to pleasure. And over the long term, we should seek to maximize utility. Mill's formulation of utilitarianism goes like this: "Actions are right in proportion as they tend to promote happiness; wrong as they tend to produce the reverse of happiness. By happiness is intended pleasure and the absence of pain."[14] As the contemporary philosopher Martha Nussbaum has observed, Mill can sound quite similar to Aristotle, who, as we shall discover just below, held that happiness (well-being) is the good or goal of human life.[15] However, unlike Mill, Aristotle did not think that happiness derives from pleasure; rather, happiness is the result of virtuous actions.

Today, we often hear utilitarian arguments when businesses engage in "cost-benefit analysis" and when advocates of free-market capitalism appeal to the slogan "let the market decide" in the face of morally difficult matters, such as the use of assisted reproductive technologies and abortion. We also hear utilitarian arguments when politicians, such as former U.S. Vice President Dick Cheney, defend "enhanced interrogation"—otherwise known as "torture"—on the basis that bringing pain to one individual provides pleasure (safety and security) for many. Similar kinds of "greatest good for the greatest number" arguments can be heard in debates over the use of nuclear power, flooding lands to further hydroelectric projects, eminent domain–expropriation cases, decisions to suspend the rule of law, and stem-cell research. In each of these cases, as with all utilitarian arguments, someone is suffering pain—often without their consent.

But is it really just or right to inflict pain on people, without their consent, to maximize the pleasures of others? This question suggests that teleological approaches to ethics consider not only the ends but also the means in achieving those ends. We now turn our attention to a teleological approach called "virtue ethics," which does in fact take into account various goods that should be achieved in striving toward an ultimate end.

Virtue ethics

Virtue ethics owes its existence in the Western intellectual tradition to the classical Greek philosophers Plato and Aristotle. For Aristotle, in particular, ethics has an internal coherency that reflects the natural order of things. He begins his famous book *Politics* with a foundational proposal, namely, everything has a natural end that it seeks. Acorns become oak trees, rivers flow toward the sea, and flowers turn toward the sun. These ends have not been created or realized by chance or by craft; rather, their existence is natural in the sense that an internal causal principle explains why things come into being and behave in a manner consistent with their ends. Like other things in nature, human beings also have an end. For Aristotle, *eudaimonia*—the Greek word meaning "happiness" or, perhaps more accurately, "human flourishing" or "well-being"—is the end that all humans seek. Even in Aristotle's day, there were those who claimed that humans ultimately seek fame, fortune, beauty, sex, or power. But Aristotle responded by noting that fame, fortune, beauty, sex, and power are just means to an end. The real end they're seeking is happiness.

For Aristotle, eudaimonia is far more than just a feeling of giddiness and joy—it is a type of happiness that goes to the core of our being. It is a state we experience as the result of living a well-ordered life, one with meaning, purpose, and direction. Additionally, eudaimonia is never fully achieved in one single action. Instead, it is achieved over the course of a lifetime. To help us achieve our natural end and to orient us continually toward the well-ordered life, Aristotle argued, we need to practise certain virtues. Virtues are dispositions, habits, and traits that enable us to engage in right action. For Aristotle, the virtues are both instrumental, because they are a means to an ultimate end, and constitutive, because they are integral to eudaimonia. As such, when we practise the virtues, we are not only engaging in right action (since each virtuous action moves us closer to our ultimate end), we are also taking part in the good life. In effect, the virtuous life is supposed to be self-generating. That is, we lead a virtuous life because we seek eudaimonia, and we know to practise the virtues because, in the process of practising the virtues, we experience well-being. Or to put it a slightly different way, the better life gets, the more we seek the virtuous life, which in turn means life gets better, and so we seek the virtuous life.

Aristotle placed the virtues into three different categories. First, the moral virtues (for example, practical wisdom, generosity, kindness, truthfulness, wittiness, modesty, and courage) are habits that help develop character. Second, the intellectual virtues (such as practical wisdom, theoretical wisdom, intellectual courage, intuition, and resourcefulness) are qualities of the mind that help us reason well. And third, from the Latin word *carde*, meaning "hinge," the cardinal virtues are the "hinge" that keeps the other virtues connected to one another. These cardinal virtues are (1) prudence (also called "practical wisdom" or, in Greek, *phronesis*), (2) temperance, (3) justice, and (4) fortitude (courage). Of all the virtues, prudence is pre-eminent, for it enables us to determine whether an action is right or wrong in a given situation. But this is not to say that prudence or any other virtue on its own is sufficient to lead us in a virtuous life. For Aristotle, we must practise all four cardinal virtues because they're interrelated. We need prudence to make wise decisions. We need temperance to keep our passions under the control of practical reason. We need justice to help us treat others according to their purpose in life. And we need fortitude to give us the strength to stand firm in our decisions, convictions, and quest for justice. For Aristotle, the person who says, for instance, "I possess all the virtues but temperance" not only doesn't possess that virtue, but doesn't possess any of the other virtues, either.

Thomas Aquinas, writing in the thirteenth century, adapted Aristotle's philosophical and moral teachings to a Christian framework. For Thomas, prudence (practical reasoning) in a Christian or a non-Christian is evidence that all people perceive a natural law. Following Aristotle, Thomas maintained that the first principle of practical reason is that human beings seek the good. As such, the first precept of the natural law is "good is to be done and pursued, and evil is to be avoided" (ST I–II, 94.2). Thomas believed that rational humans are able to know right from wrong by appealing to practical reason and the virtues, including those cardinal virtues cited by Aristotle.

While Thomas closely followed Aristotle, even to the point of giving him the honorific title "the Philosopher," Thomas did make crucial distinctions. For instance, according to Thomas, human beings are not seeking eudaimonia, but full and perfect communion with God (or heaven). By doing good and avoiding evil, the first precept of the natural law, we are both participating in and on our way toward attaining heaven. But how do we know what is good and what is evil? To answer this question, Thomas proposed four primary goods that can lead us to, but not guarantee us, the ultimate good of perfect communion with God: life, family, knowledge, and community. According to Thomas, we are social animals who are nurtured and formed by those living around us. The natural end of the community is mutual assistance. Following this good, then, our actions must preserve and enhance community bonds and the virtuous character of our communities.

In their book *Jesus and Virtue Ethics*, the Catholic New Testament scholar Daniel J. Harrington and Catholic ethicist James F. Keenan build the case for a virtue ethics based on the gospel, particularly the Sermon on the Mount (Matthew 5–7).[16] For Harrington and Keenan, the kingdom of God is the foundation on which to build a virtue ethic, since the primary virtue in the kingdom of God is love. They write, "In major ethical writings, the end in the sense of the 'goal' is where we begin. Not surprisingly, New Testament ethics starts with the kingdom of God, which is the 'end' for us all. From an ethical viewpoint, the end is the quintessential point of departure, since strong ethical systems always start with the end. The goal always defines the agenda being pursued. The agenda, from start to finish, is shaped by the end."[17]

If the kingdom of God is the beginning and end of virtue ethics, then the question becomes this: What is the primary virtue in the kingdom of God? Harrington and Keenan, as well as many other Christian virtue ethicists, point to the virtue of love as found in Jesus's statement from the Sermon on the Mount (Matthew 5:43-46): "You have heard that it was said, 'You shall love your neighbor and hate your enemy.' But I say to you, Love your enemies and pray for those who persecute you, so that you may be children of your Father in heaven; for he makes his sun rise on the evil and on the good, and sends rain on the righteous and on the unrighteous. For if you love those who love you, what reward do you have?" Paul reaffirms the priority of love among the virtues in 1 Corinthians 13:13: "And now faith, hope, and love abide, these three; and the greatest of these is love."

I have often heard both Catholics and non-Catholics express frustration at the lack of definitive conclusions that virtue ethics provides. They seem to be longing for *the* right answers to today's difficult moral dilemmas. Many Catholics turn to the Magisterium in hopes of finding those right answers. But as those early twentieth-century theologians who were critical of the Church's manualist tradition would remind us, simply adhering to rules and laws is not an accurate understanding of an ethics grounded in natural law and expressed in the virtuous life. Ethical being means that we recognize the moral ambiguity in everyday life, we seek to apply practical reason to answer moral questions, and we respond by trying to manifest the virtues in our life and help instill them in the life of our community. As we face moral dilemmas such as the definition of marriage, stem-cell research, the justice and injustice of market capitalism, the use of military force, and ecological degradation, to name just a few, we should expect diverse but fiercely faithful responses. This is the true nature of virtue ethics—an approach that has a place of prominence in the Catholic ethical tradition.

Experience

In the four hundred years prior to the Second Vatican Council, manuals dominated the Catholic moral tradition. As we discovered in our discussion of scripture, the Council sought to revitalize moral theology by infusing it with a renewed commitment to engage scripture. The Council's *Optatam totius* prescribed scripture as "nourishment" for a moral tradition starved by manuals, and the Council's *Dei verbum* attempted to highlight the importance of scripture in understanding God's continual communication with humanity. Based on the efforts of theologians calling for an end to manual dominance, and with the conciliar focus on scripture, Catholic moral theologians have increasingly turned to scripture as a valuable source of moral knowledge. This turn toward scripture has had an impact on the way Catholic ethicists prioritize the sources of Christian ethics. We now understand scripture as equally integral to the process of doing ethics as tradition and reason. While post–Vatican II moral theologians have recognized the importance of scripture, tradition, and reason, the Catholic ethical tradition has been reluctant to recognize the fourth source of Christian ethics: experience. In many ways, Catholic ethics is still working through the last vestiges of the manualist tradition. As a result, many Catholic moral theologians, myself included, contend that the Church should now work to rediscover the importance of human experience in moral theology and thereby provide further nourishment to the Church's moral teachings.[18]

Recovering Experience in the Catholic Moral Tradition

In his *Nicomachean Ethics*, Aristotle explains that experience is an essential element in the moral virtue of prudence. It is, he asserted, a virtue that can be developed only over time. Aristotle makes his case by arguing that young men may become master mathematicians, since they may possess the faculties necessary to grasp the abstract concepts in mathematics, but they are unable to amass the experience necessary to possess prudence, which can be acquired only through particular facts garnered through experience. For Aristotle, prudence "includes a knowledge of particular facts, and this is derived from experience which a young man does not have."[19] So while young men may be good at numbers, they do not have the lived experience it takes to be good at ethics.

Thomas understood the importance of experience not only in the development of prudence but also in our ability to recognize the four primary goods—life, family, knowledge, and community. According to Thomas, these primary goods are self-evident (*per se notum*: known through itself) and not the result of some process of deduction. Moreover, our knowledge of these primary goods requires experience. Over time, our understanding of these goods will become more self-evident, Thomas believed, which means our moral knowledge of the objects that correspond to those goods will increase over time.

The Second Vatican Council, as well, acknowledged the important role experience has played in the development of Church teaching. The Council's *Gaudium et spes* states: "The experience of past ages, the progress of the sciences, and the treasures hidden in the various forms of human culture, by all of which the nature of man himself is more clearly revealed and new roads to truth are opened, these profit the Church, too" (no. 44). Although much more subtle than its call for the Church's re-engagement with scripture, the Council expressed a new openness toward culture, science, and other human experiences. Breaking with nearly four hundred years of tradition, which saw the Church standing over and above these realms as judge, the Council opened the Church to dialogue with culture, modern science, and individual spiritual experiences. The Church is now in a position to listen to those voices, evaluate their insights and ideas in light of the gospel, and, to the extent that they are in keeping with the gospel, integrate them into the teaching of the Church.

A number of Catholic theologians, bishops, and conferences of bishops relished the Council's new, albeit restrained, openness toward experience. For instance, the Canadian bishops, in 1983, published a letter stating: "As Christians, we are called to follow Jesus by identifying with the victims of injustice, by analyzing the dominant attitudes and structures that cause human suffering and by actively supporting the poor and oppressed in their struggle to transform society."[20] Certain public personalities in Canada were outraged by the bishops' conclusion and denounced them for engaging in areas in which they don't belong. The bishops responded later that year with "Ethical Reflections on Canada's Socioeconomic Order," which outlined the five-step method they used in constructing their ethical reflection. The first step was "to be present with and listen to the experience of the poor, the marginalized, the oppressed in our society." In other words, the Catholic bishops made the bold argument that ethical reflection begins with human experience. The steps that followed included an analysis of the structures that create human suffering, an assessment of the situation in light of the gospel and Catholic Social Teaching, a proposal for alternative actions, and a declaration to act in solidarity with groups as they struggle to overcome injustice.

A number of Catholic moral theologians, however, disagree with ethical methods that look to experience as a primary source of moral knowledge. Sometimes called "traditionalists," these theologians maintain that human experiences must be judged by moral norms derived from moral principles alone. These principles are *not* based on empirical facts or metaphysical claims about the world, they contend, because facts and metaphysical claims are ultimately too relative to ground moral norms; rather, these principles are objective truths that human beings can deduce through reason. Consequently, they hold that the natural law provides specific rules and moral norms that should determine how we act in given situations. In making the claim that the natural law provides not just general principles but specific moral rules for specific occasions, these theologians hold on to an interpretation of the natural law that is more in keeping with the legalistic tradition that gave us the moral manuals than the natural law tradition embraced by many post–Vatican II theologians, who see experience as a vital source of moral knowledge.

On the whole, the Catholic natural law tradition teaches that the moral norms and criteria used to judge the rightness and wrongness of an act should not be reduced to specific, absolute moral principles or laws. In fact, as the *Catechism of the Catholic Church* states, "Application of the natural law varies greatly; it can demand reflection that takes account of various conditions of life according to places, times, and circumstances." In other words, reasonable people of goodwill may disagree with each other on the rightness or wrongness of moral actions because they apply the natural law differently. Yet, in spite of these differing interpretations, the *Catechism* teaches, the natural law "remains as a rule that binds men among themselves and imposes on them, beyond the inevitable differences, common principles" (no. 1957). How people of goodwill recognize the natural law amid diversity is a matter of reason and not a universal authority or law proscribing a specific action. Let's take adultery, for example. Following the natural law tradition, we know adultery is wrong not because scripture and the Church forbid it, but rather because we know, based on human experience, that such an act damages relationships between spouses, destroys families, and disrupts social cohesion.

To make a fine point, we know an act is wrong (or right) because of human experience and not because of a law or a divine command.

This point is important for at least two reasons. First, in keeping with the natural law tradition and the Church's anthropology, it preserves the dignity of the human person. It allows the human subject to use practical reason to discern right and wrong. Indeed, it recognizes the human being's essential freedom to seek and to know the good. In the words of the Second Vatican Council, "Only in freedom can human persons direct themselves toward goodness" (GS, no. 17). To demand adherence to established moral laws is to deny human beings the capacity to act in freedom. To reiterate our point, we, as rational and spiritual beings, know that acts such as adultery are wrong not because there is a law forbidding it, but rather because they undermine human flourishing.

Second, our point is important because it preserves the natural law tension between human experiences and moral norms. The traditionalist method, in stark contrast, effectively obliterates the tension by asserting that moral norms function as laws, and the proper response is for us to adhere to them. In the traditionalist approach, these norms become the bases for determining legitimate human experience. Or to put it another way, if a human experience conforms to and confirms established norms, then it is legitimate; if it doesn't, it is illegitimate. This approach to ethics is self-referential and reductionist and can lead to serious moral failures. For instance, this approach largely enabled the Magisterium to approve of slavery until the late nineteenth century.[22] So what changed, the natural law or the Church's teachings? Clearly, it was the Church's teachings. They changed because the Church rediscovered the need to preserve the tension between human experiences and moral norms, including the first precept of the natural law, namely, doing good and avoiding evil.[23] The primary challenge Catholic ethicists face as we appeal to experience as a source of moral knowledge is discerning which human experiences lead to human flourishing and which experiences impede human flourishing.

The Four Sources of Experience

Catholic ethicists generally cite four sources of human experience: culture, science, human emancipation, and individual conscience.

Cultural experience, as *Gaudium et spes* affirms, has helped the Church develop language to communicate to people within a given context. The Council recognized that, if the Church were going to speak with authority in the modern world, it needed to engage the cultures surrounding it. This engagement means the Church can learn from philosophers, social theorists, social scientists, public intellectuals, artists, activists, and other cultural leaders. As a learner, the Church can discover insights into moral truths embedded in certain cultures and can translate those truths from one culture to the next. One clear example of this phenomenon is Pope John XXIII's embrace of human rights in *Pacem in terris*. In this case, the Church discovered the moral good of human rights primarily by being in dialogue with modern social theory and cultures that guaranteed fundamental human rights. Today, human rights are an integral component of Catholic Social Teaching. Also, as a teacher, the Church may at times take positions that are countercultural. Recent statements by Pope Benedict XVI on the state of the global economy and the injustice associated with the maldistribution of wealth are instances in which the Church has criticized a socio-economic culture that hinders human flourishing.

The second source of experience is contemporary scientific knowledge. Does curing such diseases such as Parkinson's, Huntington's, or Gehrig's violate natural law or service the common good? Or what medical technologies ought we to use to keep a person alive who is in a persistent vegetative state? Having learned from its treatment of Galileo in the sixteenth century, the Church cannot simply reject scientific discoveries that fundamentally test long-held norms in the Catholic moral tradition. Instead, through our engagement with science, we may find that moral reflection rooted in human flourishing has the potential to generate new insights and lead to new moral norms.

The third source comes from the experiences of those who have suffered systemic oppression and longed for freedom from injustice. In the early 1970s, certain Latin American theologians, such as Gustavo Gutierrez and Leonardo Boff, began to develop a liberation theology that grew out of the experiences of the poor and marginalized. The gospel is contextual, they argued, and so should be our theology. They highlighted the fact that Jesus sought out the dispossessed, the despised, the alien outsiders, the powerless, and the sick in carrying out his mission. They also argued that the story of God's involvement in history has one clear theme, that is, setting the captives free (Exodus 13). Even while Pope John Paul II and then-Cardinal Ratzinger were voicing strong opposition against the various actions and theological statements associated with Latin American liberation theology during the 1980s, Catholic theologians, bishops, and even Pope John Paul himself were affirming the preferential option for the poor as an integral part of Catholic Social Teaching.[24]

Individual conscience is the fourth source of experience. According to Catholic moral teaching, "conscience is a judgment of reason whereby the human person recognizes the moral quality of a concrete act that he is going to perform, is in the process of performing, or has already completed" (*Catechism of the Catholic Church*, no. 1776). Our conscience is therefore what ultimately enables us to make moral judgments. Our conscience is where our reading of scripture, our understanding of tradition, our practical reason, and our life experiences come together to make moral judgments and to act. In Catholic moral theology, conscience appears in three senses. The first sense is the human capacity to know what is good and right. The law God has written into the human heart functions as a spark that provides light to know the good. The second sense involves moral reflection, that is, ethics. The human conscience is well-formed when we engage in the pursuit of authentic morality, values, and character, not only for ourselves but also for our communities, institutions, and societies. This process of moral reflection is not merely an abstract, rational exercise, but a process that calls us to engage in the concrete realities of life, to live the virtuous life and not simply think it. The third and final sense of conscience is the final judgment, when we finally prescribe an *ought* and act upon it.

In the Catholic tradition, conscience is the pre-eminent source in moral decision-making. Catholic theologians often refer to the "autonomy of conscience" and the "sanctity of conscience" to emphasize the point that conscience is internal to the human person and is the ultimate source of moral authority. The Vatican II document *Dignitatis humanae* (On Religious Freedom, 1965), states the Catholic position on conscience in these terms:

Man perceives and acknowledges the imperatives of the divine law through the mediation of conscience. In all his activity man is bound to follow his conscience in order that he may come to God, the end and purpose of life. It follows that he is not to be forced to act in a manner contrary to his conscience. Nor, on the other hand, is he to be restrained from acting in accordance with his conscience, especially in matters religious. (no. 3)

In other words, because conscience is how we know right from wrong, good from bad, we are obligated to follow our conscience even if it runs contrary to moral customs, laws, or norms.

However, the pre-eminence of conscience does not mean that it is a license for us to do whatever we wish. It is not the basis for an ethic of moral relativism. To the contrary, it means that we, as free moral agents in pursuit of the good, have a responsibility to understand the role of the Magisterium in promoting the Church's teaching, to engage in systematic reflection on morality, values, and character, and, in the process, to live a virtuous life. Consequently, we are morally responsible for bad judgments based on poorly formed consciences.

In sum, conscience is the ultimate source of authority in the Catholic moral tradition; however, it is not infallible. Acting on conscience doesn't guarantee a morally right and good act; but it is the basis from which we make judgments about right and wrong, good and evil. Unlike divine command ethics, the Catholic natural law tradition appeals to conscience because the moral law that is written on our hearts is internal to us. We, as free moral agents, have the capacity to know the good as well as to do the right and good. Our responsibility is to ensure that our conscience is well formed through study, habit, and ethical reflection, for the conscience is the basis on which we make judgments about right and wrong and pursue the virtuous life.

Part II

Contemporary Issues

CHAPTER 4

Sexual Ethics

In June 1958, Richard Loving married Mildred Jeter in Washington, D.C. Growing up in rural Virginia, they had known each other since she was eleven and he was seventeen. Originally they were friends, but over time they fell in love with each other. In early 1958, at the age of eighteen, Mildred became pregnant. For this young couple, marriage was the right thing to do. However, just five weeks after their wedding, on a warm July night as the couple slept in their bedroom, police deputies and dogs stormed into their house, yanked them out of bed, and arrested them because they were married.

The problem was that Richard Loving was white, Mildred Loving was "coloured" (Native American of Rappahannock and Cherokee heritage), and their marriage violated the Virginia Racial Integrity Act of 1924, which banned all marriages between a white person and any non-white person. The Lovings were charged with two counts under the Virginia Code: one that prohibited interracial couples from being married out of the state and then returning to Virginia, and one that classified miscegenation (interracial marriage) as a felony punishable by a prison sentence of between one and five years.

On January 6, 1959, the Lovings pled guilty on both counts and were sentenced to one year in prison, with the sentence suspended on the condition that the couple leave the state of Virginia and not return for 25 years. The trial judge in the case, a renowned Catholic jurist in Virginia, proclaimed:

> Almighty God created the races white, black, yellow, malay and red, and he placed them on separate continents. And but for the interference with his arrangement there would be no cause for such marriages. The fact that he separated the races shows that he did not intend for the races to mix.[1]

Following their plea agreement, the Lovings moved to Washington, D.C.

On November 6, 1963, the American Civil Liberties Union (ACLU) filed a motion on their behalf in the state trial court to vacate the judgment and set aside the sentence on the grounds that the violated statutes were in contravention of the Fourteenth Amendment of the U.S. Constitution. But little happened in the Virginia courts. So on October 28, 1964, after their motion still had not been decided, the Lovings launched a class action suit in U.S. District Court. This court ruled that the Lovings must be allowed to present their constitutional claims to the Virginia Supreme Court of Appeals. To the Lovings' dismay, the Virginia Supreme Court found that the anti-miscegenation statutes were constitutional and, for that reason, affirmed the criminal convictions. The Lovings and the ACLU decided to appeal to the U.S. Supreme Court.

On June 12, 1967, in the case of *Loving v. Virginia*, the Supreme Court unanimously overturned their convictions. Additionally, the Court ruled that Virginia's anti-miscegenation statute violated both the due process and equal protection clauses of the Fourteenth Amendment. In effect, the ruling meant that it was no longer legal to prohibit mixed-race marriages in the United States. By 1970, there were more than 300,000 interracial marriages in the United States. Today there are some 4.5 million.

The case of *Loving v. Virginia* reminds us that our sexual ethics are always, to some degree, historically and socially conditioned. Sexuality is involved in all other aspects of life, including politics, law, business, education, and recreation. We do not cease being sexual beings when we're at work, in church, at prayer, in the ballot booth, in class, with friends at the beach, or participating in a recreational soccer league. While this historical conditioning is not the determining factor in our sexual ethics, our sexual ethics are constantly affected by broader social, political, and economic changes. Here, for instance, we can think of how the Industrial Revolution changed the way we value family life, how the human rights movement led to women's liberation and interracial marriage, and how modern medicine transformed our understanding of the human body and challenged long-held beliefs about our sexuality. While it may be somewhat disconcerting to acknowledge that Catholic sexual ethics have changed over time, there is no denying the fact that they have.

In this chapter, we focus on the development of Catholic sexual ethics as they relate to the sexual body, marriage, cohabitation, and divorce, as well as the ethics of sexual intercourse, birth control, masturbation, and same-sex relationships. Our aim is to provide a context for the Church's teachings regarding sexuality and to highlight questions posed by faithful Catholic ethicists engaged in the theological pursuit of "faith seeking understanding."

The Sexual Body and the Christian Tradition

So many of today's debates in sexual ethics have to do with the big anthropological question "Who am I?" Am I (or are we) born to be monogamous? Are we naturally predisposed toward serial monogamy or multiple sexual relationships? Is my sexuality a choice? Am I born gay, straight, queer, or asexual? Are my sexual desires merely the result of biological impulses caused by hormones that have developed in our species to foster procreation?

Early Christian writers were faced with their own anthropological questions. Many of them had been posed by the Greco-Roman world from which Christianity emerged. Peter Brown, in his classic book *The Body and Society*, observed that the Greek and Roman philosophers and medical scientists had long been asking the following questions:

- What accounts for the difference between men and women? What makes men "virile" and active in sexual relations, and what makes women "soft" and passive? The second-century researcher Galen thought that the difference was due to a lack of heat girls received in the womb, which in turn made them more liquid, more clammy-cold, and eventually in need of monthly menstruation to get rid of coagulated blood. Women were, in essence, formlessly failed men—and slimy failed men at that. Men were like frothers on cappuccino machines, full of steam aching to be released. In stark contrast to women, men were hot from the time of conception through their adult years. The most virile of men were those who "kept their heat," who didn't spill their seed. Celibacy, the Greeks believed, was a way to enhance virility, to amass virile spirit.

- Is sexual intercourse at odds with the man's search for wisdom? According to the Stoics and Neo-Platonic philosophers, the appetites of the body were a hindrance to a man's pursuit of truth. Above all, sexual passion was the enemy of transcendent truth, for it demanded the focus be on the things of this world instead of metaphysical truth. For these philosophers, then, the body was nothing but a prison that stifled the spiritual quest for non-material truth. As historians of Christian thought have long noted, early Christian scholars were greatly influenced by this conception of the body.[2]

Among the educated classes, questions and answers like these formed the basis of a "taken-for-granted" approach to sexual ethics. Simply put, to those living in the first three or four centuries after the birth of Christ, the answers to these questions were simply self-evident, as natural as the sun rising in the east and setting in the west. This was the context in which Christian scholars thought about the body and sexuality.

The Body as a Site of Battle between the Spirit and Flesh

Considering Christianity to be an offshoot of Judaism, early Christian leaders looked to the Hebrew Bible to help develop a Christian understanding of the human person. The central texts were the creation stories in Genesis 1 and 2 and the story of the so-called Fall in Genesis 3. In the first creation story (Genesis 1:1–2:3), God created the man and the woman at the same time on the sixth day of creation. They were created in the image of God (*imago Dei*) and stood at the pinnacle of God's created order. The first commandment the man and the woman received from the Creator was "Be fruitful and multiply" (Genesis 1:28).

In the second creation story (Genesis 2:4-25), God created the man (in Hebrew, *adam*) first, "from the dust of the ground," and placed him in the Garden of Eden to "till it and keep it." God's first commandment to the man was "You may freely eat of every tree of the garden; but of the tree of the knowledge of good and evil you shall not eat, for in the day that you eat of it you shall die." Then God declared that the man should not be alone—the man needed a "helper as his partner." So God created out of the dust all the animals, which the man named; but still none of these animals was suitable as the man's partner. God then caused the man to fall into a deep sleep, which enabled God to take a rib from the side of the man. God made the woman from the rib of the man and presented her to him. The man said, "This at last is bone of my bones and flesh of my flesh; this one shall be called Woman, for out of Man this one was taken." The text concludes, "Therefore a man leaves his father and his mother and clings to his wife, and they become one flesh."

Genesis 3 contains the story of "the Fall." It begins with the snake asking the woman about which tree God designated for food. The woman told the snake that they could eat from any of the trees, except "the tree that is in the middle of the garden," which, according to the woman, they could also not touch. After negotiating with the snake, the woman ate from the tree and gave some to her husband. For their disobedience, God punished the woman, saying, "I will greatly increase your pangs in childbearing; in pain you shall bring forth children, yet your desire shall be for your husband, and he shall rule over you." God punished the man by sentencing him to a life of hard work and to a death that returned the man to the dust. Shortly thereafter, the man named his wife Eve, "because she was the mother of all living." God then proceeded to make clothes out of animal skins for the couple. Because the man knew the difference between good and evil, and because he might also eat from the tree of life and live forever—and be like God—God threw him out of the Garden of Eden, "to till the ground from which he was taken."

The Apostle Paul saw Genesis 1–3 as foundational for his understanding of both the nature of Jesus and the nature of all human beings. According to Paul, Jesus is a "second Adam." But unlike the "first Adam," who was primarily physical, Jesus is primarily spiritual. For Paul, sin entered the world through the physical Adam but was overcome by the "second Adam," Jesus, who was raised from the dead. "All die in Adam," Paul wrote, "so all will be made alive in Christ" (1 Corinthians 15:22).

Paul's interpretation of Genesis 1–3 rests on an anthropological assumption that was widely held in the Greco-Roman world—that is, the flesh and the soul are continually struggling against each other for supremacy over the individual. Paul wrote, for instance, "The fact is that I know that in me, that which is in my flesh, dwells nothing good, for while the desire to do good is present, in practice I cannot find the good … What a wretched man I am! Who will deliver me from this body of death?" (Romans 7:18, 24).

For Paul, the answer to his question was Jesus, who also described the human condition in terms of this battle between the flesh and the spirit. In the famous Sermon on the Mount, Jesus instructed his followers to "cut off" those parts of the body that caused them to look lustfully upon a woman. "It is better for you to lose one of your members," Jesus said, "than for your whole body to go into hell" (Matthew 5:30). So in spite of the fact that there is no dichotomy between the spirit and the flesh in the Jewish tradition, the Christian tradition has often read the spirit–flesh divide back into the Hebrew scriptures.

Consistent with many of the prominent philosophical schools of antiquity, an early Christian worldview emerged that saw spirit as transcendent, incorruptible, timeless, and unchanging. The spirit is where we find ultimate truth. By contrast, the flesh is immanently material. It is dirty, dies, decomposes, and is time-bound. The flesh is sinful. For this reason, Paul tells us, "flesh and blood cannot inherit the kingdom of God, nor does the perishable inherit the imperishable" (1 Corinthians 15:50). Only the spirit is imperishable. The danger for Christians is entangling the body with the dirty, sinful flesh. The body, as a "temple of the Holy Spirit" (1 Corinthians 6:19-20) and as a member of Christ's body (1 Corinthians 6:15), must be pure. Moreover, the body must remain clean, since God will raise it from the dead (1 Corinthians 6:14). For Paul, this meant that sexual sins, such as sexual intercourse with a prostitute, sully the body, for in the act of intercourse the two become one flesh (1 Corinthians 6:16).

The general suspicion around the sexual body in early Christianity led to widespread sexual renunciation. As Peter Brown traced in his study of sexuality in the early Church, by the second century, Christianity was distinguishable from the other religions of the day by the stringency of its sexual codes, which often entailed sexual abstinence not only for the unmarried but also for the married.[3] For early Christian scholars, sexual desire needed to be regulated. Some early Christian sects, such as the neo-Platonic Gnostics, believed that sex was evil, even within the confines of marriage. St. Augustine (354–430) repudiated the notion that sex was evil on the basis that God commanded the first human beings to engage in sexual intercourse in Genesis 1:28 and declared the creation "good." According to Augustine, sin isn't a material substance. To put matters bluntly, the physical act of a man and woman engaging in sexual intercourse isn't sinful in and of itself; rather, sin is an act of the will. Sin is the result of a choice made out of one's free will. So even when the man and the woman sinned by eating from the tree, it wasn't the flesh that caused them to sin but acts of the will and volition.

We should note that when Augustine uses the term "free will," he doesn't mean that the will is "free" from external forces or diversions. To the contrary, the will is constantly tempted to make poor decisions—indeed, the will is free to make those poor decisions. In regard to human sexuality, Augustine believed that the Fall created in human beings an "anxious grasping" (concupiscence) that draws human beings away from the love of God. It is a disordered desire focused on an object of worldly satisfaction instead of God. It is this "anxious grasping" that must be governed, Augustine argued, for it has the capacity to lead us into sexual relationships that are contrary to divine order. Although somewhat more muted than Paul, Augustine nevertheless continued to promote the idea that the flesh and spirit are fighting for the control of the body, and the primary weakness in the body is sexual pleasure.

Augustine's anthropology remained dominant throughout the Middle Ages. As the Catholic theologian Jean Porter remarked in her book *Natural and Divine Law*, Thomas Aquinas (1225–1274) and other medieval theologians did little to challenge Augustine's conception of the body as a site of struggle between spirit and flesh. Instead, if anything, medieval scholars generally reaffirmed the idea that "sexual pleasure is a corruption of nature and the pursuit of such pleasure is always more or less sinful."[4] Echoing the Stoicism of early Christianity, they argued that pleasure must be subservient to reason. Moreover, pleasure must not be a desired end of any moral action, and most certainly not of sexual relationships.

The manuals that dominated Catholic moral theology from roughly the sixteenth to the twentieth century only solidified the idea that the pleasures of the flesh needed to be tamed, even within the confines of marriage. The manuals also taught Catholics to think of sexual pleasure in legalistic terms. Too much pleasure, or pleasure that wasn't associated with a natural end, was a violation of the natural order—it was sin—and as such needed to be confessed.

Beginning in the middle of the twentieth century, a number of theologians associated with a philosophical movement called personalism began to reconsider the Church's anthropology. Rereading the work of Thomas Aquinas and other medieval scholars in light of the modern turn to the active human subject, theologians such as Jacques Maritain, John Henry Newman, Dietrich von Hildebrand, and Karol Wojtyła (the future Pope John Paul II) argued that our relationship with God involves the whole person and not just the spiritual aspects. For personalist theologians, the body is dynamic, affected by history, and relational. The Vatican II document *Gaudium et spes* (Pastoral Constitution on the Church in the Modern World, 1965) introduced the foundations of a personalist anthropology into the Church's official teaching when it declared, "man, who is the only creature on earth which God willed for itself, cannot fully find himself except through a sincere gift of himself" (GS, no. 24).

Toward a Renewed Catholic Anthropology

In spite of the mid-twentieth-century reforms just before and after the Second Vatican Council, the Catholic tradition has been reluctant to reject the anti-body teachings of early Christianity. But there have been subtle revisions. For example, between 1979 and 1984, Pope John Paul II embarked on an ambitious plan to develop a "theology of the body." Over the course of 129 lectures, John Paul addressed the body, human sexuality, and institutions such as marriage and the family, and at times implicitly invited Catholics to speculate with him on a renewed Catholic anthropology. While not completely avoiding the spirit–flesh dichotomy of the early Church, John Paul constructed a theology of the body rooted in mutuality with others and consistent with traditional interpretations of the natural law.[5]

Pope Benedict XVI's first encyclical, *Deus caritas est* (God Is Love, 2006), is in many respects a continuation of John Paul's theology of the body. But Pope Benedict took a slightly more historical approach than his predecessor. Benedict stated, "Nowadays Christianity of the past is often criticized as having been opposed to the body; and it is quite true that tendencies of this sort have always existed" (DC, no. 5). In effect, Pope Benedict acknowledged that the division between spirit and flesh in Christianity has, to some degree, contributed to theological arguments that are anti-body in nature. In this respect, the critics of the traditional Christian view of the body have a point. However, Pope Benedict doesn't believe contemporary anthropologies hold any hope for a renewed understanding of the body. For Benedict, the problem is that many contemporaries treat the body and sex as nothing more than commodities to be traded or as merely biological matters. Against these dehumanizing anthropologies, Pope Benedict maintains that we should recognize the body and sexuality as areas that allow us to exercise our freedom and to express our whole being. More specifically, we should approach sexual love (*eros*) as a divine gift to be cultivated into a selfless love of the other—it's a love that actually nourishes God's love (*agape*) of humanity (DC nos. 5, 7, 13).

In spite of Pope Benedict's claim that this positive conception of sexual love dates back to the earliest teachings of Christianity, the overwhelming evidence suggests otherwise. Try as we may, we really don't find a positive reading of *eros* in the early Church, the Penitentials of the sixth through tenth centuries, the work of influential medieval theologians, or the moral manuals of the sixteenth through the early twentieth centuries. We certainly don't find anything as radical as what Pope Benedict has suggested; namely, that erotic love and the selfless love of *agape* are united in essence but appear in different dimensions, and that both *eros* and *agape* direct us toward the love of God.

Pope Benedict's concept of love and the body in *Deus caritas est* is not new in the broad Catholic moral tradition, though it is new in papal teaching. For more than half a century, theologians and ethicists have been making this case for a connection between *eros* and *agape*. What is new here is that Pope Benedict has affirmed and clarified the relationship between erotic love—the kind of dizzying love one feels when sexually attracted to another—and the selfless love of *agape*, the love that God has for humanity. In effect, what Pope Benedict has done in *Deus caritas est* is open up the Catholic tradition, even if ever so slightly, to further theological reflection on a renewed Catholic anthropology. As we will see below, so much of the internal disagreement in the Catholic tradition regarding sexual ethics boils down to differing conceptions of the human being, the sexual body, and ongoing tensions between ethicists who tend to emphasize the classicist approach to ethics and those who emphasize the historically conscious approach. While disagreement may be unsettling to some, as a Catholic ethicist I see faithful, responsible revisiting of official Church teaching as a necessary element in the maintenance of a living tradition.

Marriage, Cohabitation, and Divorce

In his remarkable introduction to Christian sexual ethics entitled *Lily Among the Thorns*, Miguel de le Torre begins his discussion of marriage with a jarring observation. Those clamouring for a defense of "biblical marriage" should look not to the idealized nuclear family of the mid-twentieth century as their contemporary model, but rather to the polygamist compounds associated with the Fundamentalist Church of Jesus Christ of Latter-Day Saints (FLDS).[6] In August 2011, the former president of the FLDS, Warren Jeffs, was convicted by a Texas court and sentenced to life in prison for child sexual assault. The husband of some fifty wives, Jeffs was found guilty of having sex with two girls, ages twelve and fifteen.

Biblical Marriage and "Traditional" Christian Marriage

The marital practices of Mr. Jeffs are, in comparison to those found in the Hebrew Bible, seemingly tame. On the whole, marriage in Hebrew scripture is based on a patriarchal social structure. Marriage meant that a male owned his wife and could demand sexual intercourse from her, whether for his pleasure or for the purpose of increasing the size of his family. As the head of the household, the man had sexual access to a woman once she reached puberty, usually around the age of twelve. Marriages were endogamous—they occurred within the extended family. A man could have as many wives as he could afford. He could have unlimited sexual partners outside marriage, as long as his lovers weren't already married. Women who had sexual intercourse outside of marriage were adulterers. Concubinage, the practice of maintaining a long-term relationship with a woman without the possibility of marriage, was widely accepted. Men could force young girls to lie with them in bed, as King David did (1 Kings 1:13), to "keep them warm." Sex with female slaves was common. Marriage was legitimate only if the bride was a virgin. If she wasn't a virgin, her punishment was death by stoning in front of her father's house (Deuteronomy 22:13-21). Marriage could take place only with someone of the same religion (Ezra 9:12). And if a husband were to die before having children, his brother was obligated to marry the widow and father children—or, looked at another way, the widow was forced to marry her dead husband's brother and have sex with him until she bore him children (Deuteronomy 25:5-10).

So is biblical marriage what we really want, particularly if we're talking about the marital practices of the Hebrew Bible? My hunch is that we're not all that interested, especially since we tend to criminalize such sexual behaviour today.

Perhaps we're interested in a "traditional Christian marriage"? Just a warning: if we're looking for a marriage pattern that resembles the idealized nuclear family of the mid-twentieth century, where a couple falls in love, gets engaged, gets married, has sexual intercourse, and has children, we're bound to be disappointed.

Let's start with the gospels. Jesus's teaching on marriage is scant at best. When Jesus addressed the issue of marriage, it was normally in passing and almost always to make a larger point about the coming kingdom of God and the need to restore a right relationship with others (justice) and with God (righteousness). Jesus affirmed the institution of marriage in the first creation story, stating that a married couple will become "one flesh" (Genesis 1:27) and that what God has joined together should not be separated. But nowhere in scripture does Jesus reject polygamy (perhaps because the practice had waned by the first century) or the requirements for women to be virgins to get married. Indeed, Jesus never provided a definitive model for marriage. He did, however, radically redefine male adultery. The practice in Jesus's day was that a man could be accused of adultery only if he had intercourse with a married woman: another man's property. But Jesus taught that men who divorced their wives for reasons other than unfaithfulness would be guilty of adultery (Matthew 19:9), a scandalous proposition to his contemporaries and one that challenged patriarchal privilege. For Jesus, the issue of divorce was a matter of justice for women, who were being routinely cast aside by husbands who were able to obtain certificates of divorce from their lax rabbis. According to Jesus, husbands had to maintain their responsibility for their wives.

Paul's teaching regarding marriage was hardly a clarion call for the wonders of the blissful institution. With echoes of the Greeks in the background, Paul wrote to the unmarried and the widows in the Corinthian church that it is better to remain unmarried, but "if they are not practising self-control, they should marry. For it is better to marry than to be aflame with passion" (1 Corinthians 7:9). In other words, marriage is a last resort for those who can't control their passion, a necessity for those who can't maintain their "steam." And yet Paul recognized that the marriage relationship was symbolic of the relationship between Christ and the Church. He wrote:

Be subject to one another out of reverence for Christ.

Wives, be subject to your husbands as you are to the Lord. For the husband is the head of the wife just as Christ is the head of the church, the body of which he is the Saviour. Just as the church is subject to Christ, so also wives ought to be, in everything, to their husbands.

Husbands, love your wives, just as Christ loved the church and gave himself up for her, in order to make her holy by cleansing her with the washing of water by the word, so as to present the church to himself in splendour, without a spot or wrinkle or anything of the kind—yes, so that she may be holy and without blemish. In the same way, husbands should love their wives as they do their own bodies. He who loves his wife loves himself. For no one ever hates his own body, but he nourishes and tenderly cares for it, just as Christ does for the church, because we are members of his body. 'For this reason a man will leave his father and mother and be joined to his wife, and the two will become one flesh.' This is a great mystery, and I am applying it to Christ and the church. Each of you, however, should love his wife as himself, and a wife should respect her husband. (Ephesians 5:21-33)

Regrettably, Paul's exhortation to husbands and wives did little to disrupt the patriarchal social structure of antiquity, let alone Western Christendom or modernity. To the contrary, Paul's admonition to wives, in particular, to remain subject to their husbands only reinforced male privilege; it reaffirmed the idea that the man is the natural leader of the household. Furthermore, marriage remained primarily an economic institution, and entering into marriage was typically the result of economic calculation—such as expanding the family through procreation and pooling familial wealth—than any sense of romantic love.

In the twelfth century, a festering debate over marriage practices in Europe came to a head. The Roman tradition, which was widely practised in southern Europe, was that a couple needed only to make a declaration of mutual consent to be married. It didn't matter where the couple was when they made the declaration of consent—whether in front of a priest, judge, or the bride's father, or even lying together on a haystack; they were married. The northern European practice was different. There, penetrative sexual intercourse was required once consent had been given. Gratian, the legal scholar and founder of canon law, helped achieve a compromise whereby consent initiates a marriage (it becomes a *ratum*), while ensuing intercourse completes the marriage (it becomes *consummatum*). This compromise forms current Catholic teaching on marriage as defined by the Code of Canon Law: "A valid marriage between baptized persons is said to be merely ratified if it is not consummated; ratified and consummated if the spouses have in a human manner engaged together in a conjugal act in itself apt for the generation of offspring."[7]

Following Gratian's compromise, marital consent took on two forms. Consent could be given in either the future tense ("I will marry you") or the present tense ("I am married to you"). If consent was given in the future tense, the relationship was called a "betrothal" (in Latin, the *sponsalia*) and the man and woman were called "spouses." The betrothed couple would then live together. Conventionally, first sexual intercourse took place at the time of the betrothal. If consent was given in the present tense, the relationship was called a "marriage" and consummated by intercourse. In cases where the betrothal led to pregnancy, the spouses would be wedded in marriage, usually toward the end of the pregnancy. Indeed, this sequence of betrothal, sexual intercourse, possible fertility, and wedding described the marriage process in Christendom for some four hundred years.

The Council of Trent (1554–1563) drastically altered the marriage sequence and radically redefined the meaning of marriage in the Catholic tradition. Prior to Trent, marriages in the Catholic tradition and the West did not need to be performed in a church or in front of any witnesses. The Council decreed in 1563, however, that valid marriages must take place in front of a priest and at least two witnesses. Put in historical context, the Church had grown concerned by the large number of clandestine marriages, particularly in Spain and Portugal. Problems had arisen due to men marrying multiple women. Aside from the fact that this amounted to the crime of bigamy, clandestine marriages made claims to inter-family wealth difficult to sort out, especially when a husband of multiple wives died.[8] The Council also prohibited premarital sex, concubinage, and other forms of extra-marital sexual intercourse. Women who engaged in prolonged adulterous relationships could receive especially harsh punishment—they could be forcefully removed from their cities and villages by secular authorities. Regarding the theology of marriage, the Council's most significant declaration was that marriage is one of the seven sacraments of the Church, a sign of Christ's ongoing presence in the world and God's unending grace.

For the past four and a half centuries—that is, since the Council of Trent—magisterial teaching regarding the marriage sequence has remained constant: wedding, sexual intercourse, and possible fertility. Well into the twentieth century, Catholics generally adhered to this sequence. But by the mid-twentieth century, Catholic marital practices in Europe and North America had shifted. More than half of today's Catholics are adopting a sequence that closely resembles the pre-Tridentine (pre–Council of Trent) sequence of cohabitation, sexual intercourse, possible fertility, and wedding. In response, a number of Catholic authors, including the U.S. Conference of Catholic Bishops, in its report entitled

Marriage Preparation and Cohabiting Couples (1999), cite studies to show how cohabitation correlates to increased divorce rates and less marital satisfaction.[9] Recently, however, some Catholic scholars point out that these studies tend to analyze cohabitation generally, including the vague categories of "trial marriages" and "playing house," and do not account for "committed cohabitation," that is, cohabitation intended to lead to marriage.[10] When studies introduce controlling variables related to committed cohabitation, or nuptial cohabitation, the results are considerably different. These studies show that, in comparison to couples who have not cohabitated, there is actually a slight decrease in divorce rates, though the decrease is statistically insignificant.[11] Moreover, with the recent publication of the Centers for Disease Control (CDC) report *Marriage and Cohabitation in the United States* (2010), there appears to be growing evidence that the divorce rate is roughly the same for those who have and have not cohabited prior to marriage.[12] In other words, there is no definitive social scientific data to suggest that couples who engage in committed cohabitation are at higher risk of a failed marriage than those who have not cohabited.

While the social scientific data are important to help us understand the current experiences of people in intimate relationships, the morality of cohabitation doesn't rest solely or even primarily on whether cohabitation leads to an increased probability of divorce. The central ethical issue is how Catholics understand the process of marriage. For example, is it possible that people in committed cohabiting relationships are engaging in a marriage process that the Church implicitly recognized prior to the Council of Trent, a process that started with betrothal, continued through the wedding, and into married life? Those who see a strong similarity between today's marriage practices and those prior to the Council of Trent maintain that the pre-Tridentine view of marriage is more in keeping with the Church's teaching that marriage is a sacrament and sacraments are characterized by an unfolding of human relationships. They are concerned that the Tridentine approach practically reduces marriage to two legal acts: ratification followed by almost immediate consummation.[13] However, the Magisterium teaches, in effect, that any type of cohabitation is a "trial marriage" because, in large part, there is no institutional guidance for the cohabiting partners. The *Catechism of the Catholic Church* puts it this way:

Some today claim a *"right to a trial marriage"* where there is an intention of getting married later. However firm the purpose of those who engage in premature sexual relations may be, "the fact is that such liaisons can scarcely ensure mutual sincerity and fidelity in a relationship between a man and a woman, nor, especially, can they protect it from inconstancy of desires or whim." Carnal union is morally legitimate only when a definitive community of life between a man and woman has been established. Human love does not tolerate "trial marriages." It demands a total and definitive gift of persons to one another. (CCC, no. 2391)

Even with the Magisterium's clear and broad rejection of cohabitation, there must be pastoral wisdom involved in its interpretation, particularly given that as many as three quarters of all Catholics getting married first cohabited. As the U.S. Conference of Catholic Bishops stated in *Marriage Preparation and Cohabitating Couples*, "many pastoral ministers identify cohabitation as the most difficult issue they deal with in marriage preparation. They are faced with the dilemma of addressing a situation that is contrary to our moral principles while attempting to validate and sanctify the relationship of the couple through the Sacrament of Marriage."

The Ends of Marriage

The Code of Canon Law from 1917 says this about marriage: "The primary end of marriage is the procreation and education of children; its secondary end is mutual help and the allaying of concupiscence."[14] This accurately reflects the Catholic tradition's procreative model of marriage that dominated Catholic theology from roughly the second century until the mid-twentieth century. It was based on two general assumptions. First, following the Greek-influenced Christian scholars of the early Church, the procreative model assumed that sexual pleasure had to be governed. If left unregulated, the early scholars said, sexual pleasure could disrupt the social order. God provided marriage to govern sexual drives, to orient the man's active sex drive toward its appropriate end: procreation. Second, following a natural law tradition that can be traced to Aristotle, medieval Christian scholars—most notably, Thomas Aquinas—maintained that, like all things, marriage was created with a primary end. The reasoning goes like this: Human beings were created by God "to be fruitful and to multiply" (Genesis 1:28). To facilitate this activity, God provided the institution of marriage, where the two become "one flesh" (Genesis 2:24) in sexual intercourse.

Taken together, these assumptions helped provide the grounds for a marriage model that treated marriage instrumentally and as a relationship practically devoid of emotion. The instrumentality of marriage in this model is evident when we examine the two ends (or goods) of marriage. First, marriage is a good inasmuch as it leads to sexual intercourse and children. Second, marriage is a good because it provides companionship for the sexes, what Augustine called "friendship," and the necessary foundations for the family. The second creation story affirms this good, as God responded to the man's aloneness in the garden. Thomas Aquinas put it this way: "Marriage has as its principal end procreation and education of offspring ... and so offspring are said to be a good of marriage." It also has "a secondary end in man alone, the sharing of tasks which are necessary in life, and from this point of view husband and wife owe each other faithfulness, which is one of the goods of marriage" (ST, III [supp.], 65.1c).

Additionally, the procreative marriage model tended to ignore the emotional aspects of marital love. While the Catholic tradition has consistently held that love forms the basis of marriage, theologians until the mid-twentieth century usually suppressed the joys associated with erotic love in favour of reason. Augustine, for example, said that when God commanded the man and the woman to "be fruitful and multiply," the sexual act was performed without the passionate arousal normally required to engage in penetrative sex. Instead, sexual intercourse between the first two human beings, both in a state of sinlessness, occurred as an act of the will. The two original humans simply didn't need erotic passion to arouse their bodies—they could control their bodies willfully. Reason and sexual desire were perfectly aligned. According to Augustine, then, Christians who have rightly oriented their desires to please God should seek to emulate the original man and woman by engaging in sexual intercourse that manifests the willful and dispassionate control of our bodies.[15] Marriage thus helps us control concupiscence, that is, the human desire for sensual gratification.

The Second Vatican Council rejected the hierarchical language of the two ends of marriage and reconsidered the procreative model. The Council document *Gaudium et spes* describes marriage as a covenant between two persons who wish to participate in the sacrament of marriage. A number of Catholic ethicists call this the "interpersonal model of marriage."[16] This interpersonal model is, following Vatican II, based on "the nature of the human person and his acts." The model recognizes the various goods that humans experience in marriage and in marital sexual intercourse. Procreation is one of those goods, and it is one that must be realized in "the full sense of mutual self-giving" and "in the context of true love" (GS, no. 51). In marriage, a couple unites interpersonally and not just sexually or genitally. Following the Magisterium's renewed understanding of marriage, then, married couples may engage in sexual intercourse with the intention of experiencing erotic love. And yet some married couples may choose not to have children. According to Catholic teaching, these childless couples may still participate fully in the sacrament of marriage, fulfill the purpose of marriage, and become religiously, socially, culturally, and spiritually fruitful.[17]

Divorce

The *Catechism of the Catholic Church* teaches that a consummated marriage between two persons is indissoluble (CCC nos. 2382, 2397). It is permanent. To demonstrate its permanency in scripture, the *Catechism* appeals to the teachings of Jesus: "Whoever divorces his wife and marries another, commits adultery against her; and if she divorces her husband and marries another, she commits adultery (Mark 10:11-12)" (CCC, no. 1650). Unlike Eastern Christianity since the sixth century and Protestant Christianity since the sixteenth century, Catholicism does not allow for divorce in cases involving adultery. This would appear to dismiss the teaching of Jesus in Matthew 5:32, which seems to allow for divorce on the basis of infidelity: "But I say to you that anyone who divorces his wife, except on the ground of unchastity, causes her to commit adultery; and whoever marries a divorced woman commits adultery." In fact, Catholic teaching has historically dismissed the phrase "except on the ground of unchastity" as a later insertion into the sayings of Jesus, which is one reason why the Magisterium uses the version in the Gospel of Mark.[18]

Of course, marriages do break down and some couples may seek civil divorce. But according to Catholic teaching, even if a couple receives a civil divorce, both remain married under Catholic canon law.[19] Consequently, if a divorced Catholic were to remarry in a civil ceremony, he or she would be living in adultery with the new spouse. Strictly speaking, the Catholic person remarried outside the Church should seek an annulment and either remain unmarried or return to the initial sacramental marriage.

Starting in the 1960s, as laws changed to make divorces easier to obtain, and as more and more Catholics were seeking divorce, many Catholic theologians and pastors directed couples in failed marriages to seek an annulment, which involves having the marriage annulled according to canon law. An annulment means that the Church no longer validates the sacramentality of the annulled marriage. While the marriage may have been legally binding in civil courts, an annulment through canon law means that the Church recognizes the union as non-sacramental and thus not a legally binding marriage under the law of the Church. Grounds for annulment include untruthfulness about one's openness to children, coerced marriage, abuse, and no intention to be faithful. Once an annulment has been given, the man and woman are free to marry without committing the sin of adultery. As anyone who has ever gone through the experience of an annulment knows, the process can be time consuming, expensive, and emotionally demanding.

Some Catholic ethicists have noted that, since Vatican II, the Magisterium's teaching regarding divorce reflects a juridical understanding of marriage.[20] Following the model established at the Council of Trent, marriage was conceived of as a *contract*, one that was finally sealed in the consummating act of sexual intercourse. Marriage was a juridical "act" that formed a bond that existed apart from the marriage relationship. This Tridentine model of marriage as a legal contract is evident, for example, in the Code of Canon Law from 1917. But the bishops at the Second Vatican Council rejected that juridical model. According to current Catholic teaching, marriage is an interpersonal *covenant* and continually developing.[21] Indeed, one distinguishing characteristic of a covenant is that all partners in a covenant are assisting each other toward a common goal. A contract, by comparison, legally establishes the terms and conditions of the relationship. A covenant is a mutual project, while a contract stands above a relationship and demands compliance. In effect, the Magisterium has yet to work out the tension between the juridical approach to marriage, which dominated Catholic teaching for four hundred years, and the interpersonal approach developed in the twentieth century.

Until the Magisterium revisits the Church's approach to marriage, we wait. Meanwhile, we have many faithful divorced Catholics who are living unfulfilled lives, frustrated because they are unable to remarry in the Church. For example, a few years ago, I had a mature student in my course on Christian sexual ethics—I'll call her Maureen. Over the course of the semester, Maureen told her story of how, in her early twenties, she married her high-school sweetheart in the Church and had a child. After a few years, her husband began drinking heavily and abusing her. Outwardly, they kept up the appearance of a good Catholic family. They continued to attend Mass and, following the advice of their parish priest, even attended a weekend Marriage Encounter program. She put up with the abuse for a couple of years, but it was destroying her emotionally, spiritually, and physically. She filed for divorce and custody of their young son. After seven years of marriage, four of it a living hell, she was free. Drained by the experience, Maureen spent the next decade or so raising her son, working as a secretary in a small business, and avoiding intimate relationships. But then, in her late 30s, she began to fall in love with a younger man who taught at her son's Catholic school. They talked about getting married—they wanted to be married in the Church, and they were open to children. Maureen considered an annulment on the basis that her husband had destroyed a canonically valid marriage (see CCC no. 2386), but she was getting mixed messages from her local priest and her relationship with her (former) husband wasn't pleasant. Besides, money was tight and she thought it better to put any extra money toward her son's extracurricular activities and her mortgage payments. After a few more agonizing months with this man, she ended the relationship because she felt as though she was getting in the way of his happiness. Sitting in my class, in her mid-40s, Maureen told us that her son has moved to British Columbia to attend university, she has moments of loneliness in spite of having close friends, she's considering a second career in social work, and she's longing for erotic love and sexual contact, something she hasn't experienced for almost 25 years.

Pastorally, there is much work to be done to meet the needs of people like Maureen. Ethically, there are questions we need to ask. For instance, as a matter of justice, love, and human dignity, how do we account for the experiences of people like Maureen and others who, through no fault of their own, find themselves divorced and unable to remarry in the Church? These are not just questions for canon law scholars and moral theologians, but for the whole body of Christ. Surely, if the Church takes human dignity seriously, including the human desire to experience the gift of erotic love, then the Magisterium will revisit its processes, if not teaching, regarding divorce and remarriage. As it stands now, the teaching seems unfair to many people like Maureen who want to remain faithful Catholics, and yet want to move on from marriages that no longer serve the good of the human persons involved in them. In Maureen's case, she feels as though she's being punished, if not revictimized, by Church teaching for divorcing a man who abused her.

Birth Control, Masturbation, and Same-Sex Relationships

Early Christian scholars recognized and respected sexual drives as natural. But following the Greeks and a particular reading of the Genesis creation accounts, they maintained that sexual intercourse should take place only for the purpose of procreation in marriage. Adopting a biological model, they believed that sex was primarily to preserve the species, something God told not only the first human beings to do ("be fruitful and multiply"), but also the animals. For the most part, these scholars believed that the only "good" in sexual intercourse was the biological result of fertility: children.

For some early Christian scholars, though, sex had to be avoided altogether, even by married couples, because the sex act required passion, fleshly desire, and some measure of pleasure. For these scholars, anything but abstinence from sex would fall short of our calling to avoid evil. For example, Clement of Alexandria (150–215) wrote: "If we are required to practise self-control—as we should—we ought to manifest it even more with our wives ... Sexual intercourse does no one any good, except that it harms the beloved. Intercourse performed licitly is an occasion of sin, unless done purely to beget children: A hired wife shall be accounted as a sow."[22]

Augustine taught that sex is permissible only within the confines of marriage and for the purpose of reproduction. The ideal marriage should become an asexual relationship, he believed. Once a couple has become infertile or the passions have cooled, the procreative aspects of marriage would wane, allowing the good of "friendship" to flourish. But for a fertile couple, lust, sexual desire, and the "heat" of passion must be initiated by an act of volition. If those desires are initiated by an "unruly member of the body" (use your imagination here), then they must be brought under submission; otherwise, any action resulting from those desires is sinful. Also, if the sexual organs are stimulated and enjoyed without regard to the final act of procreation, then, according to Augustine, the act is sinful, for it reflects misdirected concupiscence that is associated with humanity's fallen nature. In a word, Augustine concluded that sexual intercourse, even in marriage, is a disruptive force.

Thomas Aquinas was less suspicious of sexual desire than Augustine. Writing some eight hundred years after Augustine, Thomas made a distinction between sexual desire that occurs outside marriage—he called this desire "lust"—and sexual desire that occurs within marriage. Desire that occurs outside of marriage is "non-natural" to the extent that the desire is not limited by reason or any natural institution. Without limits, Thomas argued, sexual desire has the power to overwhelm a person, to distort reason, and to cause a person to live a life devoid of the virtues. Marriage limits that desire and focuses it on the only truly unambiguous good of sexual intercourse: procreation.

Current Catholic teaching regarding the "goods" of sexual intercourse tends to follow Thomas's line of thinking. Also greatly influenced by Pope John Paul's teaching on love and the theology of the body, the Magisterium teaches that physical sexual intimacy is not merely biological but instead concerns the "innermost being of the human person." Moreover, sexuality "is realized in a truly human way only if it is an integral part of the love by which a man and woman commit themselves totally to one another until death" (CCC, no. 2361).[23] Sexual intercourse thus comes with an obligation to remain faithful to one another and, following a long-held teaching in the Church, to be open to children.

The Catholic ethicist Lisa Sowle Cahill rightly observes that so much of the current talk around sexuality has much more to do with "one's own sexual experience and that of one's partner, and the physical and affective relation of the couple, rather than the likelihood of conception." However, Cahill contends, if we are to take into account all the meanings of heterosexual intercourse, we must include its capability of procreation. But we must also take into account that, given the considerations of actual fertility, procreation need not and cannot be part of every sexual experience, even those that don't use artificial birth control. Such is the case of sexual intercourse involving post-menopausal women, spouses who, for medical reasons, are sterile, or persons who are naturally infertile. But in other cases, it is possible that the physical, emotional, spiritual, and procreative meanings of sexuality come together—"in passion, tenderness, and a love so full that sexuality mediates new being."[24]

Contraception and Natural Family Planning

Pope Paul VI's encyclical *Humanae vitae* (On Human Life, 1968) definitively established official Catholic teaching regarding the use of artificial birth control (contraception) and natural family planning (NFP). In *Humanae vitae*, Pope Paul appealed to a natural law tradition to conclude that artificial birth control is morally illicit. The reasoning goes like this: God designed men and women to engage in sexual intercourse for the purpose of procreation and the experience of marital love. Artificial birth control violates the natural law because it unnaturally prohibits the natural, divinely ordered process of procreation. By contrast, NFP (sometimes called the "rhythm method") doesn't violate the natural law because engaging in sexual intercourse during a woman's infertile periods is consistent with God's plan. Even though sex during these periods of time is not intended to lead to procreation, NFP doesn't close off the possibility that the woman might become pregnant as a result of sexual intercourse.

As Jean Porter astutely notes, Pope Paul's teaching differs slightly but significantly from Thomas's natural law argument. For Thomas, the truth of the natural law is not primarily biological but instead theological. But in *Humanae vitae*, Pope Paul bases his teaching on an "appeal to the structure of the sexual act and its inherent orientation toward procreation, as this is revealed by rational analysis prior to theological interpretation."[25] In other words, Pope Paul prioritized the goodness of the sexual-procreative act over other human actions and goods.

Pope Paul realized that his prohibition against contraception would create controversy not only in society at large but also in the Church. He encouraged a process of pastoral reflection on how to instill his teaching into the practices of Catholics. In *Humanae vitae*, Pope Paul defended his prohibition on contraception on the basis that it addressed social ills associated with artificial contraception. He said that the continued use of contraception would contribute to marital infidelity, the breakdown of marriages, and the lowering of moral standards. He was also concerned that the use of contraceptive methods might lead a man to "forget the reverence due to a woman, and, disregarding her physical and emotional equilibrium, reduce her to being a mere instrument for the satisfaction of his own desires, no longer considering her as his partner whom he should surround with care and affection" (HV, no. 17).

The issue of contraception has unfortunately created deep divisions within the Catholic Church. Even before *Humanae vitae*, there was faithful disagreement among the bishops as well as among Catholic theologians. To provide pastoral direction on the issue, which had become acute due to the invention of the birth control pill, Pope John XXIII created the Pontifical Commission on Birth Control in 1963. Shortly after Pope John's death, Pope Paul expanded the Commission over the next three years, eventually including 71 members from around the globe and from various walks of life, including medical professionals, theologians, women who worked in the medical profession, and bishops. One of the central questions facing the Pontifical Commission was whether contraception is intrinsically evil and whether it violates natural law. In a preliminary vote of theologians advising the Pontifical Commission, fifteen said "No," contraception is not intrinsically evil and does not violate natural law; four disagreed. At the end of the process, the executive committee of the Pontifical Commission, fifteen bishops, voted on three questions: (1) "Is contraception intrinsically evil?" Nine bishops answered "No," three said "Yes," and three abstained; (2) "Is contraception, as defined by the Majority Report, in basic continuity with tradition and the declarations of the Magisterium?" Nine bishops responded "Yes," five said "No," and one abstained; (3) Should the Magisterium speak on this question as soon as possible?" Fourteen responded "Yes," and one said "No." Both the Majority Report and the Minority Report from the four dissenters were forwarded to Pope Paul.

The difference between the majority and minority boiled down to their interpretation of openness to procreation. According to the minority, "each and every marriage act must remain open to the transmission of life." The majority said that marriage itself, not each and every act, is to be open to the transmission of life. In many respects, the minority report represented an adherence to the procreation model of marriage that dominated Catholic teaching until Vatican II. The majority report, which Pope Paul rejected, emphasized the interpersonal model of marriage affirmed by the bishops at Vatican II.

According to reputable research and polling data, an overwhelming majority of Catholics in North America and Europe are not adhering to the prescriptions in *Humanae vitae*. For instance, in the United States, roughly 82 percent of Catholics believe that artificial birth control is morally acceptable, only 15 percent say it's morally wrong, and 3 percent have no opinion or say that it depends on the situation.[26] Moreover, according to data gathered from the 2006–2008 National Survey of Family Growth, 98 percent of sexually experienced, self-identified Catholic women of child-bearing age have used a method of birth control other than Natural Family Planning at some point in their lives. This same set of data confirmed the findings of prior studies that showed only about 2 percent of Catholics ever used NFP.[27]

How do we respond to this situation? One of the many ways is to conclude that those not following the teachings of the Magisterium are simply living in disobedience and, perhaps, in willful disregard of official Church teaching. Those using contraception must adhere to the clear teaching of the Magisterium and immediately seek alternatives, such as NFP. Another way—perhaps a pastoral way—is to see in a good number of cases Catholic couples wrestling with a complex moral situation: namely, balancing sexual intercourse (a manifestation of conjugal love) with responsible parenthood and other responsibilities in their lives. In these cases, Catholics may understand the reasoning behind the Magisterium's proscription against contraception; the challenge is that their real-life family, work, and health conditions end up being weighed against the prospects of having additional children and responsibilities. The Catholic theologian Cristina Traina, in a profoundly personal article entitled "Papal Ideals, Marital Realities," describes how she has struggled with the tension between being open to procreation in sexual intercourse and being a responsible parent, attentive wife, and the primary breadwinner in her household. After the birth of her third child, amid work-related stress, breastfeeding, and a resulting "uninterpretable" fertility cycle, she essentially closed down the possibility of sexual intercourse. While she relished motherhood, another child would have been disastrous to her career, her family, and her mental and spiritual health. She admits that over the course of her married life, she had engaged in sexual intercourse perhaps only ten times where she could truly focus on her husband and the joys of sex. The other times, there was unhealthy fear—the fear that comes with the realization that pregnancy would undermine her capacity to provide care to her children, her husband, and her students and colleagues at her university. Even more troubling, Traina says, are the experiences of women who are poor, marginalized, and likely unhealthy. For these women, another child can be utterly devastating.

Traina's point is that *Humanae vitae* and official Catholic teaching on contraception essentially subordinate other goods—such as responsible parenthood, spousal attention, family welfare, and human flourishing that comes with one's job—to the absolute good of natural intercourse. Far from creating mutual delight in marital sexual relations, she argues, natural intercourse for some Catholics generates anxiety, suppresses sexual desire, and fosters frustration. She concludes, "This is not, in my experience, a path to happy marriage and responsible parenthood."[28]

Pastorally, there is much work to be done in communicating the moral goodness of NFP to Catholic couples. Whatever the reasons, NFP doesn't appear to be a meaningful family planning option. Ethically, there is no doubt that many Catholics turn to contraception because it's convenient and effective. But is contraception selfish? In some cases, the answer is yes. In other cases, though, the reasons why some women, in particular, turn to contraception are selfless in nature: caring for a family, meeting work-related obligations, and financial responsibility. One of the important factors sometimes lost in this moral debate is the fact that North Americans and Europeans live and work in societies that do not adequately support the type of family planning envisioned by the Magisterium. For instance, many employers do not provide paid pregnancy leave to women. In the United States, unlike Canada, there is no paid parental leave program. Many mothers experience pregnancy discrimination in the workplace, leading to lost promotions and reduced pay. And many men find that their workplace culture makes it difficult for them to take parental leaves. The underlying issue is largely the bottom line: parental leave programs are costly to businesses and, if funded in part by government, to taxpayers. Indeed, Pope Paul recognized this matter of social justice in *Humanae vitae*. Referring to his encyclical *Populorum progressio* (On the Development of Peoples, 1967), he stated:

> No one can, without being grossly unfair, make divine Providence responsible for what clearly seems to be the result of misguided governmental policies, of an insufficient sense of social justice, of a selfish accumulation of material goods, and finally of a culpable failure to undertake those initiatives and responsibilities which would raise the standard of living of peoples and their children. (HV, no. 23)

In other words, we must recognize that the Magisterium's teaching regarding the promotion of life and the family is linked to a prophetic demand for social, political, and economic conditions rooted in justice and human dignity.

The moral challenges of contraception are not limited to birth control. Since the 1980s, the scourge of HIV/AIDS has intensified the contraception debate within the Church. The official Catholic position is that condoms or any form of artificial contraception are a violation of the natural law. Still, within the Church there are theologians, bishops, and episcopal conferences that take the interpersonal understanding of sexuality and allow for individuals to appeal to conscience to balance the various goods. For instance, Bishop Kevin Dowling of Rustenburg, South Africa, insisted that "in certain circumstances the use of a condom is allowable not as a contraceptive but to prevent disease."[29] Even Pope Benedict XVI has stated that condom usage may be allowable in certain situations. The Pope said, "where the intention is to reduce the risk of infection, [condom use] can nevertheless be a first step on the way to another, more humane sexuality."[30] For both Bishop Dowling and Pope Benedict, there is a weighing of goods and intentions. In this case, they seem to acknowledge that condoms may be used if the intention is to avoid the spread of a death-dealing virus. In any case, the statements of Bishop Dowling and Pope Benedict demonstrate a recognition that the goods of protecting the health of sexual partners, providing for families, and strengthening communities are greater than the moral illicitness of prophylactic contraception.

The reasoning used by Bishop Dowling and Pope Benedict is called the principle of double effect, which holds that an act, which is morally neutral or good, may have two effects: one that is intentional and one that is unintentional. In the case of contraception, the Magisterium holds that contraceptive methods may be used if they are for therapeutic means, such as to cure diseases or relieve severe pain (HV, no. 17). For instance, some Catholic women are prescribed the pill to relieve severe menstrual pain caused by endometriosis or uterine fibroids. In this case, the primary intention and effect is therapeutic, to relieve severe pain, while the secondary effect is infertility. However, if the motive for contraception is birth control, then the Magisterium teaches that the act is morally illicit. Bishop Dowling and Pope Benedict follow this same reasoning: the motivation for using condoms is to prevent the spread of HIV/AIDS, the secondary effect is a barrier to insemination.

Masturbation

Historically, the Christian tradition has looked to scripture to find prohibitions against masturbation. The story of Onan, found in Genesis 38:1-11, is often cited as the definitive example of God condemning the act. In fact, another term for masturbation in the Christian tradition is "onanism." The story, however, has nothing to do with masturbation. It has to do with ancient familial obligations. In this case, a woman by the name of Tamar married King Judah's oldest son, Er. However, Er did something to offend God (what that was isn't clear) and died as a result. Tragically, he died childless. Following tradition, Onan, Er's brother, was obligated to have sexual intercourse with his dead brother's wife, Tamar, until she became pregnant—the child that would be born from this act would bear Er's name, even though Onan was the biological father. For whatever reason, Onan refused to ejaculate in Tamar, spilling his seed on the ground. Because Onan declined to perform his duty as the brother-in-law to the barren Tamar, God killed Onan.

Today, few biblical scholars and Christian ethicists claim that scripture provides definitive teaching regarding masturbation. Indeed, the *Catechism of the Catholic Church* acknowledges that there is no specific teaching in scripture. Instead, like many Christians who wish to prohibit masturbation based on scripture, the Magisterium holds that the act is condemned when the New Testament speaks generally of "impurity," "unchasteness," and "other vices contrary to chastity and continence."[31] The official Catholic teaching on masturbation relies primarily on a traditional understanding of the human person and the natural law. It holds that every instance of masturbation constitutes an act that is intrinsically and gravely disordered. The Magisterium defines masturbation as "the deliberate stimulation of the genital organs in order to derive sexual pleasure" (CCC, no. 2352). Consistent with the natural-biological law argument put by Pope Paul VI in *Humanae vitae*, the Magisterium says that any masturbation is morally illicit because the sexual faculties of a person have been aroused outside of marriage, the only institution in which sexual stimulation is allowed by the moral law. Moreover, the Magisterium says, masturbation denies the meaning of mutual self-giving and human procreation, the natural-biological end of the sex act. In short, the purpose of sexual stimulation is to lead to mutual, self-giving intercourse that is open to procreation. But masturbation denies both the mutuality and the natural-biological ends of sexual pleasure. According to the Magisterium, masturbation is so disordered that it may be a mortal sin—that is, so long as the act is deliberate and known to be against God's order. The seriousness of mortal sin should not be overlooked. Those guilty of mortal sin are separated from God and thus, upon death, destined to spend eternity in hell. Only confession to and absolution by a priest will put the sinner in right relationship with God.

Many Christian ethicists, both Catholic and non-Catholic, point out that traditional prohibitions against masturbation rely on anthropological assumptions that we do not share with the scholars of antiquity or the Middle Ages. For example, many Greek philosophers believed that the woman was nothing more than an incubator who provided heat and nourishment to the growing person inside her. The woman's womb added nothing to the child—it was the man's "seed" that contained the entire essence of the human person. For Aristotle, male seed was viewed as an efficient cause that changed the nutritive material supplied by the female. According to this view, every act of insemination (sexual intercourse leading to ejaculation) was of itself procreative. Based on these views of nature, it was a violation of the rules of nature for a man to waste his seed. To do so meant that a man was effectively wasting a life. Similarly, in the Middle Ages, many medical researchers, philosophers, and theologians believed that a man was not just depositing his seed into the womb of the woman, but he was depositing a human person into her. This "realization" made prohibitions against masturbation even more serious. Masturbation was, in effect, a form of homicide and had to be forbidden. On the whole, what these historical views share is the belief that masturbation is not just some youthful pleasure but a fundamental violation of nature.

Many contemporary theologians and ethicists think masturbation is morally neutral. Instead of focusing on the biological aspects of sexuality, they focus on other goods, such as justice and wholeness. In some cases, they argue, masturbation may be morally illicit. These instances might lead to psychological maladjustment, injustice toward another, or physical abuse to one's self. In other cases, masturbation may be morally licit. Examples often cited here include medical reasons, the natural inclination for youth to discover their bodies, and mutual masturbation within the confines of marriage. Indeed, as medical technologies have advanced and people are living longer, some ethicists maintain that masturbation may be the only way those suffering from sickness, injury, or age-related changes to the body can engage in sexual relationships with their spouses. As a matter of justice and human dignity, they contend, masturbation may in fact be one way of engaging in just, erotic, marital love. However, the Magisterium of the Church makes no allowances for such acts.

Questions regarding masturbation have largely focused on male masturbation and the relationship between male orgasm and procreation. But what about female masturbation? There is no doubt that the official teaching of the Church condemns both male and female masturbation.[32] However, with more research into women's sexuality and reproduction, a number of ethicists question whether the natural law tradition in Catholic teaching accounts for women's bodies and their experiences. In penetrative-procreative sexual intercourse, the male penis is essential, for it must be sufficiently stimulated to release ejaculate. However, the female clitoris serves no necessary biological role in procreation. It is certainly not the case that women must achieve orgasm or even sexual arousal to become pregnant. This has led some to question, then, the primary purpose of the clitoris. If it's pleasure, then must the clitoris be associated solely with sex, since it is unnecessary for procreation? Or is the prohibition against female masturbation merely the result of the Christian tradition's suspicion of pleasure and residue of the flesh–spirit dichotomy of the early Church? For many Catholic ethicists, these questions point to a need in the Catholic tradition for a re-examination of masturbation in light of modern understandings of the human body, recent medical discoveries, and the experiences of those for whom penetrative sexual intercourse is impossible.

Same-Sex Relationships

In general, scripture says very little about persons who engage in same-sex acts, but what it does say is not particularly affirming of either those persons engaging in those acts or the acts themselves. For example, Leviticus 18:22; 20:13 prohibits males from lying "with a male as with a woman." The penalty is death. Some point to the story of Sodom in Genesis 19:1-29 as evidence that same-sex relations are sinful. According to this story, Lot, Abraham's nephew, was hosting a group of unknown visitors (or "angels"). The men of Sodom heard of these visitors and soon surrounded Lot's house, banging on his door and demanding that Lot send the visitors out to be abused and raped by the mob. Following custom, Lot provided protection to his guests, offering instead two virgin daughters. As the mob rushed Lot's house, the angels blinded the men. The next day God destroyed the entire villages of Sodom and Gomorrah.

Paul says in his letter to the church in Rome that God gave the wicked "up to degrading passions. Their women exchanged natural intercourse for unnatural, and in the same way also the men, giving up natural intercourse with women, were consumed with passion for one another. Men committed shameless acts with men and received in their own persons the due penalty for their error" (Romans 1:26-27). In a letter to the church in Corinth, Paul declared: "Do you not know that wrongdoers will not inherit the kingdom of God? Do not be deceived! Fornicators, idolaters, adulterers, male prostitutes, sodomites [homosexuals], thieves, the greedy, drunkards, revilers, robbers—none of these will inherit the kingdom of God" (1 Corinthians 6:9-10).

Our purpose here is not to examine in detail the different ways these passages may be interpreted. However, a few words are in order. To begin, biblical scholars and theologians point out that the prohibition against and penalty for same-sex relations in Leviticus also applies to adulterers and women who have lost their virginity prior to marriage. In context, the concern was to distinguish Israel from neighbouring tribes that apparently practised such acts.

The story of Sodom and Gomorrah, biblical scholars note, was not about homosexuality. Ezekiel (16:14) interprets the story as evidence of Sodom's unwillingness to share its abundance with those who were poor. Similarly, Amos (4:1, 11) announced the destruction of Israel on the grounds that, following Sodom's example, the people oppressed the needy and crushed the poor. More problematically, we might argue today, was the willingness of Lot to offer up his two young daughters to be raped.

The meaning of Paul's statement in Romans is a source of continued debate. Paul's likely concern was, consistent with the moral values of the Greco-Roman world, with a man choosing to demean himself by taking on the role of the lower woman, thereby becoming "effeminate" or "soft." This concern is even more explicit in the passage from 1 Corinthians. The Greek terms used in this passage, which are translated as "homosexual" in some translations and "sodomite" above, connote "softness," in particular the passive role a male prostitute might assume with another man. Scholars point to the fact that pederasty (erotic relations between an older man and an adolescent boy) was a widely accepted practice in the Greco-Roman world. They also note that Roman soldiers were encouraged to have male companions in the field because the homoerotic love soldiers held for each other made them better fighters. Indeed, Roman culture recognized those relationships as generally valid, but it reaped scorn on relationships deemed "soft."

In general, scriptural writers, especially the New Testament writers, condemn homosexuality as a perversion of the heterosexual condition, which they assumed was natural and normative. Today, however, medical researchers, geneticists, social scientists, and psychiatrists, to name just a few, tend to understand homosexuality as a naturally oc-curring condition in human beings and, for the most part, reject the heterosexual norm. For instance, in 1973 the American Psychiatric Association (APA) removed "homosexuality" as a mental disorder from the new diagnostic manual, the DSM-III. In effect, the APA no longer recognizes homosexuality as a disorder that needs a cure. Moreover, since the 1940s, demographers and researchers who study sexuality have concluded that roughly 10 percent of the population in North America has had a same-sex sexual experience.[33] According to the U.S. govern-ment's comprehensive survey on sexual practices, which was conducted by the national Center for Health Statistics, 6.5 percent of men have engaged in homosexual acts, and 11 percent of women have done so. Rhetorically, some activists point out the fact that roughly 10 percent of the population is left-handed, more or less equivalent to the number of people who have engaged in homosexual acts, and that it has been only in the last century that the West has accepted left-handedness as natural.

The modern tendency to avoid seeing homosexuality as an immoral perversion of the heterosexual norm stands in stark contrast to the of-ficial teachings of the Church. According to the Magisterium, scripture firmly teaches that homosexual acts are "intrinsically disordered" and "contrary to the natural law." Homosexual acts are closed to life and "do not proceed from a genuine affective and sexual complementarity" (CCC, no. 2357). As a result, "homosexual persons are called to chas-tity." Through discipline, prayer, and counselling, homosexuals "can and should gradually and resolutely approach Christian perfection" (CCC, no. 2359).

Given the sharp differences between the modern sciences and the teachings of the Church on the naturalness of homosexual persons, critical questions have been raised, both outside and within the Church, about the anthropological foundations of the Church's teaching on homosexuality. In particular, Todd A. Salzman and Michael G. Lawler, in their provocative book *The Sexual Person* (2008), take a revisionist approach to ethics to argue that the official teachings of the Church are based on a flawed, largely medieval conception of the human body and sexuality. Although their argument is complex, let's focus on two sets of questions to get at the core of their criticism.

First, are human beings created homosexual, or is homosexuality a "lifestyle" some choose? And if certain people are born homosexual, are they born essentially disordered? This set of questions is important for Salzman and Lawler because, in traditional Catholic moral theology, human persons must be free to choose in order to be held morally accountable for their actions. The Magisterium acknowledges that, for many homosexuals, their "condition" is not a choice but a trial. It's a trial because it is "objectively disordered." Being inclined toward homosexuality isn't a sin, according to official Church teaching, but engaging in homosexual acts is. However, Salzman and Lawler maintain that this teaching effectively violates the self-integrity and human dignity of the homosexual person.

To defend their argument, they appeal to the Catholic teaching that sexuality is an essential part of one's self-integrity. They point out that the Congregation for the Doctrine of the Faith, in the important document *Persona humana* (On Certain Questions Concerning Sexual Ethics, 1975), accepts the nearly universal premise that from sex the "human person receives the characteristics that, on the biological, psychological, and spiritual levels, make that person a man or a woman, and thereby largely condition his or her progress toward maturity."[34] Moreover, Salzman and Lawler insist that any discussion of self-integrity must include an analysis of sexual orientation, a "psychosexual attraction (erotic, emotional, and affective) toward particular individual *persons*" of the opposite or same sex. By dismissing homosexuality as disordered and thus not an authentically human orientation, magisterial teaching denies homosexual persons the possibility of acting on their natural inclinations. "If what a person *is* unalterably by 'nature' and the design of God is homosexual," Salzman and Lawler write, "then both sexual integrity and self-integrity require that the homosexual orientation be embraced and integrated into the personality, and they allow expression in just and loving acts."[35] As a matter of moral reasoning, they contend, it is immoral to insist that a homosexual must go against nature and conscience to behave as a heterosexual. Furthermore, it is a denial of human dignity to demand that homosexual persons must, in effect, *never* act in accord with their natural sexual desires. To foster the self-integrity and human dignity of all persons, Salzman and Lawler propose a rethinking of "nature," one rooted in the empirical reality that there are heterosexual and homosexual persons.

Second, how is a marital relationship between homosexuals different from a marital relationship between heterosexuals who are, as a couple, permanently infertile? As we have reiterated a number of times in this chapter, official Catholic teaching holds that marriage has two ends: procreation and the good of the spouses, the latter sometimes referred to generally as "complementarity." In the section dealing with homosexuality, the *Catechism of the Catholic Church* refers to the concept of "sexual complementarity" in justifying the Church's opposition to same-sex relationships. But Salzman and Lawler ask, "What is sexual complementarity?" They note that the Congregation for the Doctrine of the Faith, in its *Considerations Regarding Proposals to Give Legal Recognition to Unions Between Homosexual Persons* (2003), offers an expansive definition involving not only marital intercourse (or reproductive complementarity) but also parenting and raising children. According to the CDF, sexual complementarity includes an openness to creation as well as a familial relationship in which the mother and father (biological or adoptive) are the ones who can best care for and nurture children. Salzman and Lawler conclude that the Magisterium's teaching essentially demands "heterogenital complementarity" and not reproductive complementarity. In the case of both the homosexual couple and the permanently infertile couple, sex acts are biologically closed to reproduction, which means that the moral choice to be "open to the transmission of life" is rendered ambiguous, if not meaningless. Yet official Catholic teaching affirms the licitness of the heterosexual relationship and forbids the homosexual relationship on the basis that the heterosexual couple is still acting according to nature because their genitals complement one another in acts open to procreation.

At the core of their argument, Salzman and Lawler maintain that the Magisterium is using a flawed approach to moral reasoning by attempting to derive a moral *ought* directly from a biological *is*. That approach to reasoning goes like this when it comes to sexuality: because the penetration of the male's penis into the female's vagina, leading to ejaculation, *is* the natural process of a sexual act open to procreation, we *ought* to engage only in heterosexual acts (within the confines of marriage). This type of moral reasoning opens the Church to charges of "physicalism," Salzman and Lawler claim, which ultimately denies the moral value of a person's intention or circumstances and naively asserts that nature interprets itself. For them, "nature" is a "socially constructed category." Consequently, "when we derive moral obligations from 'nature,' we are actually deriving them from our human attention to and our interpretation of and evaluation of 'nature.'"[36] Instead of basing the Church's teaching on socially constructed norms, they conclude, the Magisterium should look to empirical research, which confirms homosexuality as a naturally occurring condition in humans, and begin to develop a moral theology that focuses on love, justice, and human flourishing.

In response to Salzman and Lawler's *The Sexual Person*, the U.S. Conference of Catholic Bishops Committee on Doctrine issued a statement making "it clear that neither the methodology of *The Sexual Person* nor the conclusions that depart from authoritative Church teaching constitute authentic expressions of Catholic theology."[37] In general, the Committee on Doctrine objects to Salzman and Lawler's appeal to and application of the four sources of ethics: scripture, tradition, reason, and experience. First, the Committee criticizes Salzman and Lawler's "exaggerated appeal to historical consciousness,"[38] which, the Committee argues, enables them to dismiss scriptural condemnations of homosexuality as scientifically inaccurate and thus irrelevant to contemporary readers on this specific matter. While the Committee acknowledges that the Church uses historical methods to interpret texts, "in the final analysis, all interpretation of Scripture is subject to the authoritative judgement for the Church's deposit of faith," namely, the Magisterium.[39]

Second, the Committee on Doctrine claims that Salzman and Lawler effectively disregard the firm teachings of the Magisterium when they assert, "the Magisterium does not pretend to pronounce on every last detail or to impose final decisions; it understands itself as informing and guiding believers and as leaving the final judgment and application to their faithful and responsible conscience."[40] Moreover, the Committee disagrees with their view that the judgement of a particular sexual act should be determined on the basis of its impact on human flourishing. According to the Committee, this standard is "simply inadequate as a criterion for moral judgement."[41] The Committee concludes that "the chief concern of the authors of *The Sexual Person* appears to be to provide a moral justification for sexual behaviors that are common in contemporary culture but rejected as immoral by the Church."[42]

Third, the Committee contends that Salzman and Lawler have a flawed understanding of the natural law. "Where as the Church teaches that natural law is a human participation in the divine law," the Committee writes, "the skeptical presuppositions of Salzman and Lawler seem to deny the reality of such a participation."[43] Simply put, Salzman and Lawler rely too heavily on the social construction of knowledge and the premise that what we have considered "natural" is culturally specific moral actions. According to the Committee, "the root problem here is philosophical, an epistemology distorted by skepticism."[44] Because of their apparent skepticism, the Committee fundamentally rejects Salzman and Lawler's claim that "there are not absolute material norms of right and wrong actions." To be fair, the Committee does recognize that Salzman and Lawler think there is only a universal ethical norm—the ethical imperative to do good and avoid evil. However, the Committee upholds traditional magisterial teaching that the natural law provides human beings with specific material goods, and it is on this basis that the Church rejects homosexuality because it violates the basic material norm of sexual complementarity and the basic good of the family.

And fourth, the Committee on Doctrine criticizes Salzman and Lawler for presenting experience as the primary criterion for moral judgments. While the Committee recognizes that Salzman and Lawler present experience as an authoritative source, and wish to promote dialogue with scripture, tradition, reason, and experience, they ultimately understand experience "to be the determinative source of moral knowledge in matters of sexual theology," the Committee concludes.[45] The Committee comes to this conclusion on the basis that, once Salzman and Lawler have rendered scripture, tradition, and reason to be little more than social constructs, all that remains is experience to be the arbiter of moral judgment.

For many of us, no doubt, the theological conflict between the USCCB Committee on Doctrine and the authors of *The Sexual Person* may seem like an abstract debate and thus have little bearing on our individual and collective pursuit of ethical being. However, for Catholics, there is more at stake here than just winning an academic argument. The ethical issue boils down to how we understand and appeal to scripture, tradition, the natural law, and experience. Can scripture give definitive direction on sexual acts even though scriptural writers did not understand homosexuality the way most modern societies do? Are the teachings of the Magisterium based on empirical evidence regarding human sexuality and human nature? Beyond the imperative "do good and avoid evil," how specific is the natural law when it comes to material norms such as sexual acts and the composition of the family? And does the Church adequately account for the experiences of married couples, the divorced, the physically disabled who wish to engage in sexual activity and yet are unable to adhere to the Church's teaching regarding sexual intercourse, and intersex persons who were born with chromosomal abnormalities or whose anatomy doesn't adhere to the "natural" male-female body? Regrettably, these and other similar questions continue to create divisions in the Church.

CHAPTER 5

The Ethics of Life and Death

During my final year of high school, my senior English teacher made her students read Shakespeare's *Macbeth*. Back then I couldn't figure out why we were reading a bloody story of an ambitious general who, after being goaded by his wife, commits regicide to become king of Scotland and then continues on what amounts to a killing spree over the next few years to remain in power. In spite of my inability to place *Macbeth* in any context in high school, the story of the brutal, conflicted, and often cold-hearted Macbeth taking stock of his life after the suicide of his guilt-stricken wife and co-conspirator triggered something deep within me. It caused me to consider the meaning of life and death.

> To-morrow, and to-morrow, and to-morrow,
> Creeps in this petty pace from day to day,
> To the last syllable of recorded time;
> And all our yesterdays have lighted fools
> The way to dusty death. Out, out, brief candle!
> Life's but a walking shadow, a poor player,
> That struts and frets his hour upon the stage,
> And then is heard no more. It is a tale
> Told by an idiot, full of sound and fury,
> Signifying nothing.[1]

For Macbeth, life is ultimately inconsequential and meaningless in the face of death. This pessimistic view of life and death made me uncomfortable. In my final essay on the play, I concluded in so many words that Macbeth may have been a powerful king, but he was a miserable theologian.

In this chapter, we examine the ethical debates regarding life and death. To limit our discussion, we will focus on fertility treatments and assisted reproductive technologies (ARTs); the ethical handling of stem cells; abortion; and dying a dignified death. In many ways, this chapter is a continuation of our discussion of sexual ethics, especially when it comes to our anthropological assumptions and the challenges of appealing to the natural law as a basis for moral reasoning. Contrary to Macbeth, we will attempt to show that, in the Catholic ethical tradition, both life and death ought to exhibit human dignity and other moral goods that are reflective of the virtuous life.

Infertility and Assisted Reproductive Technologies[2]

Perhaps it goes without saying, but assisted fertility treatments and assisted reproductive technologies are new concerns in the Catholic ethical tradition. The first "test tube baby," Louise Joy Brown, was born on July 25, 1978, to a young couple, Lesley and John Brown, who had been unable to conceive for nine years. Lesley Brown had blocked fallopian tubes. After numerous visits to a variety of doctors and countless failed natural treatments, they met with Dr. Patrick Steptoe, a doctor working with the biologist Dr. Robert Edwards on a highly experimental technique known as in vitro ("in glass") fertilization (IVF). On November 10, 1977, Lesley Brown underwent the IVF procedure. Using a long, thin, self-lit probe called a laparoscope, Dr. Steptoe extracted an egg from one of Lesley Brown's ovaries, which researchers then mixed with John Brown's sperm. After the egg was fertilized, the research team placed it into a special solution that nurtured the egg as it began to divide. Seeing strong cell division, Dr. Steptoe placed the fertilized egg, the embryo, in Lesley's uterus. After eight weeks, the embryo became a fetus and the protocol from that moment forward was much like that in any other pregnancy.

The causes of infertility vary. For women, infertility is often due to hormonal imbalances, endometriosis, uterine fibroids, scarring from abortion, scarring from ectopic pregnancy, venereal disease, and cancer. For men, the causes may be low sperm count, weak or misshapen sperm, injuries to the testicles or the reproductive system, venereal disease, or irreversible contraceptive procedures such as a vasectomy. In most cases, doctors treat patients for infertility only after a couple has failed to conceive after twelve months of intercourse without contraception. According to the Centers for Disease Control and Prevention (CDC), about 10 percent of women (6.1 million) in the United States between the ages of fifteen and 44 have difficulty getting pregnant or staying pregnant.[3]

Regulating the Fertility Industry

Starting in the early 1980s, a fertility industry began to emerge in North America and Europe as infertile couples in large numbers began seeking out fertility treatments and ART procedures. Today the fertility industry is a multi-billion dollar business. Fertility clinics provide a host of options to people desperate for children: menstrual cycle monitoring and manipulation, 3-D ultrasounds, gene therapies, fertility drugs, procedures to clear fallopian tubes, semen extractions, ARTs, and surrogacy services. Among all of the procedures associated with ARTs, IVF is by far the most popular, accounting for 99 percent of all ART procedures. In the United States, the costs associated with ART procedures can be prohibitive. According to the American Society for Reproductive Medicine (ASRM), the average cost of just one IVF cycle is $12,400.[4] According to some estimates, the cost per live birth using ARTs in the United States is around $44,000.[5] However, in countries with heavily subsidized health care, costs can be much less. In Israel, for example, almost all ART procedures are covered under the country's universal health care plan. In England, where there is a mix between public and private health care services, fertility treatments like IVF may be covered under the United Kingdom's National Health Service plan—contingent factors include the woman's age (she must be under 40), her Body Mass Index (her infertility cannot be reasonably related to her weight), previous attempts to become pregnant using ARTs, and the number of children she already has.[6] These contingent factors, when coupled with long waiting lists, mean that many women of economic means in England choose to pay for the treatments in private clinics. In Canada, provincial health care plans usually cover only medically necessary procedures. With the exception of Quebec, where IVF is covered by the provincial health care system, these plans do not consider IVF necessary. Out-of-pocket expenses to cover lab costs, drugs, and clinic fees can run upwards of $5,000 for just one IVF cycle.

The rapid rise of the fertility industry raises questions about society's ability to regulate both the costs and the practices of fertility practitioners. In the United States, for instance, there is virtually no government regulation in place, that is, beyond the broad medical laws already on the books. This is not surprising given the general suspicion in the U.S. toward government. For many in the industry, the issue of regulation is fundamentally a matter of private-sector self-regulation. Following the logic of *laissez faire* capitalism, which we will discuss in the next chapter, the market should be left free to decide which practices violate a society's moral sensibilities and which practices are morally acceptable. As Charles Sims, co-founder and CEO of Cryobank California, said in a *New York Times* debate on the issue of regulation, "in our society the prevailing sentiment seems to be that reproductive decisions should be made by individuals (who may conceive, how and when they conceive, etc.)."[7] It is up to fertility clinics to adjust to market demands or go out of business. Sims and other defenders of self-regulation point to the guidelines published by the ASRM, which provides practitioners with a "best practices" guide to ART procedures, including guidelines to determine how many embryos to implant in any IVF procedure. This issue has become a part of public debate in recent years due to the now-famous case of the "Octomom," Nadya Suleman, who gave birth to octuplets after she had six embryos implanted in her. In spite of Sims's commitment to self-regulation, the ASRM lacks the ability to enforce its guidelines. As the well-regarded bioethics research institute the Hastings Center says in response to the situation in the U.S.,

> without governmental oversight, clinicians may practice medicine in accordance with their own beliefs. Variability in the beliefs of different practitioners permits most patients turned down by one clinic to find another where practitioners will

feel comfortable treating them … The lack of regulation and practitioner variability means that individual decisions about eligibility for ARTs may be arbitrary, biased, and inconsistent, shielding practitioner prejudices, subjecting prospective parents to great uncertainty, and avoiding public discussion of difficult policy issues in reproductive policy.[8]

The situation in Canada is scarcely different. Although the Canadian government enacted the Assisted Human Reproduction Act (AHRA) in 2004 to provide comprehensive regulation of the fertility industry, much of the Act was deemed unconstitutional in a Supreme Court ruling in 2011. The province of Quebec, with support from the provinces of Alberta, Saskatchewan, and New Brunswick, argued that the Act unconstitutionally asserted federal government jurisdiction over laws dealing specifically with fertility treatments (Quebec argued that cloning should remain under the jurisdiction of the Act). The Supreme Court ruling has had little effect on actual fertility practices since many of the provisions in the Act were never enforced or even enforceable. For instance, the regulatory agency created by the Act, the Assisted Human Reproduction Agency of Canada (AHRAC), was never empowered to provide the oversight envisioned in the legislation. As a result, when the Canadian government mounted a cost-cutting campaign in 2012, the AHRAC's $10 million budget was an easy target. The AHRAC is slated to be phased out in 2013, with all regulatory responsibilities shifting to the already overburdened offices at Health Canada.

André Picard, the acclaimed health writer for *The Globe and Mail*, says that, amid all the legal and regulatory confusion, the Canadian government should simply scrap the entire Act, get out of the business of trying to legislate health practices, and allow doctors to treat patients according to the rules established by the College of Physicians and Surgeons, which apply to all medical acts. Picard concludes that, while treatments for infertility have been a playground for fascinating ethical and legal debates, including Margaret Atwood's 1985 novel *The Handmaid's Tale*, "the reality is that families are changing in ways we could have never imagined—with foreign adoptions, same-sex couples and assisted reproduction technologies. Let's deal with it and move forward."[9] In effect, Picard wants us to leave the fertility industry alone to exist as a kind of "Wild West," where laws exist but are rendered meaningless by powerful mavericks who much prefer lawlessness.

As a society, are we willing to accept those arguments that seek to place regulation of the fertility industry in the hands of the self-regulating market or in the hands of prospective parents desperate to have children? I would hope not, for two basic reasons.

First, at a foundational ethical level, these arguments are rooted in a conflict of interest. If we were to adopt the self-regulation argument, we would be granting to those who stand to gain financially the authority to write the guidelines and enforce them. Due in part to this conflict, the fertility industry has had difficulty recognizing the inherent moral problem of effectively turning pregnancy, embryos, and life into commodities to be bought and sold on the open market. In the case of prospective parental choice, we are asking people in extenuating circumstances to limit their deepest desires to have children. As the Hastings Center has highlighted, infertile couples routinely shop fertility clinics, looking for doctors who will provide them with the fertility procedures they want, as long as they do not violate the medical code. In Canada, the 1993 Royal Commission on Reproductive Technologies, which ultimately gave rise to the 2004 Act, attempted to overcome this potential conflict by insisting that one of the guiding principles of assisted fertility practices must be the balancing of individual and collective interests. In other words, there was some recognition that individual (some might say "consumer") choice should be regulated.

Second, both the self-regulation and prospective parental choice arguments are nothing more than pleas for "moral relativism." As a society, should we not be able to ask, "How far are we willing to go with fertility?" Many of us, perhaps all of us, have sympathies for infertile couples wanting to have a child together. We might understand their desire to undergo a round of IVF. And as a society, we may approve of IVF in principle. But what if a couple wishes, say, to use ARTs and other techniques, such as gene therapy, to enhance the possibility of giving birth to a child without certain genetic defects? What if a couple wishes to use the same technologies to enhance certain traits, to produce "designer babies" or engage in so-called reprogenetics? Or to frame these two questions a bit differently, do we want the fertility industry undertaking what is, in effect, a non-coercive program of eugenics? Following the self-regulation prescription, we should let the market decide. Following the prospective parental prescription, we should, using Picard's words, "deal with it and move on." But as we know from the excesses of prior eugenic programming, including those undertaken not only in Nazi Germany but also in Alberta, Canada, (The Sexual Sterilization Act, which promoted the surgical sterilization of "mental defectives" and was in effect from 1928 to 1973), eugenic programs easily play into a society's ugliest fears and biases. Eugenic programs ultimately end up conforming to a society's racism, sexism, and ableism. Without regulations that stem from a society's norms and values, practitioners and prospective parents are free to engage in any fertility treatment they wish, so long as the medical procedures do not violate the general protocols already on the books.

Catholic Responses to Assisted Reproduction

As Pope Benedict XVI has reiterated time and again, the Catholic ethical tradition stands in opposition to what he calls "the dictatorship of moral relativism." Indeed, Catholic bioethicists generally reject and repudiate the types of arguments advanced by those favouring self-regulation and prospective parental choice. Let's now briefly examine how the Catholic tradition handles ethical challenges associated with assisted reproduction.

In general, the official teachings of the Church have concentrated on two general ethical issues. The first concerns the nature of fertility techniques and procedures in relation to sexual acts that are open to procreation within marriage (the "conjugal act"). The second is the treatment of embryos and fetuses. In 1987, the Congregation for the Doctrine of the Faith (CDF) released *Donum vitae*, an instruction on the respect for human life and the dignity of procreation. At the heart of the CDF's instruction is an ethical argument based on three goods: (1) the right to life and to physical integrity of every human being from conception to natural death; (2) the unity of marriage, which means reciprocal respect for the right within marriage to become a father or mother only together with the other spouse; and (3) the specifically human values of sexuality that require that the procreation of a human person be brought about as the fruit of the conjugal act specific to the love between spouses.

The starting point of *Donum vitae* is the anthropological premise that God has created human persons in the image of God, the *imago dei* (Genesis 1:27), and has entrusted to us humans the responsibility to have "dominion over the earth" (Genesis 1:28). To the Magisterium's way of thinking, our "dominion over the earth" means that science, medicine, and technology are not intrinsically disordered because scientists and doctors "artificially" intervene in naturally occurring events, such as sickness or even infertility. To the contrary, the responsibility of dominion assumes human intervention. The Church's concern is that science, medicine, and technology are always in harmony with fundamental criteria of the moral law: "the service of the human person, of his inalienable rights and his true and integral good according to the design and will of God."[10]

Based on the three goods (the right to life, unity of marriage, and marital procreation) and in harmony with the natural moral law, *Donum vitae* concludes that procedures that interfere with or take the place of the unitive-procreative nature of sexual intercourse within marriage are morally illicit. Those practices include artificial insemination where semen is obtained through masturbation or a non-perforated condom, in vitro fertilization, and surrogacy. Let's take a closer look at the CDF's reasoning.

As one of the least invasive and least technologically advanced procedures, artificial insemination is the practice of medically inserting semen into the uterus of a woman during her fertile period. The most common procedure is called intrauterine insemination (IUI). The CDF makes it clear that heterologous insemination, which entails the insertion of semen extracted from a "donor" who is not the woman's husband, is always and unequivocally illicit. From the Magisterium's perspective, heterologous insemination (also known as "artificial insemination by donor" or AID) fundamentally violates the unitive aspects of procreation, which take place only within the institution of marriage. The more contentious problem is the practice of homologous insemination (also known as "artificial insemination by husband" or AIH), since it meets the moral good requiring that procreation take place within the confines of marriage. The question thus becomes whether the manipulation of the husband's semen serves as a substitute for sexual intercourse. The CDF's conclusion in *Donum vitae* leaves open the possibility that homologous insemination may be morally licit:

> Homologous artificial insemination within marriage cannot be admitted *except* for those cases in which the technical means is not a substitute for the conjugal act but serves to facilitate and to help so that the act attains its natural purpose …

> Thus moral conscience "does not necessarily proscribe the use of certain artificial means destined solely either to the facilitating of the natural act or to ensuring that the natural act normally performed achieves its proper end." If the technical means facilitates the conjugal act or helps it to reach its natural objectives, it can be morally acceptable. If, on the other hand, the procedure were to replace the conjugal act, it is morally illicit.[11]

On the whole, Catholic ethicists agree that the CDF's reasoning in *Donum vitae* allows for a doctor to use a cervical spoon to push semen deeper into a woman's reproductive tract. Many fertility practitioners refer to this practice as *assisted* instead of *artificial* insemination. However, there is less agreement among ethicists on whether the CDF would allow a doctor to collect sperm from a perforated condom used in sexual intercourse between a husband and wife. The reasoning here is that the conjugal act remains open to natural procreation—the only difference is that the doctor performs a supplementary procedure by injecting the husband's semen farther into the woman's reproductive tract.

In vitro fertilization is morally illicit on two grounds, according to the CDF. First, it disassociates the procreative act from the conjugal act. IVF essentially replaces sexual intercourse. Second, the procedures used in IVF violate the human dignity of the person from the time of conception. Not every embryo is implanted in an IVF cycle. Some are destroyed or lost due to inadequate cell division, while others may be donated to research (a topic we will discuss shortly). Other embryos may be frozen and stored for a period of time.

The CDF, in *Donum vitae*, deems surrogacy morally illicit primarily because, as with heterologous insemination, the practice is "contrary to the unity of marriage and to the dignity of the procreation of the human person."[12] Furthermore, surrogacy (a) "represents an objective failure to meet the obligations of maternal love"; (b) "offends the dignity and the right of the child" to be conceived by, carried, and born to his or her own parents; and (c) undermines families by creating "a division between the physical, psychological, and moral elements which constitute those families."[13]

Finally, the CDF does point out in *Donum vitae* that a number of fertility treatments are, in principle, morally licit. These include prenatal diagnoses (that is, so long as testing isn't done for the purpose of aborting the pregnancy or does not pose unreasonable risk to the mother, embryo, or fetus) and therapeutic or medical intervention to "heal" an embryo or fetus in utero. In these cases, doctors are present to intervene in the facilitation of life.[14]

In response to the proliferation of more advanced fertility treatments, the CDF released a second instruction in 2008 entitled *Dignitas personae*. In this sequel, the CDF affirms the conclusions in *Donum vitae* regarding artificial insemination (both AID and AIH), IVF, and surrogacy. Taking the dignity of the human person as its ethical foundation (hence the title in Latin), the CDF reiterates that the human being must "be respected and treated as a person from the moment of conception; and therefore from that same moment his rights as a person must be recognized, among which in the first place is the inviolable right of every innocent human being to life."[15] This foundation, the CDF contends, prohibits us from proposing a change in the nature or a gradation in moral value of human life, even in embryonic form, "since it possesses *full anthropological and ethical status*. The human embryo has, therefore, from the very beginning, the dignity proper to a person."[16]

The CDF states that techniques aimed at removing obstacles to natural fertilization—for example, hormonal treatments for infertility, surgery for endometriosis, unblocking of fallopian tubes or their surgical repair—are morally licit. These techniques may be considered authentic, the CDF says, because they remove the causes of infertility while, at the same time, not interfering with or replacing the conjugal act. One controversial technique that the CDF considers morally licit, in principle, is gene therapy, but only as long as it's used medically to cure an inherited disease or some potential illness. Gene therapies that attempt to create or design a new human being are morally illicit, the CDF insists, since the intervention is not medically oriented but, instead, eugenically oriented to enhance human traits. According to the CDF, this type of genetic intervention is simply "*an unjust domination of man over man.*"[17]

Among the new and increasingly common techniques deemed morally illicit in *Dignitas personae* are Intracytoplasmic Sperm Injection (ICSI), freezing embryos, and freezing oocytes (immature eggs). Again, let's examine the CDF's reasoning.

ICSI is an in vitro procedure in which a single sperm is injected directly into an egg. The procedure is commonly used to help treat male infertility caused by any number of factors, including low sperm count, the inability of sperm to penetrate an egg, or the inability to release naturally (perhaps due to an irreversible vasectomy or damaged reproductive tract). Once the sperm has fertilized an egg in vitro, the embryo is allowed to develop for three or four days. Once satisfactory embryonic development has occurred, doctors will insert the embryo in the uterus. The CDF rejects ICSI for the same reason that it rejects IVF: the procedure dissociates procreation from the unitive act of sexual intercourse and it violates the dignity of the human person (e.g., if embryos are discarded due to unsatisfactory cell division).

The CDF rejects the freezing of embryos since the process of "cryopreservation" is "incompatible with the respect owed to human embryos." First, the freezing process exposes embryos to harm and serious risk of death—indeed, the freezing and thawing process often results in the loss of embryos. Second, once frozen, there is the problem of storage. In many instances, not all embryos are used in an IVF cycle. Those not used are stored in tanks, normally for later injection. But it's often the case that embryos are simply "orphaned," especially when a woman conceives or decides not to continue with another implantation procedure. The CDF bluntly asks, "What do we do with them?" The Magisterium is firmly opposed to abortion, as we will discuss shortly, so destroying embryos isn't morally acceptable. Offering embryos for prenatal adoption is morally unacceptable for the same reasons that AID is unacceptable. Giving embryos over to research cannot be justified, the CDF asserts, since research typically treats embryos as "biological matter" and not a human person.[18]

Freezing oocytes, according to the CDF, is a morally neutral act. However, the CDF says that freezing oocytes for the purpose of IVF or any other ARTs makes the practice morally unacceptable.[19]

Continuing Questions about Fertility and ARTs

While the conclusions reached by the CDF in *Donum vitae* and *Dignitas personae* are clear, the moral reasoning used by the CDF has generated a number of difficult questions. For instance, some infertile Catholic couples will find it surprising that the Church's teaching on reproductive technologies rests on certain assumptions that they do not share, which leads to questions such as these: Are children conceived using ARTs merely "products" of technology and thus in some way diminished as human beings? Can the last-resort decision to use ARTs reflect conjugal love? To answer these types of questions in light of the Church's teaching, the U.S. Conference of Catholic Bishops published a statement entitled "Life-Giving Love in an Age of Technology" (2009). The bishops acknowledge that infertility can be extremely painful and confusing to Catholic couples who hear the Church praise family life and teach that children are "the supreme gift of marriage." Implied in this acknowledgement is the reality that many infertile Catholic couples feel that the Church treats their childless marriages as inferior and deprived of God's blessings. Pastorally, the bishops are concerned by the instability that infertility can bring to a marriage and the desperation that spouses feel as they seek out medical treatments to conceive. Ethically, the bishops adhere to the teachings of the CDF. They write, "Many couples are tempted to resort to reproductive technologies because they do love each other and want to share this love with their own biological child. However, here, as in other areas of life, a good end does not justify every possible means."[20]

Also, since the publication of *Donum vitae*, a number of philosophers, bioethicists, and Catholic theologians have raised questions about the Church's reasoning when it comes to the means involved in reproductive technologies. Let me highlight three of those questions.

*If AIH (artificial insemination by husband) and homologous IVF
violate the principle of inseparability—that is, the inseparable relationship between the conjugal act and children—are AIH and homologous
IVF necessarily morally wrong?* The Catholic moral theologian Richard
McCormick, writing in response to *Donum vitae*, argues that the CDF's
emphasis on the principle of inseparability fails to recognize the complexities involved in fertility treatments. He has no doubt that conception
achieved through IVF is, using the words of *Donum vitae*, "deprived of
its proper perfection." IVF is indeed a "kind of 'second best,'" he writes.
But according to McCormick, just because IVF is a second best does
not mean that it is morally wrong in every instance. The only way it
becomes wrong in every instance is if we elevate sexual physicalism
and biologicalism, what he calls aesthetic-ecological concerns, "to an
absolute moral imperative."[21]

McCormick, who died in 2000, and some contemporary Catholic
theologians are concerned that the moral reasoning used by the CDF effectively subjugates the interpersonal aspects of sexuality, marriage, and
procreation to the physical and biological.[22] As we recall from the previous chapter on sexual ethics, the bishops at the Second Vatican Council
offered a renewed understanding of marriage, one that emphasized
interpersonal complementarity. In doing so, the Church moved away
from the teaching that there was a hierarchy of ends in marriage—with
procreation being primary and the unitive being secondary. Following
the interpersonal understanding of marriage in *Gaudium et spes* (Pastoral
Constitution on the Church in the Modern World, 1965), couples may
engage in sexual intercourse knowing full well that procreation is not
possible (e.g., in cases involving post-menopausal women or spouses
who are permanently infertile); however, couples may not engage in
intercourse where there is no interpersonal, unitive meaning. With this
understanding of the unitive-procreative relationship, some theologians
conclude, against Pope Paul VI's teaching in *Humanae vitae* (On Human
Life, 1968), that it is the marriage that needs to be open to procreation
and not each and every sexual act.

If we adopt this line of reasoning, AIH and homologous IVF become
somewhat less problematic, especially if a perforated condom is used
for the collection of semen. AIH, in particular, isn't attempting to cir-
cumvent the natural procreative process per se but instead attempting to

supplement the procreative act. Indeed, advocates of AIH and IVF note that both can be done in conjunction with the conjugal act and within the confines of marriage. In comparison to AIH, though, homologous IVF remains far more morally problematic because it involves the embryo's status and treatment in ART procedures, which leads to the second question.

How is the unintentional loss of embryos in ART procedures any more or less dehumanizing than a woman losing an embryo spontaneously? Due to modern science and medicine, we now know that natural reproduction over time involves the creation and loss of numerous embryos, many of which go completely undetected by the woman who had been carrying the embryo. The medical name for the natural loss of an embryo is spontaneous abortion (SAB), commonly called a miscarriage. An SAB is any pregnancy that ends on its own prior to twenty weeks. According to the American College of Obstetricians and Gynecologists (ACOG), studies have shown that anywhere between 10 and 25 percent of all clinically recognized pregnancies end in miscarriage. Studies that factor in hormonal testing prior to the woman's knowledge of her pregnancy have shown miscarriage rates to be around 30 percent, with some health care professionals estimating that as many as 40 percent of all pregnancies end in miscarriage. Defenders of in vitro fertilization point out that embryo loss in assisted reproduction is sometimes less frequent than in natural pregnancy, particularly among women with a history of infertility.

Michael Sandel, a philosopher known for his work on justice, observes that when people equate embryos with persons, as the Magisterium does, then this raises a practical question: How do they account for or mourn the death of an embryo? It's an intriguing question, to be sure, since the Catholic Church does not traditionally provide burial rites to spontaneously aborted embryos or fetuses, although local parish priests may occasionally offer a funeral celebration for grieving parents. Indeed, the official teachings of the Church are silent on this issue. For Sandel, the way society in general responds to the natural loss of embryos suggests that we do not regard the loss of an embryo as the moral or religious equivalent of the death of infants. Sandel concludes: "If natural procreation entails the loss of some embryos for every successful birth, perhaps we should worry less about the loss of embryos that occurs in *in vitro* fertilization and stem cell research."[23] Although his conclusion is far too shrill and rhetorical, Sandel does make a point that challenges the Magisterium's claim that IVF and cryopreservation violate the dignity of the human person because they expose the embryo to serious and life-threatening risks—risks that are, in some instances, lower than embryos created through unassisted sexual intercourse. If we follow through with Sandel's reasoning, we end up with a third question.

In the pursuit of life, the fruit of marital love, is it possible for embryos involved in the IVF process to be treated with the inherent dignity demanded of human life? A growing number of Christian bioethicists think so.[24] While some IVF practitioners may treat embryos merely as "biological matter," many practitioners understand that they are dealing with life and, as such, intend to treat the embryo with the respect and dignity owed to human life. First and foremost, this means that they treat the embryo in such a way that facilitates life—their task in the IVF process is to provide the conditions that foster life. In some cases, embryonic life cannot be sustained. In other cases, an embryo may be preserved through cryopreservation for a period of time and until the conditions are conducive to sustaining life (for example, a second round of embryonic implantation). For many prospective parents, the loss of embryos—whether in the development phases of an IVF cycle, which takes place just prior to implantation, or in the freezing-thawing phase—results in frustration, grief, and mourning at the loss of a life. For some Christian bioethicists, these experiences indicate that it is indeed possible to treat embryos involved in ARTs and cryopreservation with dignity.

It is not our place here to predict whether these and other similar questions will lead to a revisiting and further clarification of the Magisterium's teaching regarding reproductive technologies. But there are indications that the Vatican is open to broader consultation, questioning, and reflection. For instance, in February 2012, the Pontifical Academy of Life (PAV) celebrated its eighteenth general assembly with the theme "The Diagnosis and Treatment of Infertility." To help address this issue, the PAV, which is effectively a think tank created by Pope John Paul II in 1994 to promote life, sponsored a series of conferences that included participants known for challenging official Church teaching on reproductive technologies. A few members of the PAV publicly accused the president of the PAV, Monsignor Ignacio Carrasco de Paula, of violating the Academy's core values and placing it in great danger. Although it remains unclear how this public controversy will affect the PAV's work, it is evident that some members of the PAV are willing to engage with those who disagree with official Church teaching.[25]

Stem Cells

The Magisterium of the Catholic Church is *not* opposed to stem cell research; however, it is opposed to *embryonic* stem cell research. Without getting too deep into the complex science of stem cells, we need to be as clear as possible why stem cell research is such an important issue. Let's begin with a basic definition: stem cells are cells that have not yet undergone the natural process of differentiation. These undifferentiated cells contain the basic genetic elements to form anything in the human body—from the complex nervous system, to the blood and the cardio-vascular system, to our bones, skin, muscles, arms, legs, and eyes. Stems cells divide (or grow) in two ways. One way is by creating more stem cells, which are naturally used by the body to repair damaged cells. The other way is by dividing into specialized cells. These specialized cells contain the stuff to create any part of the body, but they are special because only those parts of the cell necessary to create, say, an ear, are active.

So why do researchers want stem cells? Because stem cells have the ability to develop into any part of the human body, researchers have been experimenting with the possibility that stem cell therapies could be used to treat, if not cure, cancer, Parkinson's disease, amyotrophic lateral sclerosis (ALS, or Gehrig's disease), Alzheimer's, blindness, deafness, arthritis, spinal cord injuries, and a host of other diseases and physical impairments. Since 1968, bone marrow transplants have been used to treat leukemia and Hodgkin's disease, for example, because the stem cells in bone marrow could, in some cases, be used to regenerate tissue destroyed in chemotherapy. However, bone marrow contains only about one stem cell for every thousand cells, which makes isolating stem cells a laborious and difficult task. Other sources include placental and umbilical cord stem cells, and our own body's "adult" stem cells, which can be found in blood, in fat, and in most of our organs and tissues. But researchers have had difficulties over the years developing stem cell lines from these other sources. Faced with those difficulties, many researchers see the most promise in human embryonic stem cells, which have not yet undergone any process of differentiation.

Herein lies the nub of the ethical debate. The extraction of stem cells from embryos will inevitably cause the embryos to perish—at least, that is the science up to today. The Magisterium, as we have seen, teaches that the human person's dignity must be preserved from the moment of conception through natural death. It is a violation of the embryo's dignity to destroy it, even if its destruction might eventually lead to a greater good in the future, such as finding a cure for cancer. The Magisterium believes that the type of utilitarian reasoning (the greatest good for the greatest number) used to justify embryonic stem cell research effectively dehumanizes human life by treating embryos as nothing but biological matter. According to Pope Benedict XVI, research that involves the taking of one life to enhance another is a "suppression of human lives that are equal in dignity to the lives of other human individuals and to the lives of the researchers themselves." This utilitarian approach to science has been condemned in the past and should be condemned in the future, the pope says, not only because "it lacks the light of God but also because it lacks humanity."[26] Based on the Magisterium's anthropological foundation that life begins at conception, there can be no moral argument justifying the denial of an innocent person's right to life.[27]

If live embryos must be sacrificed to harvest stem cells, the question then becomes this: What sources and methods of stem cell harvesting meet the approval of the Magisterium? According to *Donum vitae*, there are three: (1) removal of stems from an adult organism, from bone marrow, for instance; (2) the blood of the umbilical cord obtained at the time of birth; and (3) stems cells removed from fetuses who have died of natural causes. In each of these three instances, the extraction process poses no serious threat to the human person. Remarkably, the Vatican appears to be so committed to alternatives to embryonic stem cell harvesting that it has invested some $1 million in the work of the publicly traded, start-up biopharmaceutical company NeoStem, which specializes in adult stem cell research.[28] Although not a large sum of money, considering the Vatican's overall budget, the decision to invest in a private company like this one is unprecedented.

The temperature of the stem cell debate has decreased slightly over the past few years as research into adult stem cell harvesting has advanced. Still, embryonic stem cell research continues. For many Christian bioethicists, the Vatican's insistence on defining personhood at the moment of conception creates an ethical argument that is too blunt, and one that ultimately creates theological problems when pushed by other views of embryonic personhood. Ted Peters and Daniel Callahan, for example, have observed that there are three schools of thought when it comes to the personhood of an embryo.[29]

They call the first one the *genetic* school, which is exemplified by the Catholic argument for personhood at conception. According to the Magisterium, at conception—the moment in which the embryo has a genetic composition different from the mother's—the embryo is a person and has as much right to life as an infant or an adult.

The second is the *developmental* school, which holds that an embryo is life at the moment of conception, but full personhood—and thus *full* moral status—doesn't begin until a later time. While that "later time" varies, it's anywhere from fourteen days to 116 days (around the time the mother feels movement, known as the "quickening"). In any case, for the developmental school, it is clear that the blastocyte phase of embryonic development (roughly days 3 to 5, which is around the time of freezing or implantation) is too early to treat the embryo as a unique single person. As Ted Peters and Karen Lebacqz have argued, equating the creation of an embryo with a person who has a soul creates a number of theological problems, not least of which is the phenomenon of "twinning."[30] In the early stage of "embryogenesis," up to around the sixteenth day of development, an embryo may divide and create identical twins, both sharing the same genetic structure. But do these identical twins (or other multiples) share the same soul? Following the logic of the Magisterium, the embryo would have only one soul at the moment of conception. So when does the ensoulment of the identical twin (or multiples) occur? Obviously not at conception, unless we believe that twins share a soul or that an embryo actually has more than one soul. The ensoulment must come at some later stage in development—hence the basis for the development school's argument. In the end, according to the development school, we should still respect that embryo as life, but not offer the full respect we would give to an infant, for example.

The third is the *social constructionist* school, which argues that personhood is not an event but a concept based on socially constructed norms. If personhood were directly linked to the universal natural law, for instance, then one would expect to find in the world's religions a general consensus on when an embryo becomes a human subject. But there is no general consensus. Take just the Abrahamic religions, for example. Judaism, Christianity, and Islam disagree on the timing of personhood. For Jews, an embryo outside the mother's womb has no status. Once there is implantation, personhood is recognized at around 40 days. Before that time, the genetic material is "like water."[31] For Christians, the range of beliefs is from conception (the Catholic position) to birth and the first breath (a position held by a number of pro-choice Christians, who base their argument on Genesis 2:7, which states: "then the Lord God formed man from the dust of the ground, and breathed into his nostrils the breath of life; and the man became a living being"). For Muslims, the range is from 40 days up to 120 days (around the time of the quickening), depending on the teaching.

The Catholic ethicist Lisa Sowle Cahill sums up much of the ethical debate regarding embryonic stem cell research when she writes: "Public debate sometimes seems to be caught in an impasse between the value of embryos and the promised benefits of stem cell research."[32] I share Cahill's observation, as do many other ethicists. As a result, many ethicists are seeking to find areas of overlapping agreement: for example, in the areas of adult stem cell research and even embryonic protection.

Abortion

The Catholic tradition has a long history of condemning abortion as a gravely immoral act. St. Augustine, writing in the early part of the fifth century, believed that abortion was a sin because it severed the connection between marriage and procreation.[33] In 1588, in the papal bull *Effraenatam* (Without Restraint), Pope Sixtus V declared that abortion, at any stage of pregnancy, and contraception were akin to homicide and, for this reason, those who commit these acts must pay the same penalty: excommunication. Pope Pius IX, in 1869, reaffirmed the penalty of excommunication for abortion. The Second Vatican Council declared in *Gaudium et spes* that abortion is, along with infanticide, an "unspeakable crime" (GS, no. 51). And in his encyclical *Evangelium vitae* (The Gospel of Life, 1995), Pope John Paul II declared that "direct abortion, that is, abortion willed as an end or as a means, always constitutes a grave moral disorder, since it is the deliberate killing of an innocent human being" (EV, no. 62).

This is not to say, however, that the Catholic tradition has uniformly agreed on what constitutes an immoral abortion. As with the ethics of embryonic stem cell research, the Catholic debate on abortion often turns on the question of personhood: that is, when does an embryo become a person? As we just read, the official teaching of the Church today is that personhood occurs at the moment of conception. But for Augustine, the answer was different. He believed that "undeveloped fetuses" were not yet fully persons, since they were "like seeds that did not fully germinate."[34] In 1140, Gratian, the brilliant jurist who compiled the first authoritative collection of canon law, included the canon *Aliquando*, which stated, "abortion was homicide only when the fetus was formed."[35] Even Thomas Aquinas, the scholar who reconciled the natural law tradition with the teachings of the Catholic Church, believed that the fetus in the earliest stages of pregnancy was not yet a fully human person. For Thomas, following an anthropology gleaned from Aristotle, the fetus goes through various stages of "ensoulment." First, the fetus received a "vegetative soul," followed by an "animal soul," and only when the body has been fully formed in the womb a "rational soul." Only in the late stages of pregnancy, Thomas believed, does a fetus finally become a human person. Thomas's theory has become known as "delayed hominization" or "the process of becoming human."[36] And in direct response to the papal bull by Pope Sixtus V, which declared abortion at any stage akin to homicide, Pope Gregory XIV declared in 1591 that the Church should use the quickening test (at around 116 days) to determine when abortions would become murder.

There is little doubt that the definitiveness of the Vatican's position today on embryonic personhood is due in large part to Pope John Paul II's tireless efforts to advance a culture of life. The pro-life campaigns that energized not only Catholics, but people of all faiths and none, in the 1970s and 1980s also played an important part in developing the concept of embryonic personhood. If we were to read only Pope John Paul II and literature produced by pro-life organizations, we could quite easily conclude that the Catholic Church has a long history of continuous agreement regarding personhood beginning at conception. But even the Magisterium has not always been as definitive as Pope John Paul or pro-life advocates in making the case for personhood at the time of conception. For instance, in the CDF's text *Declaration on Procured Abortions* (1974), released just shortly after the controversial U.S. Supreme Court decision *Roe v. Wade* (1973), the writers of the declaration note the following regarding the Catholic tradition of ensoulment and personhood:

> This declaration expressly leaves aside the question of the moment when the spiritual soul is infused. There is not a unanimous tradition on this point and authors are as yet in disagreement. For some it dates from the first instant; for others it could not at least precede nidation [implantation]. It is not within the competence of science to decide between these views, because the existence of an immortal soul is not a question in its field. It is a philosophical problem from which our moral affirmation remains independent for two reasons: (1) supposing a belated animation, there is still nothing less than a human life, preparing for and calling for a soul in which the nature received from parents is completed, (2) on the other hand, it suffices that this presence of the soul be probable (and one can never prove the contrary) in order that the taking of life involve accepting the risk of killing a man, not only waiting for, but already in possession of his soul.[37]

In other words, the authors could not agree on when a fetus is ensouled. Since they could not definitively establish a time in which the fetus obtained a soul, they concluded that the Church should oppose abortion, even in the early stages when the fetus is not yet physically viable outside the body (which was the anthropological conclusion drawn in *Roe v. Wade*), because it may well be that abortion is killing an ensouled human person.

While it is certainly true that the official teachings of the Catholic Church reject abortion, they also allow for exceptions when the life of the mother is in jeopardy. Catholic theologians refer to this exception as an "indirect abortion." The ethical reasoning is based on the principle that the primary intention in the procedure is to save the life of the mother. The "secondary effect" is the termination of the pregnancy. Although specific health conditions are not clearly spelled out in any official documents of the Church, indirect abortions have been used to terminate ectopic pregnancies, which are pregnancies that occur outside the womb, and pregnancies involving women with life-threatening heart conditions, uterine tumours, and certain types of cancer. In general, the Magisterium has limited indirect abortion solely to conditions where the direct, physical act of carrying a pregnancy to term puts the mother's life at risk. Pope Paul VI, in his encyclical *Humanae vitae* (1968), states: "the Church does not consider at all illicit the use of those therapeutic means necessary to cure bodily diseases, even if a foreseeable impediment to procreation should result there from—provided such impediment is not directly intended for any motive whatsoever" (HV, no. 15).

In spite of the Magisterium's clear teaching regarding the moral licitness of indirect abortion, some anti-abortion hardliners in the Church reject it. In November 2009, for example, Bishop Thomas J. Olmsted of Phoenix, Arizona, publicly criticized the ethics board at St. Joseph's Hospital and Medical Center in Phoenix for allowing doctors to perform an abortion to save the life of a mother of four suffering from pulmonary hypertension. Bishop Olmsted said that, while efforts should be made to save a pregnant woman's life, abortion cannot be justified as a means to that end. "There are two patients in need of treatment and care; not merely one," the bishop said. "The unborn child's life is just as sacred as the mother's life, and neither life can be preferred over the other."[38] According to this line of reasoning, then, other factors, such as the pregnant woman's responsibility to her other four children, are, in effect, morally irrelevant when it comes to weighing the risks associated with a potentially life-threatening pregnancy.[39]

Part of what makes abortion so tendentious in public debate is the fact that it involves two competing rights claims: the rights of the pregnant woman and the unborn child's right to life. In modern liberal societies such as those in North America and Europe, who we are as human subjects is characterized primarily by our capacity to make decisions for ourselves. Whom we marry, where we work, what we do with our lives is, we believe, up to us to decide. Prior to the women's movement in the twentieth century, Western societies looked upon women as second-class citizens. They couldn't vote, couldn't own property, and couldn't work in professions reserved for men. In short, the women's movement brought to light the injustices associated with a system of male privilege, otherwise known as patriarchy. By the late 1960s, women in the Western world were asserting their rights as equals to make decisions regarding their health and well-being. For many women, the idea that the state, the Church, or society could force a woman to carry a fetus against her will was a fundamental violation of her right to privacy and her rights over her body.

The U.S. Supreme Court ruling in *Roe v. Wade* (1973) decided that a woman does indeed have a right to privacy, which meant she has the right to an abortion; but that right has to be balanced with the life of the unborn child—once again, raising the issue of personhood. The Court decided that abortions only in the first trimester would be permitted. Since that landmark ruling in the U.S., the debate has shifted to late-term abortions, including the abortion of fetuses that could be viable outside the mother's body.

In Canada, abortions have been legal since passage of The Criminal Law Amendment Act, 1968–1969, which included the provision that a committee of doctors had to agree that the abortion was for the physical or mental well-being of the mother. In 1988, the Supreme Court of Canada ruled in *R. v. Morgentaler* that the provision in the 1969 law violated a woman's rights to the security of person under section 7 of the Canadian Charter of Rights and Freedoms. Since then, Canada has had no abortion laws.

In the wake of both *Roe v. Wade* and *R. v. Morgentaler*, public debate in the U.S. and Canada has been monopolized by two camps: the "right to life" movement and the "pro-choice" movement. Unfortunately, these two camps are defined more by their politics than their ethical reasoning. Lost in this polarized public debate are those who are *both* pro-life and pro-choice. In a 2011 survey by the Public Religion Research Institute, 70 percent of Americans said the term "pro-choice" describes them well or somewhat, while 66 percent also identify with the term "pro-life." Among Catholics in particular, 77 percent said "pro-life" describes them well or very well, and 70 percent said "pro-choice" describes them well.[40]

Are these people just confused? I don't think so. More likely, people today recognize the need to balance the claims of women, who have been historically marginalized and objectified, with the unborn child's right to life. Their aim, I believe, is to dramatically reduce the need for abortions. Unlike the hardline pro-life stance (which accepts only the legal prohibition of abortions) and the hardline pro-choice stance (which reduces the issue simply to the right of a woman to choose), those in the middle of the fray want to focus on creating the social and economic conditions that give women options other than abortion, including adequate sexual health education, adoption alternatives, and meaningful work, all important factors in reducing unwanted pregnancies. In virtue ethics, we would call this an act of prudence.

Take the case of sex-selective abortions, for example. In June 2012, the Canadian Broadcasting Corporation ran a series of reports on the lack of girls being born in Southeast Asian areas of Toronto.[41] Consistent with a trend seen in a number of urban centres in Canada and the United States, these reports found that some women were using 3-D ultrasounds to discover the sex of their children early in the pregnancy. The implied conclusion in these reports was that these women, mostly Hindus or Sikhs, were then choosing to abort girls. To this situation, the hardline pro-life stance has little to offer women seeking to overcome the injustice of patriarchal bias against girls. Similarly, the hardline pro-choice camp finds itself in the contradictory position of upholding the right of women to choose to abort a girl. As this case illustrates, there must be ethical nuance beyond the politicized rhetoric of the pro-life and pro-choice camps. For the most part, we find that nuance in ethical arguments for cultural, social, and economic support and reasonable regulation, all of which is beyond our scope in this introduction.

Dying a Dignified Death

In 2005, Steve Jobs, the CEO of Apple Computer and Pixar Animation, stood before the graduating class at Stanford University and talked about dying:

Remembering that I'll be dead soon is the most important tool I've ever encountered to help me make the big choices in life. Because almost everything—all external expectations, all pride, all fear of embarrassment or failure—these things just fall away in the face of death, leaving only what is truly important. Remembering that you are going to die is the best way I know to avoid the trap of thinking you have something to lose. You are already naked. There is no reason not to follow your heart.

About a year ago I was diagnosed with cancer. I had a scan at 7:30 in the morning, and it clearly showed a tumor on my pancreas. I didn't even know what a pancreas was. The doctors told me this was almost certainly a type of cancer that is incurable, and that I should expect to live no longer than three to six months.

He continued:

No one wants to die. Even people who want to go to heaven don't want to die to get there. And yet death is the destination we all share. No one has ever escaped it. And that is as it should be, because Death is very likely the single best invention of Life. It is Life's change agent. It clears out the old to make way for the new. Right now the new is you, but someday not too long from now, you will gradually become the old and be cleared away. Sorry to be so dramatic, but it is quite true.

Unlike Macbeth, Steve Jobs found meaning in the face of death. An agnostic, Jobs thought "Life" had a built-in renewal plan. Death prompts us, he believed, to get rid of people's opinions that "drown out your own inner voice." And most importantly, Jobs concluded, death ought to compel you to "have the courage to follow your heart and intuition. They somehow already know what you truly want to become."[42]

In the past few years, the highly publicized illnesses and deaths of Steve Jobs, Christopher Hitchens, Terri Shiavo, and Pope John Paul II have sparked a new round of public debate regarding the care we owe to those with terminal illnesses or medical conditions. Two questions typically frame this debate. First, what measures should physicians take to keep a person alive? Second, do terminally ill patients have a right to assisted suicide? Let's see how the Catholic ethical tradition answers these questions.

Ordinary/Proportionate and Extraordinary/Disproportionate Means

We don't die the way we used to. At the turn of the twentieth century, the primary causes of death in the United States were pneumonia, influenza, and tuberculosis. In 2010, heart disease and cancer were by far the major causes of death. In 2010, pneumonia and influenza combined accounted for a slightly higher number of deaths than suicide, but less than Alzheimer's disease and diabetes—tuberculosis was virtually eradicated in the U.S. by the 1950s.[43]

Not only have our causes of death dramatically changed in the past century, but also our places of death have changed. According to the Centers for Disease Control and Prevention, in 2010, roughly 70 percent of Americans died in hospitals, long-term care facilities, or nursing homes. In 1900, only about 30 percent died in medical institutions.

Also, we're living longer. In 1900, life expectancy was about 49 years of age, while a person born in 2010 is expected to live to be near 80 years old. Advances in medicine, science, and technology have extended life—and they have added to the moral complexities associated with death and dying, particularly in acute situations where a patient is on "life support." Simply put, these advances have made it possible to keep people alive well beyond what was possible a few generations ago.

Catholic teaching on extending the life of a patient is based on a moral distinction first made in the sixteenth century between ordinary and extraordinary means. As moral categories, ordinary means are those that *do not* require excessive physical, mental, financial, or spiritual burdens primarily on the patient and secondarily on the patient's family and caregivers. Extraordinary means *do* cause an excessive burden on the patient, the patient's family, and the patient's caregivers. On the whole, this is a distinction that has been adopted by the medical profession, where "ordinary means" is synonymous with "standard treatment" and "extraordinary means" is equated with "experimental treatment." But as a matter of ethics, the adoption of this distinction for actual medical procedures is problematic. It reduces a moral distinction used for prudential moral judgment to specific medical treatments. In its 1980 *Declaration on Euthanasia,* the Congregation for the Doctrine of the Faith prefers to use the language of "proportionate means" and "disproportionate means" to emphasize the prudential character of the distinction. The *Catechism of the Catholic Church* uses both the older distinction between ordinary/extraordinary and the newer language of proportionate/disproportionate: "Discontinuing medical procedures that are burdensome, dangerous, extraordinary, or disproportionate to the expected outcome can be legitimate" (CCC, no 2278).

The moral distinction between ordinary/proportionate and extraordinary/disproportionate means functions as a basic ethical framework that helps us in our decision-making. In the Catholic tradition, there are several criteria that we consider when evaluating relative benefits of life-extending treatments. The CDF, in the *Declaration on Euthanasia*, says we should "study the type of treatment to be used, its degree of complexity or risk, its cost and the possibilities of using it, and [compare] these elements with the result that can be expected," all while taking into account the patient's overall medical condition and physical and moral resources.[44] In other words, there's no Catholic template or checklist that we apply when dealing with end-of-life questions. Instead, the Catholic tradition requires that we use our prudential judgment to determine, on a case-by-case basis, the proper course of action.

Consider this example. Imagine that you're sitting in my classroom listening to two guest lecturers talk about the meaning of life. One is a 30-something professor, physically fit, and openly proud of her husband and three young children. The other is a retired, elderly professor who jokes about his smoking habit and the fact that he has more stents in his heart than teeth in his head. Now assume that the young professor collapses to the ground, grabbing her chest. What should we do? Proportionate means would likely entail us calling 9-1-1, checking for a pulse, and locating and using an automated external defibrillator (AED) to restart her heart. We would expect the emergency medical technicians (EMTs) to work feverishly to resuscitate her, to restore vital signs, and to get her to the hospital as quickly as possible. We would reasonably expect the emergency room staff to continue resuscitation measures. Assuming she survives, but with a badly damaged heart and with neurological damage, we would likely expect her cardiologist to perform exploratory surgery and tests to figure out what caused the cardiac arrest, all with an eye to a cure. And we would likely expect her health care providers to keep her on life support until such time as her physicians determine that she is, for example, unresponsive, lacks the ability to sustain life on her own, and is in a persistent vegetative state. Disproportionate means might entail extending her life with mechanical ventilation and a pacemaker.

Now consider what we should do if it were the old professor who went down grabbing his chest. Proportionate means would likely involve us calling 9-1-1, checking for a pulse, and looking for the AED. Before using the AED, though, we might check the professor's wallet and wrists to see if he has a "do not resuscitate" (DNR) order. If he has one, we might wait for the EMTs to show up to perform basic medical procedures, such as ensuring that his throat and air passages are clear, checking for a pulse, and so on. Disproportionate means would likely entail the Emergency Room staff attempting to resuscitate, inserting a feeding tube, placing him on a ventilator, and using cardiac stimulation.

In general, Catholic ethicists want to avoid two extremes when it comes to questions of extending the life of a patient: vitalism and subjectivism. Vitalism holds that the patient, the family, and health care professionals have an obligation to extend life at all costs. With the emphasis on the culture of life in the Catholic Church since the 1990s, some Catholics have demonstrated a tendency toward vitalism. For instance, in his statement "Life-Sustaining Treatments and Vegetative State" (2004), Pope John Paul II teaches that providing food and water to a patient in a vegetative state "always represents a *natural means* of preserving life, not a *medical act*."[45] In other words, withholding food and water is, in effect, an act of euthanasia, which the Magisterium prohibits. Richard McCormick thinks that conclusions like those drawn by Pope John Paul are inconsistent with the Catholic Church's anthropology, which recognizes death as part of the human condition. McCormick wrote: "Imagine a 300-bed Catholic hospital with all beds supporting PVS [persistent vegetative state] patients maintained for months, even years, with gastrostomy tubes … An observer of the scenario would eventually be led to ask: Is it true that those who operate this facility actually believe in life after death?"[46]

The other extreme is subjectivism, which often involves the appeal of a terminally ill patient claiming he or she has an absolute right to terminate his or her life without regard to the public interest. As we will see when we discuss assisted suicide, subjectivism is the result of a modern, liberal understanding of the human subject as one who has complete autonomy over his or her body. For many Catholic ethicists, this type of radical subjectivism can all too easily mask a patient's alienation and dehumanizing living conditions. The concern here is that the patient is making a choice to terminate his or her life in a compromised state, perhaps fearing that "life is no longer worth living" or that a prolonged death might become an excessive burden on family members.

Finding an ethical balance between the commitment to life and the autonomy of the patient is at the heart of Catholic teaching on extending life. In a carefully worded statement entitled *Ethical and Religious Directives for Catholic Health Care Services* (2009), the U.S. Conference of Catholic Bishops (USCCB) offers these directives to Catholics caring for the dying. First, "a person has a moral obligation to use ordinary or proportionate means of preserving his or her life." It's important to note the USCCB does not claim that artificially delivered water and food are ordinary or proportionate. Second, the USCCB says that "a person may forgo extraordinary or disproportionate means of preserving life," which means not putting an excessive burden on the patient, family, or community. And third, the U.S. bishops maintain that, "*in principle*, there is an obligation to provide patients with food and water, including medically assisted nutrition and hydration for those who cannot take food orally. This obligation extends to patients in chronic and presumably irreversible conditions (e.g., the "persistent vegetative state") who can reasonably be expected to live indefinitely if given such care."[47] Revisiting the teaching of Pope John Paul II, which stated that providing food and water "always represents a *natural means*," the USCCB's conclusion is that providing food and water is *in principle*—not *in practice*—an obligation. In other words, withholding medically provided food and water is not necessarily an act of euthanasia. According to the USCCB's reasoning, when a patient is near death, or when the artificial means of providing food and water create an excessive burden on the patient, the physician may determine that withholding food and water is morally justifiable.

Many of us may be left scratching our heads, wondering why the Catholic tradition doesn't provide a clear and concise list of what constitutes morally licit and illicit life-extending treatments. Such bewilderment may be warranted, especially if we consider the level of detail that the Magisterium goes into in dealing with sexuality, marriage, procreation, ARTs, and the treatment of embryos. While the Magisterium may eventually end up developing such a list, I would hope that it refrains from doing so largely because any list would inevitably hinder, if not replace, moral judgment. The way the Catholic ethical tradition currently addresses extending human life is consistent with both the natural law precept "do good, avoid evil" and the tradition of virtue ethics that requires us to consider how our actions foster our sense of who we wish to be, even in the face of death.

Euthanasia and Physician-Assisted Suicide

In Catholic bioethics, there is a difference between choosing to withdraw life-sustaining procedures (sometimes mistakenly referred to by ethicists as "passive euthanasia") and choosing to die as the result of a direct action intended to cause death. According to the USCCB's *Ethical and Religious Directives for Catholic Health Care Services*, health care professionals should always respect a patient's decision to withdraw life-sustaining procedures—that is, as long as those decisions are based on the adult patient's "free and informed judgment" and are not contrary to Catholic moral teaching.[48] Moreover, the U.S. bishops state that Catholic health care institutions "may never condone or participate in euthanasia or assisted suicide in any way."[49] Following the official teachings of the Church, euthanasia (literally, "good death") and assisted suicide are fundamental violations of human dignity and can never be morally justified. As the *Catechism of the Catholic Church* states: "We are stewards, not owners, of the life God has entrusted to us. It is not ours to dispose of" (CCC, no. 2280).

In Catholic bioethics, there is also a difference between performing a procedure with the *intention* to hasten a patient's death and performing a procedure that *unintentionally* hastens a patient's death. This difference is based on the Catholic principle of double effect. In sum, the principle of double effect holds that an act, which is morally neutral or good, may have two effects: one that is intentional and one that is unintentional.

The prime example involves pain management, in which case treating a patient with pain reliever medication for the purpose of relieving pain (the primary effect or intention) may hasten the patient's death (the secondary effect). The USCCB ascribes to this moral reasoning in its directive to health care professionals:

> Patients should be kept as free of pain as possible so that they may die comfortably and with dignity, and in the place where they wish to die. Since a person has the right to prepare for his or her death while fully conscious, he or she should not be deprived of consciousness without a compelling reason. Medicines capable of alleviating or suppressing pain may be given to a dying person, even if this therapy may indirectly shorten the person's life so long as the intent is not to hasten death.[50]

The Magisterium's prohibition against euthanasia and assisted suicide is increasingly at odds with public opinion and public policy. For example, in 1994, voters in Oregon approved the Death with Dignity Act, which permits doctors to prescribe, but not administer, a lethal dose of drugs. The Oregon law contains rules that reasonably ensure the mental competency of patients seeking assisted suicide. Between 1997, when the law was finally passed, and 2010, 525 patients died from ingesting medications prescribed under the Death with Dignity Act. Of that group, 96.9 percent of patients died at home, the median age was 72, and 78.5 percent had cancer. In 2010, 96 people died under the provisions of the Act. Consistent with the annual numbers since 1997, the most frequently mentioned reasons for ending their lives were autonomy (93.8%), decreasing ability to participate in activities that made life enjoyable (93.8%), and loss of dignity (75.8%).[51] In the state of Washington, voters approved legislation in 2009 that resembles Oregon's. In 2009, the Montana Supreme Court ruled in *Baxter v. Montana* that, since there is "nothing in Montana Supreme Court precedent or Montana statutes indicating that physician aid in dying is against public policy," the state could not arbitrarily charge a physician who participated in the act with a crime.

In Canada, suicide is not a crime; but assisting with a suicide is (e.g., prescribing drugs or directly administering lethal doses of drugs). The Criminal Code of Canada outlaws suicide assistance, with penalties of up to fourteen years in prison. But a 2012 decision by a British Columbia Supreme Court judge declared Canada's laws against physician-assisted suicide unconstitutional because they discriminated against the physically disabled. Like all Canadians, Gloria Taylor, a woman with ALS, is free to commit suicide, the judge concluded; but because she is disabled, she would be unable to do so—a violation of Section 15 of the *Charter of Rights and Freedoms* that guarantees equality. Should the ruling hold up under appeal, Canada would join the Netherlands, Belgium, Luxembourg, and Switzerland, as well Oregon, Washington, and Montana, as a jurisdiction where assisted suicide is legal.

In general, advocates of euthanasia and physician-assisted suicide make a two-pronged rights-based argument. First, they hold that human persons are autonomous and have a right to make decisions regarding their health, quality of life, and, in the cases of terminal illnesses or medical conditions, how and when they die. This right is often framed in terms of a person's "right to die" in peace and with dignity. Second, they insist that, in rights-based societies, human persons have the right to privacy, including the right to make health care choices with the assistance of a medical professional. Policies that seek to interfere with the doctor–patient relationship are, they argue, violations of this right.

For doctors, physician-assisted suicide poses its own set of problems. First and foremost among them is that physician-assisted suicide clearly violates the Hippocratic Oath: "I will neither give a deadly drug to anybody if asked for it, nor will I make a suggestion to this effect." Indeed, the American Medical Association (AMA) and the Canadian Medical Association (CMA) have rejected moral arguments in favour of physician-assisted suicide. The job of the physician, the AMA and CMA conclude, is to work with the patient as a facilitator of life. To ask physicians to facilitate death places them in a confusing situation—and patients must never be confused about what role doctors are playing in providing health services.

The growing support for euthanasia and assisted suicide should compel Catholics to ask again the difficult question: Why do we exist? How we answer this question matters. Do we exist merely so that our vital physiological functions can be maintained? Or do we exist for more holistic reasons—so that we can experience love, friendship, community life, meaningful work, joy in nature, humour, and yes, even dying? A holistic understanding of ordinary/proportionate and extraordinary/disproportionate means, and a holistic understanding of life beyond the physical and biological goods of extending life, may provide answers not just to Catholics but to a growing part of society that doesn't see the good in prolonged "redemptive suffering."[52] With a holistic understanding of human life, the physical good of bodily integrity must be balanced against other goods—including social, psychological, and spiritual goods. In my judgment, Catholic theologians have a lot of work to do in developing a more holistic approach to preserving life and to dying a dignified death. In doing that work, we should seek out those advocating for a "good death," for in dialogue with them we might be reminded of something we should already know: death doesn't have the final word.

CHAPTER 6

The Ethical Challenges of Capitalism

On October 17, 1996, Canadians tuned into their nightly newscast to hear CBC news anchor Peter Mansbridge say: "Good evening. A blistering attack on governments across the country today, from Canada's Roman Catholic bishops. The issue is poverty. The bishops accuse governments of using the most vulnerable people in society as human fodder in the battle against deficits. And the bishops weren't the only ones speaking out." The Canadian Conference of Catholic Bishops (CCCB) was using the fourth annual United Nations International Day for the Eradication of Poverty as the occasion to release their pastoral letter called *The Struggle Against Poverty: A Sign of Hope for Our World* (1996).[1] The CBC report continued:

> In Canada, more than five million people are poor. More than a million of them are children. The Canadian Conference of Catholic Bishops issued a sharp attack against government policies it says hurt Canada's poor, especially the children ... The bishops quote a report from Church groups, which says, "In our society, if a parent denies a child food, clothing and social security, it is considered child abuse; but when our government

denies 1,362,000 children the same, it is simply balancing the budget."

As the former director of Social Affairs at the CCCB, Joe Gunn, recalled, "That statement caused a bit of a stir."[2]

The 1996 pastoral letter of the Canadian bishops was not the first or most controversial CCCB statement on the economy. That designation goes to a seven-page paper called "Ethical Reflections on the Economic Crisis," released on New Year's Day, 1983. The bishops claimed that the government of Prime Minister Pierre Elliott Trudeau had put business interests above the interests of those suffering from poverty and unemployment, which was 12.8 percent at the time. Their paper criticized the Trudeau government's pro-business strategy for putting a "renewed emphasis on the 'survival of the fittest' as the supreme law of economics." The bishops argued that priorities had to be on controlling profits, increasing taxes on the rich, allowing for a larger role for labour unions, and establishing a government-backed jobs creation program. The bishops stated, "The goal of serving the human needs of all people in our society must take precedence over the maximization of profits and growth." The bishops' criticism of the Canadian government was a front-page story in most daily newspapers in Canada and was also covered in *The New York Times*, *The Washington Post*, *Los Angeles Times*, *Newsweek* and *Time*. Eventually, the CCCB sold 200,000 copies of "Ethical Reflections on the Economic Crisis" and had it translated into seven languages. In spite of the enthusiasm and interest generated by the paper, Prime Minister Trudeau flippantly dismissed the bishops with a terse statement: "I don't think their economics are very good." It was, he believed, all he needed to say to make his case to Canadians that religion and ethics are private matters and, for that reason, Catholic bishops have no business meddling in the economy.

In this chapter, we show that Christian ethics does have an integral role to play when it comes to addressing the social consequences of economic arrangements. The reason why this is the case is that any economic system operates with certain assumptions about the human person (anthropology); a particular view of reality (worldview); a set of norms and values, loyalties, and prior experiences (prejudices); and an internal logic that justifies how the economy handles moral decisions (approaches to ethical decision-making). Our focus in this chapter is capitalism because, starting in the late eighteenth century, the pursuit of capital accumulation radically changed social relations, the nature of work, and social values. Today, we live in societies with globalized economies, where actors, from individuals to societies, tend to define success by purchasing power. Arguably, consumer capitalism has become *the* defining force in developed countries. As individuals, we're in danger of becoming consumers first, citizens second. As societies, we're treating our governing bodies as businesses, restructuring our social services to maximize efficiencies, and refashioning education, including university education, to meet the needs of the job market. This latter change is important to many Catholic and other Christian universities that have seen their liberal arts budgets cut in favour of programs that are more vocationally oriented. In a word, we are, as Pope John Paul II intimated in *Centesimus annus* (The Hundredth Year, 1991), in danger of prioritizing "having" over "being" (CA, no. 36). But is this the kind of person we want to become, the kind of community and society we wish to be? As we will show in this chapter, the Catholic social tradition provides an alternative to the alienating and dehumanizing tendencies of unfettered capitalism.

Industrial Capitalism and Catholic Social Teaching

Catholic Social Teaching has its origins in the great social and economic upheavals of the nineteenth century. Across Europe, the old medieval economic system, which was characterized by feudal estates, peasant farming, household production of goods such as clothes and furniture, and local markets, was disappearing. In its place, a new, larger, and more complex business economy began to emerge—an economic system known as industrial capitalism. At the foundations of this economy was a new anthropology. Adam Smith, the author of *The Wealth of Nations*, published in 1776, believed that we are creatures who desire to better our material conditions in life. According to Smith, it is a "desire that comes with us from the womb, and never leaves us till we go into the grave."[3] In essence, human beings are naturally self-interested, fiercely competitive, and in search of ways to accumulate capital (that is, wealth that could be used to generate even more capital, which in turn creates an endless cycle of capital-wealth accumulation). We are no longer just *Homo sapiens* (the "Man of Knowledge"); we are *Homo economicus* (the "Economic Man"). Based on this anthropological view, this new economic system did not want to artificially restrict the human desire to make money or to compete against others who were also seeking to make money. To the contrary, competition was encouraged because, in theory, it would foster ingenuity, provide more efficient ways of producing goods, and create more wealth. Indeed, capitalism relies on the assumption that every able-bodied person is naturally a "capitalist" who seeks to purchase goods at the lowest price and to sell their goods to the highest bidder.

In the early part of the nineteenth century, few had any goods of economic value to sell, and even fewer had any money to purchase goods to sell. What they did have, though, was their labour, which they could offer to a new class of people that owned factories. This situation presented a serious problem to would-be labourers—factories were rarely in rural areas. So in search of factory work, many young men living in rural areas, and in some cases entire families, left their villages to seek jobs in the factories sprouting up in urban centres, such as London, Leeds, Manchester, Paris, and Hamburg, in Europe, and New York, Philadelphia, Pittsburgh, Boston, and Chicago, in the United States. Also, many poor Canadian men, including Alfred Bessette—the future St. André Bessette from Montreal—made their way to New England to work in factories humming at full speed to meet the demands of the new economy and the U.S. Civil War. But many were unable to find jobs, which resulted in a large number of "wandering poor," as they were called, living on the streets of these burgeoning industrial cities. There were few options for these "wandering poor." In England, for instance, the land they had lived on as peasants, traditionally known as a "commons," had been reclaimed by landowners so they could raise sheep for wool production and other livestock that could be sold on the market. For these landowners, it had become far more profitable to use the land to produce material that could be sold on the open market than it was to have peasants maintain the land to sustain the local community.

For those "lucky" enough to find jobs in nineteenth-century factories, the working conditions were horrific. Shops were poorly ventilated. Workers in steel mills had few breaks from the blast furnaces that turned their workplaces into infernos. Textile and grain workers routinely passed out on the job because they would breathe in dust particles, which clogged their airways and cut off oxygen to their brains. Children often had the most dangerous jobs, such as crawling into hot machines or wriggling into tight crawl spaces below factory floors to repair or reset a malfunctioning part. Those children who stood at assembly lines were often chained to their work for fourteen hours at a time. Lost fingers, limbs, and even lives were not uncommon in the factory. In the words of the English poet William Blake, these were nothing but "dark Satanic mills."[4]

The German social theorist Karl Marx famously observed that there were two aspects of capitalism. One aspect is that capitalism created miserable, dehumanizing working conditions for labourers, a class of people Marx called the proletariat. The other aspect is that capitalism generated a tremendous amount of capital and wealth for those who controlled the means of production, the so-called bourgeoisie. Friedrich Engels, one of Marx's closest allies, confirmed Marx's observation after a meeting with a wealthy industrialist in Manchester, England. Engels remarked to the industrialist that he had never seen such a horribly built city as Manchester, with its hideously grimy and unsanitary worker slums. After listening patiently to Engels, the wealthy gentleman retorted, "And yet there is a great deal of money made here. Good morning, sir." Engels concluded bitterly, "It is utterly indifferent to the English bourgeois whether his working-men starve or not, if only he makes money. All the conditions of life are measured by money, and what brings no money is nonsense, unpractical, idealistic bosh."[5] For the bourgeoisie, though, this situation was just short of ideal. There was cheap labour, and still there was a labour force energized by dreams of economic success and promises of a better life for those who worked hard. Business and factory owners used this situation to make large profits, which, as economic historians note, were rarely shared proportionally with the working class.

Marx and Engels were not alone in criticizing the implementation of an unregulated market economy. In his encyclical *Rerum novarum* (On Human Labour and Capital), published in 1891, Pope Leo XIII wrote that an unconstrained economy had led to an unjust situation in which a "a small number of very rich men have been able to lay upon the teeming masses of the labouring poor a yoke little better than that of slavery itself" (RN, no. 3). To prevent this injustice, the pope insisted, workers must be guaranteed a living wage, human working conditions, the right to organize and strike, and governmental protection from exploitation (RN, nos. 28–34, 36–38). These were practical actions that would help overcome the injustices associated with unfettered capitalism. But these actions alone could only go so far in reforming capitalism's practices.

The pope believed there needed to be a radical reassessment of the moral and philosophical foundations underpinning capitalism. First, Pope Leo thought that the proponents of the unregulated market were mistaken in their claim that capitalism was essentially a natural institution and that the economy should be governed solely by market forces, what Adam Smith called the "invisible hand of the market." As Donal Dorr remarked in his magnificent introduction to the Catholic social tradition entitled *Option for the Poor*, Pope Leo "challenged the current assumption that the 'laws' of economics should be treated as though they were laws of nature, and therefore the basis for morality."[6]

Second, Pope Leo not only rejected but repudiated one of the primary tenets of capitalism, namely, that labour could be treated merely as a commodity that could be purchased at a price determined by the laws of supply and demand. Instead, the pope argued, the value of labour, which appears in the form of wages, must be based on the needs of the worker. He wrote, "there underlies a dictate of natural justice more imperious and ancient than any bargain between one person and another, namely that wages ought not be insufficient to support a frugal and well-behaved wage-earner" (RN, no. 45). Yet, by placing labour on the open market, capitalism effectively turns the worker into a victim who must, "through necessity or fear of a worse evil" (RV, no. 45), agree to an unjust wage and often dehumanizing working conditions. The lamentable situation of the nineteenth-century working class in Europe and North America was that the labour pool was vast, which enabled factory and business owners to offer cheap wages to workers. The result was a working class that remained poor while wealthy owners became even wealthier.

And third, Pope Leo held that the state ought to play a role in protecting workers from unfair labour practices and the maldistribution of wealth. According to one of the fundamental principles of capitalism, an employer's primary, if not sole, obligation to the worker is to pay the worker the agreed-upon wage. Against this principle, the pope insisted that employers have an initial obligation to pay workers a *dignified wage*. This wage may often be more than the lowest labour price in a market, especially if the labour supply is greater than the demand. But a dignified wage is a matter of justice and recognition of a worker's human dignity. For Pope Leo, a just wage should enable a worker to save money and, in time, purchase private land (RV, no. 46). The state has an obligation, the pope insisted, to ensure that employers are offering such wages and that a tax system is in place that effectively redistributes wealth. In this respect, the state has an obligation "to promote to the utmost the interests of the poor" and "to serve the common good" (RV, no. 32).

As Dorr has noted, Pope Leo's remedy to the labour problem of the nineteenth century was very much a "top down" approach. There's no denying that it was. Some might add that the pope's remedy appears to be somewhat contradictory. On the one hand, the pope held that government should not be involved in the affairs of business—it should be neutral and above economics. To supporters of capitalism, this may sound like an absolute rejection of Marxist socialism and a subtle affirmation of *laissez-faire* economics, which teaches that the state intervenes in economic matters only to protect private property and the free trading of goods. On the other hand, the pope maintained that the state must intervene, albeit in limited ways, in the economy to protect the poor. To some, this may sound like veiled Marxist socialism, which holds that the state should control the economy. Neither extreme is the case. In fact, Pope Leo was trying to find a middle path between unfettered capitalism and Marxist socialism. He rejected the underlying anthropology and worldview of capitalism, but he could not accept the revolutionary aspects of Marxist socialism, which, to the pope's way of thinking, was tantamount to lawlessness. Although siding with the poor, Pope Leo was not willing to support worker movements that disrupted the civil order. Instead, he hoped *Rerum novarum* would spark a moral conversion on the part of those benefiting from capitalism, namely, the industrial capitalists and others in the owning class.

The Globalization and Exploitation of Labour

The story of the little Pakistani boy Iqbal Masih is well known to many Catholics. At the age of four, Iqbal's mother sold him into bonded labour to a carpet factory to pay a $12 debt. For six years, Iqbal worked at a loom, at least fourteen hours a day, six days a week. Once his year-long apprenticeship was over, he was paid about 60 cents per day, most of which went to pay for his lodging, food, and any mistakes he made at the loom. At the age of ten, he was freed from the factory with the help of the Bonded Labour Liberation Front (BLLF). Soon after his release, he worked with the BLLF to help other children gain their freedom, which resulted in the forced closing of the carpet factory where he once toiled. His story grabbed international attention—but he upset a number of factory owners by shedding light on Pakistan's unjust labour practices. At the age of thirteen, on Easter Sunday in April 1995, Iqbal was shot and killed under mysterious circumstances.[7] In the fifteen years since his death, there has been a significant reduction of children in bonded labour. Yet it is estimated that some 250,000 children in South Asia are still forced to work in carpet factories. And according to a 2011 report from the United Nations Children's Fund (UNICEF), an estimated 12 percent of children in India between the ages of five and fourteen are engaged in child labour activities, including carpet production.[8]

In January 2012, the U.S. sports network ESPN reported that the Dallas Cowboys, one of the most iconic sporting businesses in the world, has been using sweatshop labour factories in Cambodia and in other countries with cheap labour and lax labour laws to manufacture its sports apparel. Operating under the name Silver Star Merchandising, the Cowboys apparel company made roughly $90 million in 2009. In spring 2011, Silver Star signed a ten-year agreement with the University of Southern California, with the USC Trojan being one of the most highly recognizable and valuable university mascots in the United States. According to Forbes, the Dallas Cowboys football team was worth an estimated $2.1 billion in 2012, and the Cowboys owner, Jerry Jones, was worth $2.7 billion. Meanwhile, according to the ESPN report, garment workers in the Cambodian sweatshop where Dallas Cowboy gear is produced make only 29 cents per hour, are forced to work 60 hours per week, are scolded for taking washroom breaks, and are sometimes physically abused if a daily quota is not met.[9] In the late 1990s, Nike and other name-brand apparel companies came under similar scrutiny, prompting in the U.S., Canada, Europe, and elsewhere a widespread campaign against sweatshop labour.

Child labour and sweatshop labour did not vanish in the twentieth century. For the most part, it just moved from Europe and North America to poor countries around the globe. While no longer prevalent in Europe or North America, economically developing countries in the global South—countries in Latin America, South and Southeast Asia, and Africa—openly recruit foreign businesses by offering them a large and cheap labour pool. For these countries, foreign investment is central to their manufacturing and agricultural exports economy. Poor young men often end up in agricultural work, while young women typically find factory work. In a capitalist economy, everything from cellphones, to celery, to computer processors, to clothes must be produced as cheaply and efficiently as possible. Shareholders demand profit. In the nineteenth century, industry and manufacturing attracted cheap labour from the vast pool of unemployed living in urban slums. With a 21st-century globalized economy, though, industry and manufacturing based in economically developed countries like the United States, Canada, and England seek cheap labour in countries like Cambodia, Vietnam, Bangladesh, Pakistan, Myanmar, Ghana, and Nigeria as a means of maximizing profits. Cheap labour is no longer in the Ardwick district of Manchester or in the Bowery district of New York City, as it was during the heyday of the Industrial Revolution, but on the outskirts of Phnom Penh, Lahore, and other cities in economically troubled countries. Indeed, the globalization of labour preys on countries recovering from war, despotic governments, social upheavals, natural disasters, and other catastrophes that have left them desperately poor and with few jobs. As Pope John Paul II said in 1997, "The globalized organization of work, profiting from the extreme privation of developing peoples, often entails grave situations that mock the elementary demands of human dignity."[10]

Pope John Paul II first addressed the issue of labour in his encyclical *Laborem exercens* (On Human Work), published in 1981. He was particularly attuned to labour issues. He had worked closely with the emerging Polish Solidarity Movement (*Solidarnosc*) in its struggle for independent labour unions, political reforms, freer markets, and the right to free speech under a communist government. *Laborem exercens* was a remarkable contribution to the Church's teaching on labour and provided a new development in Catholic social thought: it rooted the Church's teachings regarding labour in scripture and a renewed anthropological understanding. John Paul II noted that, in the creation story found in Genesis 1:1–2:4, the first human beings were commanded by God "to be fruitful," "to multiply," and "to fill the earth and subdue it." These creative actions are linked to our essential nature as beings created in the image of God (*imago dei*). In our work, the pope says, we participate in the activity of God, our Creator. Moreover, the gospel preached by Jesus Christ, a craftsman, is a gospel of work. It calls us to continue God's creative work, which through our different forms of work reveals particular facets of our likeness with God. In essence, then, human beings are workers. The pope writes in *Laborem exercens* (On Human Work, 1981), "Work is one of the characteristics that distinguishes humans from the rest of creatures, whose activities for sustaining their lives cannot be called work, and in doing so occupy their existence on earth" (LE, Introduction). Work must preserve human dignity. "Workers not only want fair pay," the pope says, "they also want to share in the responsibility and creativity of the very work process. They want to feel that they are working for themselves—an awareness that is smothered in a bureaucratic system where they only feel themselves to be 'cogs' in a huge machine moved from above" (LE, no. 15). Child labour, sweatshops, and similar working conditions are dehumanizing because they disregard the subjective aspects of work, that is, the human desire to be creative and to be responsible for the objects (or goods) that our work produces.

So what action is required of us? As ethical beings rooted in Catholic Social Teaching, we have a moral imperative to resist dehumanizing economic relationships. In *Centesimus annus*, which celebrated the hundredth anniversary of *Rerum novarum*, John Paul II said, "It is right to struggle against an unjust economic system that does not uphold the priority of the human being over capital and land" (CA, no. 35). Resistance may take various forms: political action, social activism, social justice education initiatives, purchasing fairly or directly traded goods, or participation in alternative economic structures, such as the slow economy movement. Whichever form of resistance we take, we do so knowing that our participation in the global market economy means that we are in a relationship with those who produce the goods we purchase. We may not meet them or know them, but our actions impact their lives. In all of our relationships, God has called us "to do justice, and to love kindness, and to walk humbly with your God" (Micah 6:8). We should pay close attention to Micah's prophetic moral imperative. Doing economic justice is linked to our relationship with God. Doing justice has spiritual consequences. As Pope John Paul II stated in his visit to Canada in 1984, "Poor people and poor nations—poor in different ways, not only lacking food, but also deprived of freedom and other human rights—will sit in judgment on those people who take these goods away from them, amassing to themselves the imperialistic monopoly of economic and political supremacy at the expense of others."[11]

Preferential Option for the Poor

In 1968, the Latin American Bishops Conference (CELAM) met in Medellín, Colombia, with an agenda to apply the teachings of Vatican II to church life on their continent. As Gregory Baum has observed in his book *Amazing Church*, the Church was still echoing the reformist hopes of *Rerum novarum*. For example, the conciliar document *Gaudium et spes* (Pastoral Constitution on the Church in the Modern World, 1965) expressed confidence in so-called welfare capitalism, the economic system that enabled Western nations to establish a strong middle class after World War II, with the help of social safety nets, all while expanding economic output. Inspired by the British economist John Maynard Keynes, welfare capitalism had the support of the West's major parties, including, though to a lesser degree, pro-business parties. In Medellín, however, the bishops did not share the Western view on the economy. "They looked at the existing capitalist system not from the centre," Baum writes, "where it produced great wealth but from the margin, where it undermined the subsistence economy on which ordinary people depended and destabilized the social relations that sustained their cultural and religious identity."[12] The widespread poverty and misery in Latin America was, the bishops proclaimed, "an injustice that cries to heaven."[13] This injustice was due primarily, though not exclusively, to a capitalist economic system centred in the global

North. The bishops argued that their countries were dependent on a centre of economic power, around which they gravitate. "Our nations frequently do not own their goods," the bishops wrote, "nor [do] they have a say in economic decisions affecting them."[14] While corruption and local incompetence are partially the reasons for the injustice, "the principal guilt for the economic dependence of our countries rests with power, inspired by uncontrolled desire for gain, which leads to economic dictatorship and the 'international imperialism of money' condemned by Pope Pius XI in *Quadragesimo anno* [On the Reconstruction of the Social Order, 1931] and Pope Paul VI in *Populorum progressio* [On the Development of Peoples, 1967]."[15]

The importance of the Medellín Conference was not that it addressed the issues of poverty and the injustices of capitalism, for that had been done by bishops and popes since *Rerum novarum*; rather, it was that, for the first time in the Catholic social tradition, the Church hierarchy affirmed that the starting point of theological reflection is the lives of those suffering on the margins of society. Alfred Hennelly put it this way in his introduction to the Medellín Conference documents: "Its importance was to institutionalize in its decrees the experience and practice of a significant number of Catholics in every stratum of the church from peasants to archbishops. It thus provided legitimation, inspiration, and pastoral plans for a continent-wide preferential option for the poor, encouraging those who were already engaged in the struggle and exhorting the entire church, both rich and poor, to become involved."[16] In other words, the Medellín Conference rejected the top-down economic reformism favoured by Western leaders and it called the Church, as an institution, to reorient its loyalties toward those on the margins of society.

Although the bishops at the Medellín Conference did not use the term "preferential option for the poor," they did lay the institutional groundwork for it in Catholic Social Teaching. The term was in wide usage in the 1970s among Latin American liberation theologians such as Gustavo Gutierrez, Juan Luis Segundo, and Leonardo Boff. These liberation theologians (and pastors) learned from scripture that the justice of a society is determined by its treatment of the poor. For instance, God's covenant with Israel was dependent on the way the community treated the poor and unprotected—the widow, the orphan and the stranger (Deuteronomy 16:11-12; Exodus 22:21-27; Isaiah 1:16-17). Throughout Israel's history and in the New Testament, the poor are agents of God's transforming power. In the gospel of Luke, Jesus proclaims that he has been anointed to bring good news to the poor (4:1-22). And in the Last Judgment, we are told that we will be judged according to how we respond to the hungry, the thirsty, the prisoner, and the stranger (Matthew 25:31-46). Moreover, these theologians found in scripture that God's own identity, "I AM WHO I AM," is connected to God's liberating work of setting the Israelites free from the bondage of Egyptian slavery (Exodus 3). In light of scripture, then, liberation theologians posed this question to the Christian tradition: If scripture reveals a God who is primarily concerned with the poor and oppressed, and the gospel is directed especially toward the poor, then should not the Church now look to the experiences of the poor, the marginalized, and the oppressed as the initial act of pastoral, theological, and moral reflection?

In spite of concerns about the political actions of certain liberation theologians, especially during the 1980s, the Catholic social tradition has embraced "the option for the poor." For example, following the Medellín Conference, the Latin American bishops met in 1979 in Puebla, Mexico, where they used the liberation theology vocabulary of "option for the poor" to describe the Church's obligation to read scripture and interpret society from the perspective of the poor, as well as to convey the Church's pastoral duty to be in solidarity with the poor as they struggle for justice. The Canadian bishops drew on the option for the poor in the development of their 1983 paper "Ethical Reflections on the Economic Crisis," the one that Pierre Trudeau brusquely dismissed, and their 1996 letter *The Struggle Against Poverty*. The U.S. bishops stated in their pastoral letter *Economic Justice for All* (1986), "As individuals and as a nation, therefore, we are called to make a fundamental 'option for the poor.' The obligation to evaluate social and economic activity from the viewpoint of the poor and the powerless arises from the radical command to love one's neighbour as one's self. Those who are marginalized and whose rights are denied have privileged claims if society is to provide justice for all."[17] And although not always consistent in his use of the "option for the poor," Pope John Paul II held that the option for the poor, or "love of preference for the poor," as he sometimes called it, is "a special form of primacy in the exercise of Christian charity, to which the whole tradition of the Church bears witness. It affects the life of each Christian inasmuch as he or she seeks to imitate the life of Christ, but it applies equally to our social responsibilities and hence to our manner of living, and to the logical decisions to be made concerning the ownership and use of goods" (*Sollicitudo rei socialis* [Social Concern of the Church, 1987], no. 42).

In essence, the option for the poor calls on us to understand sin not just in individualistic terms. Instead, the option for the poor reminds us that sin has a social component. The Latin American bishops at the Medellín Conference understood that individual sin did not explain the miserable conditions endured by the poor and oppressed. They concluded that there were social, economic, and political structures that dehumanized the poor. Catholic moral theologians refer to this sin as "social sin." In *Reconciliatio et paenitentia* (On Reconciliation and Penance, 1984), Pope John Paul describes the nature of social sin in these terms:

> Whenever the church speaks of situations of sin or when she condemns as social sins certain situations or the collective behaviour of certain social groups, big or small, or even of whole nations and blocs of nations, she knows and she proclaims that such cases of social sin are the result of the accumulation and concentration of many personal sins. It is a case of the very personal sins of those who cause or support evil or who exploit it; of those who are in a position to avoid, eliminate or at least limit certain social evils but who fail to do so out of laziness, fear or the conspiracy of silence, through secret complicity or indifference; of those who take refuge in the supposed impossibility of changing the world and also of those who sidestep the effort and sacrifice required, producing specious reasons of higher order. (RP, no. 16)

For John Paul II, the ultimate responsibility for social sin resides with individuals. We are indeed challenged as individuals to respond to economic structures that, for instance, enable some 900 million people around the globe to live in hunger while developed countries such as the United States, Canada, and England regulate and limit the production of food crops—all to maintain a supply-and-demand balance that will yield handsome profits for the agricultural industry.

So what are relatively well-off Christians to do when faced with the complex issues of social sin? Simply retreating into guilt and despair is not the answer, if we follow the teachings of Pope John Paul. What is demanded of us as ethical beings is that we actively work to overcome the structures that make us complicit in the dehumanization of the poor and oppressed. Given that many of us reading this book right now are likely the "birds" who soar above a sea of economic injustice, we must make decisions as individuals, communities, institutions, and societies to be in solidarity with the fish, who, as Filipino peasant Mang Juan said, swim in a sea "of usury, and tenancy and other unjust relations." This is the essential ethical demand of the preferential option for the poor.

Global Finance and the Great Recession of 2008

On the afternoon of October 13, 2008, the U.S. Treasury Secretary Hank Paulson was locked in a room with nine of the leading investment bankers in the United States. Paulson was there because he, along with New York Federal Reserve Bank chair Tim Geithner, was orchestrating a plan to inject $250 billion into the U.S.'s largest banks. Just a few months earlier, one of Wall Street's most iconic banks, Bear Stearns, had been forced to sell its assets to JP Morgan/Chase bank because it lacked liquidity—the bank had simply run out of money. In September 2008, the fourth largest investment bank in the United States, Lehman Brothers, had filed for bankruptcy, which created tremendous anxiety in the stock markets and fear among policymakers that not only was the U.S. economy on the verge of total collapse, but also quite possibly the global economy. The finance markets were frozen, Paulson believed, because there wasn't enough money in the system to lend or to pay off immediate debts. Shortly after his meeting with the Wall Street bankers, Paulson confessed that pouring billions in public money into the banks was "objectionable," but, in his opinion, unavoidable—the U.S. government absolutely had to restore confidence in the markets and persuade the banks to start lending again. By the end of the week, the U.S. Treasury department announced further capital infusions into the finance market, totalling close to $2.25 trillion. By the end of 2011, the U.S. government had injected an estimated $29 trillion into the economy on the whole, through bank bailouts, loans guarantees, and asset purchases.

As the former head of Goldman Sachs, the largest investment bank on Wall Street, Paulson was, by his own admission, an avowed laissez-faire capitalist. He believed in Adam Smith's invisible hand of the market: markets ought to be left alone to regulate themselves. According to classic theories of self-regulating capitalism, one of the primary ways the markets regulate themselves is by punishing those who make bad investments, sell inferior products, or fail, for whatever reason, to compete on the open market. Punishment in a self-regulating market comes in the form of economic loss. The threat of punishment/economic loss is what keeps owners and investors from being too risky in the marketplace. What Paulson feared by the government giving banks money, buying up stock in General Motors, and enacting other so-called economic stimulus measures was "moral hazard," that is, a situation where a party engages in overly risky behaviour because the costs are not borne by the party taking the risk. In other words, without the fear of economic punishment, or even failure, banks, insurance companies, manufacturers, and others receiving "bailouts" would be free to engage in even riskier economic activity. Moral hazard is partly why Mitt Romney declared in the earliest days of the Great Recession, "Let Detroit Go Bankrupt."[18] The market should be allowed to take its course and punish risky or bad businesses. Indeed, moral hazard is what happens when "banks are too big to fail," when governments find it necessary to intervene to keep banks afloat, or else risk bringing down a country's economy.

In 1991, just shortly after the collapse of the Soviet Union, and amidst a tide of pro–free market euphoria, Pope John Paul II addressed the question of whether the failure of communism means that capitalism was truly the victorious social system, and, if so, whether capitalism should be the goal of the countries now making efforts to rebuild their economy and society in Eastern Europe and in the Third World. The pope's answer was prophetic:

> If by "capitalism" is meant an economic system which recognizes the fundamental and positive role of business, the market, private property and the resulting responsibility for the means of production, as well as free human creativity in the economic sector,

then the answer is certainly in the affirmative, even though it would perhaps be more appropriate to speak of a "business economy," "market economy," or simply "free economy." But if by "capitalism" is meant a system in which freedom in the economic sector is not circumscribed within a strong juridical framework which places it at the service of human freedom in its totality, and which sees it as a particular aspect of that freedom, the core of which is ethical and religious, then the reply is certainly negative. (*Centesimus annus*, no. 42)

The Great Recession beginning in 2008 is precisely what Pope John Paul warned against—an economy without adequate regulation, without a commitment to place the good of the human community above economic gains, and without the recognition that human freedom springs from an ethical and religious core.

While there were a number of causes that contributed to the Great Recession beginning in 2008, one cause is clear: the global financial market was woefully under-regulated. This under-regulated financial market enabled banks to expand the amount of credit available in the consumer market by bundling together home mortgages and other assets for the purpose of securing repayment on financial instruments known as Mortgage-Backed Securities (MBS). When the housing market began to plummet, the mortgages that were bundled together to "securitize" the MBS loans decreased in value. Homeowners experienced the loss directly. The drastic drop in home prices meant that, in many cases, the amount a homeowner owed on a mortgage was greater than the value of the home they lived in. This was particularly problematic for Americans who had adjustable-rate mortgages (ARMs), which required periodic mortgage renewal at a new rate of interest. Because they owed more than the house was worth, it was impossible for many homeowners with ARMs to refinance when their mortgage term expired. Those who could refinance found themselves paying a much higher rate of interest, which meant many homeowners could not meet their monthly mortgage payments. For those banks that had created or purchased large bundled-MBS packages, and these were among the largest banks in the United States and Europe, the housing market crash meant they were now without enough money to cover the losses incurred in their mortgage lending operations.

In October 2011, the Pontifical Council for Justice and Peace (PCJP) released a bold statement on the economic crisis entitled *Towards Reforming the International Financial and Monetary Systems in the Context of Global Public Authority*.[19] The pretext for this statement was Pope Benedict XVI's encyclical *Caritas in veritate* (Charity in Truth, 2009). In this social encyclical, Pope Benedict says that the global financial crisis "obliges us to re-plan our journey, to set ourselves new rules and to discover new forms of commitment, to build on positive experiences and to reject negative ones. The crisis thus becomes *an opportunity for discernment, in which to shape a new vision for the future.* In this spirit, with confidence rather than resignation, it is appropriate to address the difficulties of the present time" (CV, no. 21). The ultimate objective of the PCJP statement was to set out a new vision, one rooted in ethical and religious values, to shape the future of the global economy.

The PCJP understands the crisis as a structural injustice created primarily by unfettered capitalism. The Pontifical Council recalls that Pope Paul VI, in his encyclical *Populorum progressio* (1967), has "already clearly and prophetically denounced the dangers of a liberalist conception of economic development because of its harmful consequences for world equilibrium and peace." The liberalist, or liberal, concept of the economy is one that resists government interference and believes the market should be self-regulating. But the PCJP counters that the Catholic social tradition has long noted that unregulated markets do not provide for the common good and do not operate with any ethical commitments to a community or a society. Indeed, from *Rerum novarum* in 1891 to *Caritas in veritate* in 2009, the Catholic social tradition has criticized liberal capitalism for its appeal to supposed economic laws, which effectively supersede the moral values of a community, and for its often virulent individualism, which in capitalist economies is little more than greed operating under the guise of competition. Lost in all of this is the foundational premise that the economy must be predicated upon the common good and not on loyalties to shareholders and the business classes.

By far the most audacious proposal offered by the PCJP is the formation of a central world bank that would regulate the flow of monetary exchanges. Fulfilling a role similar to the United Nations, this central bank would have "a realistic structure and be set up gradually," the Council wrote. It should ensure "free and stable markets overseen by a suitable legal framework," provide "support of sustainable development and social progress of all," and be "inspired by the values of charity and truth," recalling Pope Benedict's encyclical *Caritas in veritate*. One significant benefit of this central bank would be that it involves developing countries. Global economic decisions must not be left to those with the greatest power. Instead, "the governance of globalization must be marked by subsidiarity," the Council argued, "articulated into several layers and involving different levels that can work together." Rooted in the principle of subsidiarity, then, the bank could avoid bureaucratic isolation, further risk of delegitimization, and threats of takeover by powerful countries or economic blocs.

While the possibility of a global central bank remains unlikely in the near future, Pope Benedict XVI and the Pontifical Council on Justice and Peace have offered a bold vision of what an economic system could look like if it were oriented to serve the common good.

CHAPTER 7

The Ethical Use of Force and the Quest for Peace

B y early 312, the Roman Empire had fragmented to the point where conflict between rival factions threatened to lead to protracted civil war. With the impending collapse of the imperial governing system, known as the tetrarchy, and with the death of the senior emperor Galerius in Rome, in 311, a power vacuum existed at the centre of the Empire. Two factions vied for control: one led by Constantine, the leader of the western provinces, and the other by Maxentius, a formidable emperor who had governed the important Roman sector of the Empire since 306. The war that loomed ahead in the spring of 312 looked ominous. The two sides had roughly equivalent armies and neither side had a definite strategic advantage. The difference-maker, military historians will say, was Constantine's tactical brilliance.

Having made quick work of Maxentius's forces in northern Italy, Constantine set out for Rome. Maxentius thought that, if he remained in Rome, he would be facing the full brunt of Constantine's army. The only winning option, he concluded, was to leave Rome, rally the largest force possible, and face Constantine on a battlefield of his choosing. That battlefield was an area just north of Rome, on the Tiber River, known as the Milvian Bridge.

On the evening of October 27, 312, Constantine and his army hunkered down to prepare for the following day's battle. Constantine knew he was going to encounter an army that was larger, fresher, and better equipped than his. But according to the Christian historian Eusebius (263–339), Constantine was growing in confidence because earlier he had received a sign of impending victory while marching into the sun. In Latin, it read *in hoc signo vinces*, "in this sign, conquer." Based on conversations he claimed to have had with Constantine, Eusebius reported that Constantine was initially unsure of the apparition's meaning. The explanation came later that evening in a dream in which Jesus Christ appeared to him and explained that he should use the sign against his enemies. Eusebius then went on to describe the labarum, the military standard used by Constantine, showing the Greek letters Chi (which resembles the letter X) and Rho (which resembles the letter P). The X would be superimposed on the P, resulting in ☧.

The following day changed the course of history. Constantine's forces quickly broke through Maxentius's lines, forcing Maxentius's bloodied and exhausted troops against the Tiber. Rumours quickly spread that Maxentius had died in the desperate retreat. The next morning, Maxentius's body was pulled from the Tiber. To demonstrate that the emperor had met his demise, Constantine had Maxentius decapitated and his head sent to Rome. Just hours after claiming his victory at the Milvian Bridge, Constantine entered Rome, where he was welcomed as the de facto leader of the Empire's western sector.

While the historical veracity of Constantine's conversion to Christianity just prior to the Battle of Milvian Bridge is open to much debate, it is certain that his decision to link his victory over Maxentius to his conversion forever changed the nature of Christianity and the Christian Church's relationship to the state. No longer was Christianity a marginal, though widespread, religion in the Roman Empire; it was now the religion of the emperor. In time, it would become *the* religion of the Empire.

Christian theologians found themselves scrambling to make sense of this change. How would they adapt the teachings of a minority religion based on the sayings of a first-century Jewish radical to being the religion of a superpower? Answers to this question meant that theologians had to consider Christianity's teaching regarding governing authority, patriotism, pacifism, the use of force, the differing moral standards for clergy and laity, the sanctity of war and peace, and the treatment of enemies, to name just a few.

Although we are far removed from Constantine's fourth-century Roman Empire, a similar question remains with us: How do we relate the teachings of the Christian tradition to contemporary political and military issues? Or more specifically, how do we Catholics relate our Church's teachings, based on the sayings of a first-century Jewish radical, but largely developed within the context of Christendom, to 21st-century issues such as nuclear weapons, war by remotely controlled weapons, international terrorism, and the responsibility to protect vulnerable populations? Sketching out an answer to this latter question is our task in this chapter.

Pacifism and the Early Church

For the first three hundred years of its existence, Christianity was a minority religion with relatively little doctrinal uniformity. Questions about the nature of Jesus and Church governance created massive rifts in the Church. In spite of these significant differences, though, Christian theologians were virtually unanimous in their rejection of war. Roland Bainton, in his classic *Christian Attitudes Toward War and Peace* (1960), observed: "The age of persecution down to the time of Constantine was the age of pacifism to the degree that during this period no Christian author to our knowledge approved of Christian participation in battle. The position of the Church was not absolutist, however. There were some Christians in the army and they were not on that account excluded from communion."[1] Many of them had been soldiers before their conversion. Others, though, became soldiers thinking that an immediate death meant more time to spend with God in eternity. In any case, Roman generals were not always delighted to have Christians among their ranks. Their apprehension wasn't based on any theological bias, but rather on a practical military concern. Too many Christian infantry were breaking ranks and charging headlong toward the enemy, where they met a quick and certain death. Not only did this lack of battlefield discipline create holes in infantry lines, but it also made advancing on and retreating from the enemy more difficult, because armies needed to navigate the dead Christian soldiers. Simply put, Roman generals couldn't rely on Christian soldiers because of their penchant for needlessly getting themselves killed.[2]

There were theological reasons for early Christianity's pacifism. Many Christians believed that the use of force was contrary to the teachings of Jesus. For instance, Clement of Alexandria (150–215) stated:

> If you enroll as one of God's people, heaven is your country and God your lawgiver. And what are his laws? You shall not kill; you shall love your neighbour as yourself. To him that strikes you on the one cheek, turn to him the other also [Matthew 5:38] … The Church is an army that sheds no blood.[3]

Tertullian (160–225), one of the most outspoken opponents of war in the early Christian Church, thought that the teachings of Jesus prohibited Christians from fighting for the Roman Empire, or any governing authority, for that matter, because they established a different set of moral and spiritual principles. He argued:

> There can be no compatibility between an oath made to God and one made to man, between the standard of Christ and of the devil, between the camp of the light and the camp of darkness. The soul cannot be beholden to two masters, God and Caesar. Moses, to be sure, carried a rod; Aaron wore a military belt and John had a breastplate. If one wants to play around with the topic, Joshua led an army and the Jewish nation went to war. But how will a Christian do so? Indeed how will he serve in the army even during peacetime without the sword that Jesus Christ has taken away? Even if a soldier came to John and got advice on how they ought to act, even if the centurion became a believer, the Lord, by taking away Peter's sword, disarmed every soldier thereafter [Matthew 26:53]. We are not allowed to wear any uniform that symbolizes a sinful act.[4]

Roughly half a century earlier than Tertullian, Justin Martyr (100–165) opposed war on the grounds that the conversion to Christianity marked a radical departure from the Empire's worldview, norms and values, loyalties, and ethical decision-making. He said:

We who [once] delighted in war, in the slaughter of one another and in every other kind of iniquity have in every part of the world converted our weapons into instruments of peace: our swords into ploughshares, our spears into farmers' tools [Isaiah 2:4], and now we cultivate piety, justice, brotherly charity, faith, and hope, which we derive from the Father through the crucified Saviour.[5]

For these early Christian theologians, the gospel of Christ was fundamentally inconsistent with the moral and political ideologies of the Roman Empire. Not only had the teachings of Jesus led them to eschew violence as a morally legitimate act, but the "other-worldliness" in Christ's teachings led them to the conclusion that they should prioritize the "kingdom of God" over Caesar's already present kingdom. Roman officials stationed in urban centres where Christianity thrived clearly understood this theological stance, which caused the Empire enough concern to monitor the activities of the Christian churches in areas that could be easily destabilized.

Origen (185–254) took a more nuanced position regarding Rome. In response to the charge that Christians were undermining the Empire because they refused, on the whole, to serve in the military or government, Origen said that Christians could support the Empire, but not through the use of force or by serving in the government. Instead, Christians could pray for divine assistance:

To be sure, the more pious a man is, the more effectively does he assist the emperors—more so than the troops that go out and kill as many of the enemy as possible on the battleline…. The Christians fight through their prayers to God on behalf of those doing battle in a just cause and on behalf of an emperor who is ruling rightly in order that all opposition and hostility toward those who are acting rightly may be eliminated. What is more, by overcoming with our prayers all the demons who incite wars, who violate oaths and who disturb the peace we help emperors more than those who are supposedly doing the fighting…. We do battle on [the emperor's] behalf by raising a special army of piety through our petition to God.[6]

Origen thus concluded that Christians may support wars, provided they are for just reasons, but the teachings of Jesus prevent Christians from picking up arms.

Other Christians adopted pacifism because they objected to the imperial protocol that required troops to pledge allegiance to the emperor, the *Pontifex Maximus*, who, according to Roman custom, was recognized as a god. Also, many Christian soldiers objected to a common practice in the imperial military that required periodic animal sacrifices to the Roman gods. For these early Christians, such requirements were forms of idolatry.[7]

By 312, then, attitudes among Christians still tended toward pacifism. But as Origen demonstrated in his response to the charge that Christianity was undermining the Empire, attitudes among Christians toward the Empire were not wholly negative. Indeed, the Church and its quickly forming governance structure, which was based largely on a Roman political template, facilitated the transformation from a small community-based religion to a religion at the centre of the Empire. In 314, at the Council of Arles, the Church formally recognized the need for governing authorities to engage in armed conflict. By 380, Christianity (as spelled out in the First Council of Nicaea in 325) had become the official religion of the Roman Empire. Practically speaking, no empire can have its official religion and its religious leaders promoting an ethic of pacifism. Thus, in spite of three centuries of pacifism, the Christian tradition began the process of blunting its theological resistance to state-sanctioned violence to meet the demands of the Empire. In effect, Christian theologians in the late fourth and early fifth centuries had to develop a Christian ethic of empire, which included the formulation of a Christian just war theory.

The Development of a Christian Just War Theory

The concept of a just war is not exclusively Christian. Ancient warring societies often had honour codes, war protocols, and conventions that established the proper conduct of war. The Hindu epic *The Mahabharata*, for example, refers to a list of laws that are intended to make war as humane as possible. It prohibited warriors from attacking those who are unarmed and engaging other warriors who are at a distinct disadvantage due to their lack of arms. Underlying these laws is a principle of fairness. Indeed, many societies, including those influenced by Greco-Roman military thought, appealed to commonly held conventions. Among these conventions was the principle that war contracts between enemy states should be in place prior to the first battle. These contracts would establish the terms of engagement and provide some criteria for determining victory. Although these conventions may have been routinely disregarded once war broke out, there remains in many societies the moral principle that war must be limited. In the Greco-Roman tradition, it was largely through the work of Plato, Aristotle, and the Roman philosopher Cicero (106–143 BC), who had been influenced by the Stoic school of philosophers, who provided a framework for a just war theory.

St. Ambrose

The first theologian to begin formulating a Christian just war theory was St. Ambrose (339–397), who was the bishop of Milan from 374 to 397. For Ambrose, the overriding question was this: if Christianity is to be protected from foreign invaders and from internal forces opposed to orthodox Christianity, do Christians have a responsibility to fight for the governing authority that is providing the protection? Ambrose's response was a resounding "Yes." Christians have a civic obligation to fight when called upon.

Ambrose's principal sources in laying the groundwork for a Christian just war theory were the Hebrew scriptures (which often has God championing a "holy war" to defend religious orthodoxy), the writings of Cicero, Roman law (which holds that parties have a legal obligation to abide by the terms of a contract), and the natural law tradition of Plato and Aristotle. Following the natural law tradition in particular, Ambrose argued that war must be virtuous. Justice must be the aim of war, but it must also fundamentally include wisdom, temperance, and fortitude. One of the mistakes made by earlier pacifist theologians, he contended, was that they focused too much on the spiritual and eschatological (end times) aspects of the kingdom of God. They were still expecting the imminent return of Jesus Christ. Their otherworldly perspective led Christians to shirk their worldly (or temporal) responsibilities, Ambrose believed, including their civic responsibilities to ruling authorities.[8]

To emphasize the Christian's worldly responsibilities, Ambrose claimed that the virtues are not only spiritual dispositions but also moral obligations that should be infused in every part of our life. Another way of putting it is that, for Ambrose, the virtuous life has not only a vertical disposition (God and eternal salvation) but also a horizontal disposition (worldly responsibilities to family, neighbours, and political bodies).[9] For this reason, governing authorities, soldiers, and all others involved in war have an absolute moral obligation to conduct themselves in ways that manifest justice.

The groundwork Ambrose laid for a Christian just war theory had three basic elements. First, war has to have just reasons, what the just war tradition calls *jus ad bellum* ("the right to war" or "justice toward war"). Ambrose held that war is never a divinely sanctioned act. It is a political act, directed by men who have been entrusted by God to be God's servants on Earth (Romans 13) and who must resort to political means in the pursuit of justice. Those governing authorities who pursue justice act in accordance with God's will. But merely possessing the wisdom to engage in conflict for morally justifiable reasons does not mean governing authorities are in a position to declare a "holy war."

Second, Ambrose held that justice must guide the conduct of war, what the just war tradition calls *jus in bello* ("justice in war"). Citing King David as his example, Ambrose believed that combatants have an obligation to respect their enemy. Captured soldiers must be treated with respect, non-combatants must not be targeted, and enemies who are found innocent of any crimes must be released and treated as non-combatants.

The third element of this nascent Christian just war theory was an exemption for Christian clergy. Ambrose believed that violence stains the human spirit. Although Christians have an obligation to fight for a governing authority, the act of fighting is a worldly act that is ultimately tainted by sin, even if for just reasons. Consequently, Christian soldiers are forbidden to fight for themselves—they fight only to defend others. Clergy, however, are forbidden to fight, even in the defence of others, because the primary task of clergy is to celebrate the sacrament of the Eucharist, which requires clergy to be pure in spirit.

St. Augustine

St. Augustine of Hippo (354–430) was one of Ambrose's most capable students. Baptized by Ambrose in 387, Augustine used Ambrose's groundwork to develop a Christian just war theory. It was not a systematic theory, but rather a theory that emerged over the course of Augustine's lifetime. Because he was the first Christian thinker to provide a thorough definition of just war, theologians today sometimes refer to Augustine as the father of the Christian just war theory.

Augustine's thinking on war evolved over time. Initially, Augustine introduced to Christianity a distinctly theocratic understanding of war. In contrast to Roman thinking on war as an act aimed at restoring the rights of an injured party, Augustine believed war could serve to punish wrongdoers. In the case of non-Christian enemies of the Roman Empire, this meant that war could be used to punish enemies for their non-belief. Augustine looked to the persecution of the Israelites to make his case. Both Pharaoh and Moses persecuted the Israelites, Augustine argued, but Pharaoh did so out of unrighteous hatred, while Moses was motivated by love. Also, early on, Augustine didn't make a moral distinction between offensive and defensive wars. Wars were wars—what determined their moral value was largely the disposition of those engaged in the conflict. War undertaken out of hatred was both unrighteous and unjust, while a war conducted out of love was both righteous and just. Citing Hebrew scripture, especially the case of God ordering Joshua to lay ambushes for his enemy (Joshua 8), Augustine observed that God had occasionally authorized acts of offensive war, that is, acts that violated established political agreements and war protocols.

By the end of the fourth century, Christianity was entrenched as the Empire's religion. Many Christians believed that the Roman Empire was God's political arm and, as such, the Empire needed finally to rid itself of Roman gods and idols, which were an affront to God's ultimate authority. In spite of his reputation for being a staunch defender of Christian orthodoxy, Augustine began to raise concerns about the moral absoluteness, if not self-righteousness, involved in Christian actions to cleanse the Empire of the Roman gods and so-called paganism. He recalled that, during a sermon he preached in 401 in the city of Carthage in North Africa, he had to stop in the middle of it to quiet a rambunctious crowd that had begun to shout, "Down with Roman gods, down with Roman gods." For Augustine, the exuberance was a sign that Christians had equated the power of the Empire with God's power and that they believed the Roman emperor was God's worldly warrior. Augustine could draw this conclusion because he, too, had been caught up with the idea that the demise of paganism in the Empire was a fulfillment of prophecy and a sign that God was using the Empire in a special way. But Augustine had started to distance himself from the idea that, through the outworking of the Empire, the "whole world has become a choir praising Christ."[10] By 410, Augustine's thinking on the Roman Empire, the Church, and the nature of citizenship had effectively matured. He became convinced that God's will and order cannot be realized through human thought or action. The power of human sin is simply too strong and too pervasive. Consequently, Christians should disavow any idea that governing authorities and soldiers are carrying out a divine command when they fight and kill in the name of righteousness. The relationship between worldly institutions and God has been so marred by sin, Augustine concluded, that it is simply impossible for God to give divine sanction to any worldly institution, even the revered Roman Empire.

Augustine's mature thinking on war and political theology began to emerge in the cataclysmic years following the fall of Rome in 410. In the summer of 410, after a long siege, Rome opened its gates to the Visigoths. For three days, they plundered Rome, taking valuables from wealthy families, desecrating churches, raiding mausoleums, and kidnapping influential aristocrats. Militarily, the fall of Rome was only a minor setback, and within a few months the balance of power would swing back toward the Empire. But spiritually, the fall of Rome resulted in a crisis of faith that would forever change Christian theology's stance toward the state.

In the wake of Rome's sacking, citizens began to ask penetrating questions. Why would the Christian God allow Rome to fall at the hands of the pagan Goths? Is the Christian God impotent? Rome was strong while it was under the protection of the Roman gods, so should we not return to the gods? Are the Roman gods punishing us for abandoning them? What is the appropriate response to attacks such as those carried out by Alaric's forces? And should we even defend governing authorities who are, based on their defeat, evidently outside of God's will? In his sweeping work, *City of God*, which he wrote between 413 and 423, Augustine set out to answer these and other similar questions.[11]

On the issue of the Church's relationship to governing authorities, as well as the Christian's responsibilities to government, Augustine had to address three basic questions. First, is it right for Christians to defend a relatively just society from a relatively unjust attack? Second, how does Christian theology reconcile war and killing in war with the teachings of Jesus in his Sermon on the Mount? And third, assuming both that it is right to defend a relatively just society and that Christian theology can reconcile war with the teachings of Jesus, what are the conditions or criteria of a just war? Augustine doesn't pose or answer these questions in a systematic way. Instead, his views on war and the Christian faith come to us in *City of God* under a variety of topics, from the nature of citizenship to the nature of love. Let's briefly summarize Augustine's responses.

(1) Defending a Relatively Just Society from a Relatively Unjust Attack

With questions lingering about the fall of Rome and the apparent inability of the Christian God to protect Rome, Augustine mounted a theological argument in *City of God* that transformed the Christian tradition's understanding of political authority. His argument is based on a redefined worldview. According to Augustine, those who believed that the fall of Rome was an indication of God's impotency or that the Roman gods were punishing them for abandoning their traditional beliefs were basing their beliefs on an incorrect worldview. They had effectively conflated the Roman Empire with the kingdom of God, resulting in the mistaken belief that the Empire was the kingdom of God on earth. Or to put this in context, they had equated an earthly city, the city of Rome, for a heavenly city, the City of God. For Augustine, the fall of Rome actually clarified the fact that the Roman Empire never operated with God's absolute authority. The only authoritative body that has God's absolute approval, he argued, is the kingdom of God, and that kingdom will remain a heavenly kingdom until the return of Christ. Thus God was not defeated when the Empire fell, because God was not in control of the Empire. And there would be no reason for the Roman gods, if they existed, to inflict destruction on the Empire, because Roman citizens were more than capable of wreaking havoc on their own.

The difference between Augustine's earthly city and the City of God is stark. The earthly city is tainted by sin, leading to greed, lust, arrogance, pride, and fear. Left to their own devices, human beings would eventually destroy themselves, Augustine asserted. But God has given human beings governing authorities to restrain the impulse of sin by creating and enforcing laws, punishing law-breakers, and resorting to force, if necessary, to maintain the "tranquil order" (*tranquillitas ordinis*, one of Augustine's favourite terms). This government is not, however, a theocratic state, Augustine claimed, because government itself is tainted by sin. Ruling authorities inevitably impose laws and act in ways that manifest greed, lust, arrogance, pride, and even fear. Always to some degree at odds with the City of God, which offers true peace and justice, government and the earthly city can only achieve relative justice and peace.

Although Augustine was pessimistic toward government, he did not allow his pessimism to lead to complete despair and passivity. To the contrary, he insisted that, as corrupt and depraved as it was, the Roman Empire provided relative order, justice, and peace. In particular, the Empire had allowed the Church to flourish and Christians to live in relative peace. In comparison to the Empire, the Goths and other potential rivals to the Empire offered only inferior forms of order, justice, and peace. Augustine believed that their unjust attacks on the Empire, including the scandalous sacking on Rome, only demonstrated their propensity toward disorder, injustice, and violence. To Augustine's way of thinking, then, attacks from relatively unjust aggressors must be met by force, for order, justice, and peace must be defended, even though they are imperfect.

(2) Reconciling War with the Sermon on the Mount

Augustine believed that Christians hold dual citizenship. On the one hand, Christians are, through their baptism, citizens of the City of God. As a result, Christians will spend eternity in the City of God, in fellowship with God. But on the other hand, Christians are also citizens of the earthly city, in this case the Roman Empire, where they live out their earthly lives. The question was how we make sense of living in both cities. To answer this question, Augustine turned to St. Paul, who in his letter to the Roman church said:

> Let every person be subject to the governing authorities; for there is no authority except from God, and those authorities that exist have been instituted by God. Therefore whoever resists authority resists what God has appointed, and those who resist will incur judgment. For rulers are not a terror to good conduct, but to bad. Do you wish to have no fear of the authority? Then do what is good, and you will receive its approval; for it is God's servant for your good. But if you do what is wrong, you should be afraid, for the authority does not bear the sword in vain! It is the servant of God to execute wrath on the wrongdoer. Therefore one must be subject, not only because of wrath but also because of conscience. For the same reason you also pay taxes, for the authorities are God's servants, busy with this very thing. Pay to all what is due to them—taxes to whom taxes are due, revenue to whom revenue is due, respect to whom respect is due, honour to whom honour is due (Romans 13:1-7).

Based on Paul's instruction to the church in Rome, Augustine concluded that Christians have a duty to pay taxes, follow the law, and, with the exception of clergy, fight for one's governing authority. What remained to be established, however, was the extent to which Christians could reconcile the pacifist teachings of Jesus with the earthly obligation to fight. Was there not a contradiction in scripture?

By the time Augustine was writing *City of God*, the Church had largely settled on a canon of Christian scripture. In fact, Augustine had been one of the driving forces behind a movement in the Church to close the canon. Unlike Ambrose, who was actively writing just a few decades earlier, Augustine had to contend with a greater sense of scriptural authority in the Church. In making the case for the ethical use of force, he had to explain an apparent contradiction between the gospel teachings of Jesus, on the one hand, and, on the other hand, the Church's tradition of instructing Christians to fulfill their obligations to governing authorities, which would include fighting and killing for Rome.

The primary scripture Augustine had to address concerns the teaching of Jesus in Matthew 5:38-48, the final few lines of the so-called Sermon on the Mount:

> You have heard that it was said, "An eye for an eye and a tooth for a tooth." But I say to you, Do not resist an evildoer. But if anyone strikes you on the right cheek, turn the other also; ... You have heard that it was said, "You shall love your neighbour and hate your enemy." But I say to you, Love your enemies and pray for those who persecute you, so that you may be children of your Father in heaven....

Tertullian and other early Christian theologians maintained that this teaching of Jesus categorically prohibited Christians from taking up arms against enemies. But Augustine offered two important nuances. First, he claimed that Jesus was speaking specifically to individual Christians and not to governments. Pacifism is an individualistic ethical stance. But governments may still use limited force for just reasons. Second, he argued that, although Jesus's pacifist teaching was aimed at individual Christians, it was not intended to prevent Christians from protecting their neighbours from harm. It was, rather, intended to prohibit Christians from using violence for their own self-interest, including their own self-preservation.

So how, then, does Augustine morally justify war in light of Jesus's instruction to "turn the other cheek"? The short answer is that Augustine understands war as an act of neighbourly love leading to peace. Or to put it another way, love is what motivates us to protect our neighbours, while peace is the goal.

Let's consider a crude and unpleasant example. Suppose you are invited over to a friend's apartment for dinner. Toward the end of the evening, you hear an argument break out in the apartment next door. You ask your friend if this is a normal occurrence. She says it isn't, because the neighbour just recently moved in. But she knows the neighbour has a restraining order against her former husband, who was recently released on bail, pending a charge of assault with a deadly weapon against his wife. Within minutes, the argument dramatically escalates. Amidst crying and objects slamming against the apartment walls, you hear a man shout, "I'm going to kill you right now!" What is the Christian response?

If you're in a part of town where the police respond quickly, either you or your friend will undoubtedly call 9-1-1. Given the rapidly escalating nature of the conflict, and your knowledge of previous violent activity, one of you is also likely to run next door to intervene. Let's say it's you. Upon entering the apartment, you find an enraged man with a knife heading toward a dazed and bruised woman. Out of the corner of your eye, you see a baseball bat. You pick up the bat and swing hard, striking the attacker across the back of his head. The attacker has been subdued. The neighbour's life has been saved. But is your use of violent force ethically justified? Following Augustine's thinking, the answer is "Yes," if your motivation was love. The answer is "No" if you swung the bat in anger, hostility, or hatred, or you somehow took pleasure in the act itself. In this case, although you used violence, according to Augustine's line of reasoning, you still met the conditions of Jesus's teaching in the Sermon on the Mount. You acted not out of self-interest or self-preservation. Instead, you acted out of neighbourly love.

Now suppose the attacker had come toward you upon seeing that you had picked up the bat. Should you not at this point drop your weapon and "turn the other cheek"? Again, an Augustinian answer would depend on the motivation. If you're intending to engage the knife-wielding attacker out of self-interest or self-preservation, you should follow the teachings of Jesus in the Sermon on the Mount and drop your weapon. Self-defence isn't an adequate reason for the use of force. However, if you're intending to fend off the attacker to subdue him before he can once again attack an innocent, defenceless victim, then you are not only morally justified in fighting, but you are also morally obligated to fight.

Augustine believed that thinking on war could follow a similar line of reasoning. War undertaken by a governing authority to gain more power, to take land, or to torture a rival government and its population is never morally licit, he argued. Those reasons for war are rooted in aggression, self-interest, and love of violence. Consequently, war fought for those reasons must be considered unjust. However, governing authorities still have an obligation to fight on the basis of neighbourly love, that is, to protect a relatively just society's vulnerable populations from unjust attacks.

Although war may be at times justified, according to Augustine, war is nevertheless a product of sin *and* a sin itself. War involves killing, and when a Christian kills another person, either in defence of a neighbour or on behalf of a government fighting to achieve peace, it adversely affects the Christian's soul. Killing is, after all, a sin. Indeed, this is the tragedy of war, according to Augustine: Christians may have to engage in limited, but horrible, acts of violence and killing to prevent greater evils. War is therefore not a virtue, and warriors themselves can claim no specific virtue in their victories. To the contrary, war is to be lamented and warriors are to be cared for spiritually in a special way. In fact, based on Augustine's thinking on war, the medieval Church required all soldiers returning from battle to confess their sins and to ask for forgiveness, even though they may have performed their duties out of love of their neighbour and without violating Jesus's "turn the other cheek" teaching.

(3) Criteria for a Just War

Augustine realized that war needs ethical limits. Drawing on Cicero, Ambrose, and scripture, Augustine highlighted three criteria of a just war. First, war must have a *just cause*. War, as we've just discussed, must be waged to protect vulnerable populations, to defend a relatively just state from an unjust attack, and always to pursue peace. Second, war must be declared by a *legitimate authority*. War is a political act and, as such, can only be declared by someone who has the political authority to do so, such as an emperor, a king, or another sovereign. And third, war must have *right intention*. The only legitimate end of war is the peace that comes from order, the essence of the *tranquillitas ordinis*. Those involved in war must not fall prey to the baser human passions, including greed, lust, arrogance, pride, and fear. Additionally, Augustine referred to two other criteria of just war: it must be fought with *proportionality* and soldiers must *discriminate between combatants and non-combatants*.

St. Thomas Aquinas

Writing in the thirteenth century, St. Thomas Aquinas (1225–1274) addressed war at a time when Christian Europe was, arguably, at its most vulnerable stage politically and militarily. The crusades brought war to the forefront of European culture in the high Middle Ages. Yet it had been nearly eight hundred years since a theologian, Augustine, had addressed the issue of war within the context of a comprehensive theological work. Thomas changed this by including war as a topic to be discussed under the category of charity in his voluminous work *Summa theologica* (ST), which he wrote from 1265 to 1274.

Thomas looked to Augustine as his guide. He agreed with Augustine that just wars must be declared by a legitimate authority, have a just cause, and be fought with right intention. He also agreed that peace must be the goal of war (ST, II–II, 40.1). But he departed from Augustine in a number of important areas.

First, Thomas argued that war is not essentially sinful. The state has an obligation to defend the common good and, as Ambrose and Augustine claimed, citizens have a civic responsibility to fight as well in defence of the common good. The act of fighting in a just war should not therefore be construed as an evil for which an individual is held responsible or accountable; rather, it should be viewed as a non-moral evil that occurs when individuals carry out their natural duties to protect the common good. In this case, soldiers and others involved in war are not guilty of sin (a moral evil) because the evil of killing in war is not the result of individual choice. Instead, the evil of killing is chalked up to a natural, though tragic, consequence of an otherwise virtuous act of protecting the common good.

Second, Thomas did not consider war an act of neighbourly love. Unlike Augustine, who claimed that a Christian soldier should love an aggressor even as the aggressor kills him, Thomas removed the biblical love command from the just war theory and placed killing in war within the context of natural order, natural justice, and the defence of the common good. For Thomas, to demand that we love our aggressor suggests a level of moral perfection that is neither attainable nor obligatory (ST, II–II, 25.8).

Third, Thomas disagreed with Augustine's premise that law and order must be maintained regardless of the injustice perpetuated by governing authorities. Following Aristotle, Thomas held that rulers who make laws that violate the natural law and stifle the virtues are promoting tyranny, and tyranny cannot stand. "A tyrannical government is not just," Thomas wrote, "because it is directed, not to the common good, but to the private good of the ruler" (ST, II–II, 42.2.).

The fourth difference from Augustine concerns the matter of killing in self-defence (ST, II–II, 64.7). According to Augustine, killing in self-defence is morally illicit. However, according to Thomas, it is permissible because it is the unintended consequence of the natural act of self-preservation, assuming that proportional force is used. In making his case, Thomas introduced the principle of double effect. As we recall from our discussions of sexual ethics and bioethics, the principle of double effect is based on the premise that a single act may have two effects: one that is intended and one that is unintended. The act of self-defence, then, may have two effects: one, to save one's own life; the other, to kill an attacker. In sum, Thomas thought that moderate force should always be the presumption in self-defence. But if mortal force is required to defend ourselves, and if our intention is to save our lives (that is, the primary effect), then killing an attacker is an ethically justifiable act, for it occurs as a secondary effect.

Francisco de Vitoria and Francisco Suarez

For some three hundred years following Thomas's discussion of war in *Summa theologica*, Catholic theologians all but left the issue of war to the warriors and the leaders of the Church. But by the early sixteenth century, European civilization had begun to show signs of change. Explorers had found new civilizations around the globe. New markets were beginning to emerge in the Americas. And the Church had started to experience splinter movements that eventually led to the Protestant Reformation.

Europe's involvement in the Americas led to new thinking on war. Francisco de Vitoria (1486–1546) was a Spanish Dominican priest who had been observing the Spanish conquest of native populations in the Americas. He expressed concern that Spain had not respected the Native American's natural claim to the land. He dismissed the prevailing argument that, since these people were uncivilized pagans, Christian civilizations were not required to recognize their land claims. In response, Vitoria proposed a set of guiding principles to deal fairly with other peoples—in doing so, he was laying the foundations for modern international law. Among those principles were just war criteria: non-combatant immunity, proportionality, and a prohibition against using religion as a basis for war.

Francisco Suarez (1548–1617) was a Spanish Jesuit and a close reader of Vitoria. Suarez defended the Thomistic tradition that war is not inherently evil, as long as certain conditions are met. War must be declared by a legitimate authority, have a just cause, be proportionate (including factoring in the cost of war), and have a probability of success. Additionally, a just war must include non-combatant immunity and in-war proportionality. And although not in a specific way, Suarez raised the issue of punishing war criminals and the lawfulness of victor nations taking the treasure of vanquished nations.

We should note in the thinking of Vitoria and Suarez a shift toward the legal application of just war criteria. For Ambrose, Augustine, and Thomas Aquinas, just war theory remained largely a matter of moral theology. There were no laws that obligated governing authorities to abide by just war criteria. In practice, the criteria were occasionally used by clergy and rulers to justify the actions of Christian authorities. Moreover, there is little evidence that the criteria actually limited war or caused any ruler to pause when engaging in battle. By framing just war criteria in primarily legal terms, Vitoria and Suarez were part of a late-medieval intellectual movement that would lead to the formulation of international law. Although very rudimentary, emerging principles of international law would require states to comply and to be accountable for their actions. Protestant thinking on war was experiencing a similar shift, moving from the theological approaches of Martin Luther and John Calvin to the work of the Dutch Protestant and so-called father of international law Hugo Grotius (1583–1645), who provided the just war tradition with the two basic categories: *jus ad bellum* and *jus in bello*.

Reassessments of the Just War Theory

It was not until the twentieth century that the just war tradition once again fell under theological scrutiny, both in the Catholic and Protestant churches. At least three factors have come together to create a need for this reassessment in the Catholic tradition.

First, there was the disestablishment of Catholicism in formerly Catholic countries. By the late nineteenth century, Catholicism was declining as a social and political force around the globe. A number of governments, including those in Germany, France, and certain Latin American countries, had become hostile toward clerical privilege and Catholic political power. In response to the Mexican government's violent anti-clericalism in the mid-1920s, for example, Pope Pius XI (1922–1939) encouraged lay organizations to mobilize under the banner of "Catholic Action" to provide passive resistance against state aggression.[12] By the 1930s, and in response to violations of religious freedom in Nazi Germany and Mussolini's Italy, Pope Pius XI had effectively revived the Thomistic argument that civilian resistance may, under certain circumstances, trump the claims of a legitimate authority. Because the Vatican was claiming that Catholics have the right to resist modern political authorities hostile to the Church, questions began to arise about the legitimacy of political authorities and their capacity to declare war. In international conflicts, the Church typically adopted a position of neutrality. But when it came to internal conflicts between a state and the Church, the Vatican often questioned the legitimacy of the government, even as Vatican diplomats attempted to negotiate with government officials for Catholic religious freedom.

Second, in the early part of the twentieth century, a peace movement began to emerge in the Church. Although still quite marginal, a sizeable number of Catholics, particularly in France and Germany, had already joined lay peace groups prior to the outbreak of World War I, which raged from 1914 to 1918. Following tradition, Pope Benedict XV (1914–1922) and the Vatican took a neutral position on the war. But Benedict thought the Church should intervene as a neutral party to bring the war to an end. As a result, he issued a seven-point peace plan in August 1917 that encouraged the leaders of the warring countries to negotiate a peace that preserved the common good. The plan, however, went nowhere. Dismayed but not defeated by the lack of support for the plan, Pope Benedict turned the Church's efforts toward caring for prisoners of war, facilitating prisoner exchanges, providing humanitarian assistance, and working with countries to help re-establish peaceful diplomatic relations. Although Benedict never specifically cast his peacemaking efforts within the just war theory, his "pacifist papacy" provided legitimacy to a growing number of peace organizations that all but ignored the Church's just war teaching.[13]

The third and most significant factor leading to a reassessment of the just war theory was the modern nature of warfare. The carnage of World War I was a devastating blow to the ideology of human progress. The bloody battlefields of Europe were proof that "enlightened" and "Christian" peoples were still capable of wreaking havoc on one another. But the mayhem of World War I was not the tipping point for a thorough reassessment of the Church's just war teaching. Only after World War II did the Vatican begin to address specific elements of the Church's just war teaching.

To begin, Pope Pius XII (1939–1958) affirmed the argument that the just cause principle refers solely to defensive wars—this had been the position of the Church since the sixteenth century. However, the nuclear weapons strikes on Hiroshima and Nagasaki and an ensuing nuclear arms race between the United States and the Soviet Union caused Pope Pius to question the moral justification of defensive wars. He concluded that the Church needed to re-examine the just war tradition, since even defensive wars were likely to be too destructive and disproportionate to be morally legitimate. With the advent of nuclear weapons, a war between nuclear powers, even if it met the defensive war criterion, would be without justification because victory and post-conflict justice would be impossible in countries completely destroyed by nuclear weapons. While Pius XII was able to identify the basic problems facing the Church's traditional teachings on the ethical use of force, it was his successor, Pope John XXIII, who provided many of the answers.

Pope John XXIII and *Pacem in terris* (1963)

Pope John XXIII (1958–1963) was committed to bringing the Church "up to date" (*aggiornamento*) in the modern world. To start this broad process of renewal, he called the Second Vatican Council (1962–1965). At the same time, he made a concerted effort to address the Church's duty to work toward social justice and peace. In his encyclical *Pacem in terris* (Peace on Earth, 1963), Pope John declared that peace is the calling and aim of the Church. A practical element of the Church's calling in the world is the support of any political order that serves the common good, which he defined as the defence and promotion of human rights. Though *Pacem in terris* was criticized by some leading theologians of the day, including the noted Protestant theologian Reinhold Niebuhr, for not focusing enough on justice, Pope John's vision of peace brought back to life a theological tradition of peace that had its roots in the teachings of Jesus (e.g., Matthew 5:38-48) and the non-violent practices of the early Church. According to Pope John, the Church is called to peace, while governing authority is called to justice—and through an interdependent relationship, they should promote and protect the common good.

Pope John XXIII was a contextual thinker. The context for *Pacem in terris* was the Cuban Missile Crisis of 1962. This game of high-stakes nuclear poker signalled to Pope John that international relations, conceived of as anarchy, had to be reconsidered and then recast in favour of the common good of all humanity. To his dismay, the dominant political philosophy of the Cold War—"political realism" (or *realpolitik*)—was a destructive, dehumanizing ideology. Passed down from Hobbes, Machiavelli, and Clausewitz to Cold War strategists on both sides of the East–West conflict, political realism operated with the presupposition that politics must inevitably be a violent struggle over power and based on self-interest. Peace is not a moral value but a political situation in which power is balanced and violence is absent. In other words, peace is the result of governments recognizing no strategic political or economic advantage to armed conflict. To political realists, ethics in politics is an unwarranted intrusion at best. At its worst, ethics is the enemy of good politics. Pope John understood that this political ideology contradicted the Church's doctrine of the "universal common good" and its corresponding political ethic that the human community could and should foster the virtuous life (PT, nos. 132–35). Instead of giving priority to violence, then, Pope John envisioned an alternative political system based on the peaceable virtues of faith and hope, courage and compassion, as well as justice and peace.

According to Pope John, one of the defining features of a properly functioning political system is its commitment to human rights. Political authorities have a duty, he said, to "ensure that these [individual] rights are recognized, respected, co-ordinated, defended and promoted, and that each individual is enabled to perform his duties more easily"

(PT, no. 60). Though there are many ways that political authorities can enable individuals to perform their duties, chief among them is providing necessary housing, drinking water, medical care, and other essential services. Conversely, political authorities that fail to preserve the common welfare, to protect and promote the rights of citizens, and to defend against injustice have neglected their responsibility. As a result, the pope concluded, "any government which refused to recognize human rights or acted in violation of them, would not only fail in its duty; its decrees would be wholly lacking in binding force" (PT, no. 46).

To Pope John XXIII, the increasing demands of modern politics and the growing disparity among nations has highlighted the obligation that states have to pool their material and spiritual resources. Based on the principle of "active solidarity," the collaborative efforts of states should enable weaker states to achieve a more just and a more peaceable society. These efforts mean that states, particularly the more affluent states, must at times forgo self-interest, economic expediency, and political ambitions to "join forces whenever the efforts of particular States cannot achieve the desired goal" (PT, no. 99). In practice, this active solidarity depends on a commitment to vibrant international relations, which in turn promotes understanding and fosters mutual responsibility for the welfare of the human community and the universal common good.

Two specific themes emerged in Pope John's vision of international relations based on the doctrine of active solidarity. First, to develop a sustainable geopolitical climate, fundamental steps were required in the areas of arms control and the demilitarization of international politics. Second, Pope John concluded that individual states had largely failed in their obligation to conduct international relations in the defence and promotion of the universal common good. The range of global issues— from nuclear escalation to widespread immigration to dehumanizing economic practices—had simply gone beyond the scope of individual states to protect and promote the common good. In general terms, Pope John proposed a "public authority of the world community" (PT, no. 139) to handle these issues. In more specific terms, he believed that the United Nations could serve not only as a catalyst for peaceful coexistence among states, but also as a mechanism to hold states accountable for their own domestic actions (PT, no. 145).

Against the backdrop of nuclear escalation, the pope insisted that conflicts between states must be conducted politically and diplomatically. The indiscriminate and devastating nature of nuclear weapons simply means that military conflict between nuclear powers would be beyond moral legitimacy. Simply put, wars involving nuclear weapons can never be just. The term ethicists often use to describe this moral position is "nuclear pacifism," and it is evident that Pope John XXIII understood Catholic teaching regarding war to be nuclear pacifism.

The Vatican II document *Gaudium et spes* (Pastoral Constitution on the Church in the Modern World, 1965) reaffirmed the primacy of the peace ethic in the formation of just societies. It states, "Peace is not merely the absence of war; nor can it be reduced solely to the maintenance of a balance of power between enemies; nor is it brought about by dictatorship. Instead, it is rightly and appropriately called an enterprise of justice. Peace results from that order structured into human society by its divine Founder, and actualized by men as they thirst after ever greater justice" (GS, no. 78). It also adopted Pope John's nuclear pacifism, along with other wars that would include indiscriminate killing and the annihilation of large populations. "With these truths in mind, this most holy synod makes its own the condemnations of total wars already pronounced by recent popes, and issues the following declaration: Any act of war aimed indiscriminately at the destruction of entire cities or extensive areas, along with their population, is a crime against God and man himself. It merits unequivocal and unhesitating condemnation" (GS, no. 80).

A Challenge to Peace (1983)

To commemorate the twentieth anniversary of Pope John's prophetic encyclical *Pacem in terris*, the bishops of the United States Conference of Catholic Bishops drafted the pastoral letter *A Challenge to Peace* (1983). Consistent with the general themes of Pope John's encyclical, the U.S. bishops affirmed the spirituality and ethics of peacemaking. God is, above all, the "God of peace" (Romans 15:33) who seeks peace for all people far and near (Psalm 85; Isaiah 57:19). Based on this understanding of God's working in history, the U.S. bishops encouraged the Church to emphasize peacemaking as an essential element of faith, and peace as the foundational calling of each and every Christian's life (Matthew 5:44-48;

John 14:27). The Church should do this by continually reminding the world that Jesus has called the Church and believers everywhere to be peacemakers. Moreover, the U.S. bishops, inspired by the teachings of John XXIII and facing yet another round of nuclear escalation in the Cold War, came to the conclusion that Catholic teaching contains a "presumption against war."[14]

But the "presumption against war" doctrine does not mean that war can always be avoided. There are occasions when the moral use of force is necessary. To place limits on the use of force, the U.S. bishops appealed to a list of criteria that has become the basis for the just war theory. The *jus ad bellum* criteria are the following: (1) just cause (e.g., in defense of an unjust attack), (2) comparative justice (i.e., the fight for justice must be comparatively more just than the injustice that necessitated war), (3) legitimate authority, (4) right intention (i.e., force may be used solely for re-establishing conditions for just social, political, and economic relations), (5) probability of success, (6) proportionality (the overall harm expected from the use of force must be outweighed by the good to be achieved), and (7) last resort (i.e., force may be used only after all diplomatic, peaceful alternatives have been seriously attempted and exhausted). These *ad bellum* criteria must be met *before* an authority may override the strong moral presumption against war. In addition to the *ad bellum* criteria, the bishops highlighted these *jus in bello* criteria: (8) non-combatant immunity, (9) combat proportionality (e.g., limit damage to civilian populations and property), and (10) right intention (i.e., even in the midst of conflict, the aim of political and military leaders must be peace with justice).

The U.S. bishops also made it clear that the use of nuclear weapons is a violation of the principles of just war. They not only rejected their use in war but also their existence as a sustainable deterrent to war. While they recognized that deterrence could be an effective strategy to avoid war, the nature of nuclear weapons makes deterrence an unjust means. Their implicit argument is that the threat of unjustifiable violence (nuclear attack) is not morally permissible because the threat may be actualized, and that actualized threat would far outweigh any tenuous peace. Additionally, threatening to slaughter (hundreds of) thousands of innocent people simply violates human dignity. Accordingly, the bishops called for immediate nuclear test bans, the formation of nuclear non-proliferation treaties, enhanced participation of the United Nations to help with enforcement, and a renewed emphasis on mutual security instead of mutually assured destruction.

Humanitarian Intervention and the Responsibility to Protect

The end of the Cold War marked a radical shift not only in the geopolitical balance of power but also in the nature of military conflict. After the collapse of the Soviet Union, international politics moved from the bipolar tensions that defined the Cold War to a new situation in which the United States was the sole superpower. In the early 1990s, a number of political theorists began to consider the creation of a "new world order," one in which the United States could exert its power globally to open up economies to the free market and to bring democracy to countries formerly under the sway of Communism.[15] Others thought that the new political situation would lead to new forms of conflict along well-defined civilizational boundaries, resulting in a simplistic mentality that pitted the "West" versus the "rest."[16] While both theories gained popular support, each having books on bestseller lists around the globe, they largely failed to predict the types of conflicts that flared up just shortly after their publication.

Ethnic conflicts in the Balkans demanded the attention of western political leaders to stabilize a region once governed by Soviet-style ideology and military force. The ethnic conflicts in the Balkans (1992–1996), the Kosovo intervention (1999), and the humanitarian emergencies in Somalia (1991–1993) and Rwanda (1994) brought to light the ambiguous, but politically popular, idea of humanitarian intervention. While intervention has long been a part of international relations, humanitarian intervention developed only in the early 1990s. It emerged as states realized that they must at times violate another state's sovereign boundaries to protect a population against severe threats—namely, genocide and other gross human rights violations. In theory, humanitarian intervention offered a new normative standard in international relations. Instead of intervention being based primarily on state interest, humanitarian intervention presupposed that states have an overriding moral obligation to protect vulnerable populations. In practice, however, humanitarian intervention remained fundamentally political. And because it involved international political relations, humanitarian intervention remained under the jurisdiction of international law and the two fundamental tenets of international relations—that is, the principle of state sovereignty and the doctrine of non-intervention.[17] In the wake of the Rwandan genocide and the ethnic conflicts in the Balkans, international bodies, international non-governmental organizations (NGOs), and religiously affiliated development organizations found themselves increasingly hesitant to use the language of "humanitarian intervention."

With the release of the 2001 report from the International Commission on Intervention and State Sovereignty (ICISS) entitled *The Responsibility to Protect*, the prevailing language regarding interventions has been "the responsibility to protect" (R2P).[18] On the one hand, the framers of R2P embraced the principle of non-intervention codified in the U.N. Charter as a way to protect weaker states from the predations of the strong. On the other hand, the framers elevated international humanitarian law, including respect for human life and human rights, to a level on par with border sovereignty. The net effect is that, if a state is unwilling or unable to protect its citizens, then the international community has a *legal* responsibility to intervene militarily in that state, as long as certain conditions are met. The framers called these conditions "precautionary principles." Catholics and many others would recognize these principles as just war criteria (e.g., just cause, comparative justice, legitimate authority, right intention, probability of success, proportionality, and last resort).

The Catholic Church has followed this shift from humanitarian intervention to the responsibility-to-protect framework. For example, in his 1999 World Day of Prayer for Peace Message, Pope John Paul II summed up the Catholic tradition's understanding of military force when he stated, "war is the failure of all true humanism."[19] Over the course of his papacy, John Paul presented war as a force that destroys communities, pits neighbour against neighbour, weakens the moral foundations of society, and severs lines of global solidarity. Despite this negative view of war, in his 2000 World Day of Prayer for Peace Message, Pope John Paul II avowed the right of humanitarian assistance and the necessity of what was then called humanitarian intervention.[20] He stated, "Clearly, when a civilian population risks being overcome by the attacks of an unjust aggressor and political efforts and non-violent defence prove to be of no avail, it is legitimate and even obligatory to take concrete measures to disarm the aggressor."[21]

In an address to the U.N. General Assembly in 2008, Pope Benedict XVI publicly embraced the R2P framework. Observing that the principle of the "responsibility to protect" has a long history in the Western tradition, the pope linked the human rights emphasis in R2P to the Church's concept of human dignity. He stated:

> Human rights are increasingly being presented as the common language and the ethical substratum of international relations. At the same time, the universality, indivisibility and interdependence of human rights all serve as guarantees safeguarding human dignity. It is evident, though, that the rights recognized and expounded in the [Universal] Declaration [on Human Rights] apply to everyone by virtue of the common origin of the person, who remains the high-point of God's creative design for the world and for history.[22]

Consistent with Pacem in terris, Benedict reiterated R2P's basic premise: The state has the primary duty to protect its own population from human rights violations, as well as from the consequences of humanitarian crises, whether natural or created by human injustice. But if states are unable to guarantee this protection, the international community has an obligation to intervene within the limitations of international law.

In February 2011, the United Nations Security Council cited principles associated with R2P in drafting a resolution to deal with attacks on the civilian population in Libya.[23] Clinging to power, Libya's autocratic ruler Moammar Gadhafi ordered military forces still loyal to him to start firing on cities and villages that had supported his overthrow. Libya was, in effect, in the midst of a civil war, but Gadhafi had far superior weapons and he was using them on unarmed civilians. Initially, the U.N. Security Council approved a resolution placing economic sanctions and other punitive diplomatic measures on Libya. By March 2011, however, the Security Council determined that the just-cause threshold of R2P's precautionary principles had been met. This triggered a second resolution authorizing an enforced no-fly zone and a military intervention into

Libya. The mission, under the direction of NATO command, quickly shifted from the protection of innocent civilians to regime change. Operationally, the mission shift meant NATO forces, including Canadian and U.S. forces, were no longer primarily enforcing no-fly zones but were instead involved in bombing runs targeting Gadhafi military assets and convoys. On October 20, 2011, shortly after being hit by a NATO strike, Gadhafi was captured by Libyan rebels in his hometown of Sirte and subsequently killed, allegedly by a gunshot to the head.

For many advocates of the R2P framework, the use of force in Libya was a first test for R2P. The jury is still out whether R2P passed the test. For some observers, such as the well-regarded Princeton scholar of international affairs Anne-Marie Slaughter, R2P was a success because it did what it was supposed to do—protect vulnerable populations. But for other observers, such John Siebert, Director of the Canadian peace organization Project Ploughshares, a "poor precedent has been set in this operationalization of the principle of protecting vulnerable civilians … The failure of the operationalization of [the second U.N. Security Council resolution] through the military focus on inappropriate means (bombing from the air) and inappropriate ends (regime change) created an unfortunate precedent that has the potential to fatally weaken the concept of the R2P for future acceptance and use by the international community."[24]

The "War on Terror" and Preventative War

The terrorist attacks of September 11, 2001, sparked a new round of thinking on the just war tradition. The conscience-shocking horror of the attack caused even long-time advocates of peace to support the use of military force. Almost from the outset, voices across the political spectrum began to describe the U.S.-led assault on Afghanistan as "just war." One long-time peace advocate, Richard Falk, wrote that war in Afghanistan was "the first truly just war since World War II."[25] Pope John Paul II also affirmed the right of the U.S. to use military force in Afghanistan.

In spite of widespread support for the Afghanistan mission, particularly in the early days, there are those, myself included, who objected to the just war argument on a number of points. First, the attack was not an act of war by a state actor—it was an act of terrorism by an international non-state actor, namely, al-Qaeda and its leader, Osama bin Laden. My concern was that, by calling the response to the terrorist attacks a "war," countries were going to go into "war mode," which would mean the use of certain weapons, the suspension of certain liberties, and the promotion of a national war mentality. It would also mean that many innocent men, women, and children in Afghanistan would be injured or die as a result of misguided bombs and bullets. The likely outcome of a war in Afghanistan would be increased hostility toward the U.S. and a protracted presence in a country long known for defeating great powers by waiting them out. In short, a war in Afghanistan would lead to the exact opposite of the objectives given at the time. Thus, while the attacks on the U.S. may have met the *ad bellum* threshold of a just cause, the military response failed to meet other criteria—including both the *ad bellum* and *in bello* proportionality criteria, as well as the last resort and non-combatant immunity criteria.

Second, the war in Afghanistan was quickly subsumed under the banner of a broader "war on terror." On September 16, 2001, President Bush responded to a reporter's question with the following warning: "This crusade—this war on terrorism—is going to take a while."[26] Bush later apologized for the use of the word "crusade," realizing after the fact that crusades are associated with Christian holy wars against Muslim forces. The term was never again used by the Bush White House. While "crusade" might have just been an unfortunate term used by a rhetorically challenged president, the use of that term nevertheless highlights the emotional aspects of the U.S. response—in the president's mind, the war on terror (or terrorism) was virtually a holy war. On September 20, 2001, during a televised address to a joint session of congress, Bush launched the war on terror when he said, "Our 'war on terror' begins with al-Qaeda, but it does not end there. It will not end until every terrorist group of global reach has been found, stopped and defeated."[27] From a just war perspective, Bush's declared war on terror violates the *ad bellum* principle of reasonableness of success. Bluntly put, there is no way to defeat terror in a sinful world. Terror is an evil, and to overcome terror we would first have to eradicate evil. But following the Christian tradition, only the return of Jesus will bring an end to evil. In effect, then, the "war on terror" as framed by the Bush administration is nothing less than an apocalyptic war. It is one that will end only when history ends, when Jesus Christ returns to retrieve the faithful. Such a war can never be just.

And third, on March 23, 2003, the U.S. and coalition forces invaded Iraq on the premise that Iraq had been harbouring al-Qaeda terrorists and that, under the direction of Saddam Hussein, Iraq had been developing nuclear weapons. U.N. inspectors had been monitoring Iraq since November 2002, but by early 2003 they had found no evidence of a nuclear program, nuclear weapons, or other weapons of mass destruction (WMDs). On February 5, 2003, General Colin Powell, the U.S. Secretary of State, appeared before the U.N. to make the case for the war by presenting U.S. intelligence that seemingly proved that Saddam Hussein had weapons of mass destruction. Military critics argued from the outset that the evidence was hardly convincing. Already in January 2003, Pope John Paul II had spoken out against what appeared to be an imminent invasion of Iraq. In an address to the diplomatic corps at the Vatican, he said, "War is never just another means that one can choose to employ for settling differences between nations" and reiterated that "war cannot be decided upon ... except as the very last option and in accordance with very strict conditions."[28] According to the pope, those conditions had not yet been met. Just a few days after the invasion, it had become clear to the international community that, in fact, Iraq didn't have any WMDs and was not developing any WMD program.

The Iraq War was essentially a war of choice, a preventative war devised, perhaps, to forestall any future attack. In the just war tradition, preventative war is considered an unjust war—the U.S. had not been attacked, there was no imminent threat to the United States, and the stated objectives (to eliminate the threats of terrorism and WMDs) were inconsistent with the means employed. Even those who supported the Afghanistan mission on the basis of a just war argument found themselves declaring the Iraq war unjust.

The Continuing Challenge to Peace

The Catholic Church is not one of the historic peace churches—a group that includes the Church of the Brethren, the Mennonites, the

Amish, and the Quakers. In fact, many people are inclined, whether fairly or unfairly, to identify the Catholic Church with the violent excesses of the crusades, European imperialism, and totalitarian rulers such as Spain's Francisco Franco. But in spite of the Church's association with religiously sanctioned military campaigns, militaristic foreign policies, and even certain strong-armed dictators, a number of Catholics rank among the most widely recognized peacemakers in the Christian tradition: St. Martin of Tours, St. Francis of Assisi, Dorothy Day, Franz Jägerstätter, Daniel Berrigan, and Mother Teresa, to name just a few. Though pacifism and the just war tradition are apparently incompatible, they have co-existed in the Catholic Church over the centuries. And while there is often disagreement between pacifists and those who appeal to the just war tradition on specific issues, there are also areas of overlapping consensus. For instance, in response to modern forms of warfare, including those that threaten mass destruction, the pacifist and just war traditions often find themselves in unison as they call for dialogue and diplomacy as ways to avoid the use of military force.

Another area where there is overlapping consensus is in their support of various peacemaking initiatives. Above, in our brief discussion of the "war on terror," we asked whether war was the only appropriate response to the terrorist attacks of September 11, 2001. We argued that, following just war theory, war was not the appropriate response. So what would have been an appropriate alternative?

I would suggest an approach called "just peacemaking." First proposed by the Protestant theologian Glen Stassen and later refined by an ecumenical group of Christian theologians, just peacemaking attempts to avoid the idealism of pacifism and the fatalism of political realism (*realpolitik*). Followers of just peacemaking may still use just war theory to determine the morality of war once war is inevitable. What just peacemaking provides is a series of alternative practices that help avoid war: (1) support direct nonviolent action, (2) take unilateral action to reduce war, (3) use cooperative conflict resolution, (4) acknowledge responsibility for conflict and injustice and seek forgiveness while repenting, (5) advance democracy, human rights, and religious liberty, (6) foster sustainable development, (7) work with cooperative forces in the international system (e.g., prioritize cooperation over competition in the global market), (8) strengthen the United Nations, (9) reduce offensive weapons and weapons trade, and (10) encourage grassroots peacemaking groups and voluntary associations.[29]

While we should have no illusions that these practices will bring everlasting peace in a sinful world, we have to conclude that just peacemaking is consistent with Catholic Social Teaching, the Church's "presumption against war" doctrine, and the continuing challenge to peace. Moreover, the just peacemaking framework is a long-overdue complement to the just war theory, which is, as we argued here, a theory that is ultimately a theory suited for empires. Indeed, many countries today, including Canada, do not possess the military capability to engage in war on their own; or if they do, they would be able sustain the conflict only for a short period of time. Many of these countries, particularly in the developing world, are not even able to handle policing on their own. In these countries, private policing is paid for by wealthy homeowners and well-established businesses. Also, the just war language doesn't apply particularly well to the churches that do not have enough political sway to hold political leaders to just war principles. Instead, countries and religiously based humanitarian organizations alike can and do engage in peacebuilding in ways that align with the practices of just peacemaking.

CHAPTER 8

Ethics and the Environment

I n early August, Iowa farmland is jam-packed with acre upon acre of corn. Travelling down Iowa's farm roads this time of year can lead to tunnel vision, as you begin to feel hemmed in by walls of corn stalks reaching 10 to 12 feet high. Corn seems to be everywhere. In 2012, Iowa farmers planted corn on nearly 14 million acres of land. To put that in some perspective, imagine almost the entire province of Nova Scotia or the state of West Virginia as a cornfield—that's Iowa in August.[1]

So what are Iowans doing with all of this corn? According to the United States Department of Agriculture, around 15 percent of Iowa's corn was used in 2011 for livestock feed in the U.S. Another 15 percent went toward the production of food products such as cornstarch and high-fructose corn syrup, which is widely used as a sweetener in beverages, candy, and processed foods. Roughly 16 percent of Iowa's corn was exported, mostly to Japan, Mexico, Korea, Russia, and Egypt, to be used mainly for livestock feed. And approximately 53 percent of Iowa's corn went in to the production of ethanol, or grain alcohol, which can be used as a biofuel or a fuel additive in combustible engines. Yes, you read those numbers correctly: the majority of Iowa's corn isn't being used for food, but instead for fuel to be burned in cars and trucks on our roadways.

Since 2005, domestic production of ethanol fuel in the United State has increased by almost 500 percent, and Iowa produces almost 30 percent of all ethanol in the United States. This spike in ethanol production is due to two major factors. The first factor is the widespread ban of a fuel additive called MTBE (for the scientifically minded, that's methyl tertiary butyl ether). MTBE had been used for more than a decade to help the fuel industry meet the standards imposed by the Clean Air Act, which were intended to reduce carbon monoxide emissions. While the additive was effective in reducing carbon emissions, there were unintended consequences. In the late 1990s, scientists discovered that MTBE levels in water wells were abnormally high, and likely high enough to be harmful to humans. In 2000, the state of California enacted legislation to phase out MTBE over a four-year period. Other states soon followed suit, bolstered by further studies conducted by the Environmental Protection Agency, which found high levels of MTBE in other water supplies. With MTBE being phased out, researchers looked to ethanol, a clear and relatively clean fuel, as a replacement. Ethanol could be added to current fuel mixtures to increase octane levels and reduce carbon emissions. The problem facing the fuel industry back in 2004, just after MTBE bans started to take effect, was how to produce enough ethanol to meet demand. It was at this point that Iowa farmers and the biofuel industry partnered to ramp up the supply of ethanol.

The second factor has to do with the U.S. government's desire to create a domestic renewable energy source. This desire stems from foreign policy and national security concerns. Simply put, the U.S. government wants to reduce America's dependence on oil rich, but also politically unstable, countries in the Middle East, Africa, and Latin America. To provide support to the biofuel industry, and in the process try to rid the U.S. of its "addiction to foreign oil," the U.S. government began offering large subsidies to corn-ethanol producers.[2] The initial subsidy in 2005 amounted to $10 billion, but subsidies eventually levelled off to around $6 billion a year by 2011, before being cut in 2012. Moreover, to help further spur on the biofuel industry, the U.S. Congress passed an energy bill in 2007 that required fuel blenders to use 15 billion gallons of conventional biofuels, mainly corn ethanol, by 2015 and an additional 21 billion gallons of so-called second-generation or advanced biofuels by 2022. In other words, ethanol production has become a government-mandated industry in the United States.

The net effect of the snap-turn toward ethanol has been an economic bonanza for agribusiness and rural economies in the U.S. Corn Belt. In Iowa alone, the ethanol industry accounted for nearly 74,000 jobs in 2011 and $6 billion in gross domestic product. On the outskirts of Cedar Rapids, a town of about 125,000 people, Archer Daniels Midland (ADM), one of the world's largest producers of biofuels, recently completed work on the largest ethanol plant in the United States, capable of producing upwards of 420 million gallons of ethanol a year.[3] Rural Iowa is now home to some 41 ethanol plants. The Iowa Corn Promotion Board summed up the importance of ethanol to Iowa's economy in a recent advertising campaign, "We grow jobs by the bushel. Keep jobs green in Iowa. Buy ethanol."[4]

While ethanol and the biofuel industry have revived economies in the Corn Belt, they have had disastrous effects elsewhere. The rapid expansion of biofuels production has threatened food sovereignty and aggravated the problem of world hunger. In early 2008, a global food crisis emerged as price hikes in grains used in the production of biofuels drove up food prices. According to a World Bank report published in 2008, biofuels had increased global grain prices by nearly 75 percent.[5] In Mexico, for example, the increase of corn exports in early 2007 to sustain the ethanol market in the U.S. resulted in a 400 percent spike in the price of corn, the population's main food source. The price spike spawned the Mexican "Tortilla Riots," as people took to the streets to protest the government's unwillingness to set price caps on food commodities essential to the Mexican diet.[6] In the Arab world, the food crisis set off a wave of bread riots in Bahrain, Yemen, Jordan, Egypt, and Morocco. It is no coincidence that by 2011, with the rise of the "Arab Spring," these countries had suffered political uprisings. However, the media in North America chose not to focus on food and agricultural concerns, such as the fact that Arab countries import more than 50 percent of their food. Instead, the North American media concentrated on the emergence of Islamist political parties and the struggle for democratic reforms. Lost in this analysis was the reality that skyrocketing food prices, impending famines, and the inability of regimes to respond to these crises played a significant role in fueling the Arab Spring. As *The Economist* noted in one of its retrospective analyses of the Arab revolutions, "It is sadly appropriate that Mohamad Bouazizi, the Tunisian whose self-immolation triggered the first protest of the Arab spring, should have been a street vendor, selling food. From the start, food has played a bigger role in the upheavals than most people realize."[7]

The cornfields of Iowa are, I believe, a good example of why we should treat our relationship with the environment as a central ethical concern. First, they ask us to consider how we understand God's creation. Does the natural world have an intrinsic value or goodness? Or is the natural world valuable only inasmuch as human beings are able to use it to better our lives? What is our relationship to God's creation—are we a master, manager, steward, servant, or slave of creation? Second, Iowa's cornfields cause us to reflect on how we live in God's creation. Are there general ethical principles or virtues that should guide our actions? Or should we simply let the market decide? And third, Iowa's corn—which the locals sometimes call "money trees"— compels us to ask about the connection between environmental practices and social, political, and economic justice. How are the poorest and most vulnerable among us affected by our environmental policies and practices? In this chapter, we briefly address these questions in light of the Catholic social tradition.

The Good of Creation

The very first words in scripture proclaim the good news of creation: "In the beginning when God created the heavens and the earth, the earth was a formless void and darkness covered the face of the deep, while a wind from God swept over the face of the waters. Then God said, 'Let there be light'; and there was light. And God saw that the light was *good*; and God separated the light from the darkness" (Genesis 1:1-4). The goodness of creation is a theme that continues throughout the first creation story in Genesis, culminating in the words "God saw everything that he had made, and indeed, it was *very good*. And there was evening and there was morning, the sixth day" (Genesis 1:31).

The Christian tradition has typically understood the good in creation in Genesis 1 as a state of paradisaical perfection. Creation is good because the Creator, God, declares it to be so. As a result, the good in creation is not contingent upon how humans use creation—there is no *instrumental value* in Genesis 1; rather, the good in creation is an intrinsic element of creation itself. In the Christian tradition, this *intrinsic good* of creation is not due to God being *in* creation (a belief known as "panentheism") or God existing as the totality of nature (a belief known as "pantheism"). God is not, for instance, *in* a tree, a river, a mountain, or a non-human animal. However, God *is* in the human person in some form, since God created humanity in the image of God (*imago dei*) and the body is a temple of the Holy Spirit (1 Corinthians 6:19). Also, traditional Christian views of nature depart from many other ancient religions by rejecting the pantheistic notion that God is everything and everything is God. Instead, the Christian tradition most often portrays the Creator as one who wishes merely to enjoy the perfection of the handiwork in the Genesis creation stories. Unfortunately, though, the Creator's wishes don't always come true.

As we know from our previous discussions of the Genesis creation stories, the Christian tradition finds in Genesis 3 the story of creation gone awry. The original man and woman sinned, and the consequences of that sin had a ripple effect on all human relationships. First, the sin of the man and the woman disrupted the relationship between humanity and God. Sin meant that humanity would no longer be in right relationship with God, that is, until Jesus's life, death, and resurrection brought redemption to a fallen world. Second, because of sin, humanity is no longer in a state of social harmony. Sin redefined social relationships broadly. Mistrust, deceit, jealousy, and hubris (an extreme form of pride or arrogance) are realities that keep us from living in peace and harmony with one another. According to tradition, the story in Genesis 4 of Cain killing his brother Abel out of jealously confirms that animosity and violence are forever a part of the human condition. And third, the sin of the man and woman disrupted humanity's relationship with nature. In Paradise prior to the Fall, all of creation was in harmony, with the human persons carrying out their duties according to the order of divine creation. God granted the man and woman "dominion" over the fish of the sea and the animals (Genesis 1:26, 28). God told the man and woman to be "fruitful and multiply, and fill the earth and subdue it" (Genesis 1:28). In the second creation story, God puts the man in the Garden of Eden "to till it and keep it" (Genesis 2:15). But with the first sin, there is enmity between nature and humanity. The natural act of procreation (to "be fruitful and multiply") becomes painful for the woman (Genesis 2:16). The natural act of physical labour becomes a burden for the man, who must toil at odds with the natural world. The fields will be littered with "thorns and thistles," God told Adam, and "by the sweat of your face you shall eat bread until you return to the ground" (Genesis 2:18-19).

A number of early Christian scholars, including the second-century apologist St. Irenaeus, believed that the disruption caused by sin in the Garden had actually been overcome by the redemptive work of Jesus Christ. Because Jesus played an integral role in the original acts of creation (John 1:1-3) the material world ought to be treated as a redeemed world, one that reflects the original harmony of God's creation. For Irenaeus, in particular, his view of creation was a defence against a dichotomous worldview held by some Greek philosophers and Gnostic-Christian sects. These followers of a dichotomous view of reality believed that the material world was a lesser reality, while the non-material world of ideas and wisdom was a more authentic reality. Gnostics, for example, thought that an evil god had accidentally created the material world; consequently, they believed that humans should strive to flee this material world and seek truth in authentic, non-material *gnosis* (knowledge).

In the Western Christian tradition, however, the theological argument for a redeemed creation was eventually eclipsed by the teaching that sin created an ultimately impassable barrier between humanity and the natural world. Although not as radically dichotomous as some Greek philosophical schools or Gnostic sects, the early Church maintained a split between spirit and flesh as well as between the spiritual world and the material world. For example, St. Augustine, in the fifth century, saw a fundamental tension between the spiritual world and the material world. On the one hand, Augustine could write glowingly of the essential goodness of creation:

> The earth is good by the height of its mountains, the moderate elevation of its hills, and the evenness of its fields; and good is the farm that is pleasant and fertile; and good is the house that is arranged throughout in symmetrical proportions and is spacious and bright; and good are the animals, animate bodies; and good is the mild and salubrious air; and good is the food that

is pleasant and conducive to health; and good is health without pains and weariness; and good is the countenance of man with regular features, a cheerful expression, and a glowing colour; and good is the soul of a friend with the sweetness of concord and fidelity of love; and good is the just man; and good are riches because they readily assist us; and good is the heaven with its own sun, moon, and stars.[8]

But on the other hand, he could not accept the idea that human persons could live in harmony with creation, for sin remained a barrier to earthly perfection. Moreover, in Augustine's theology any love of the material world tends to lead humanity away from the unity of God, who is the fountain of life.[9] Ultimately, Augustine thought the love of God and the love of the material world were at odds with one another—either you love God or you love the material world. Framed in terms of this either/or, he drew the conclusion that we should seek God. Those who pursue good in the natural world "nibble at empty shadows," Augustine said.[10] By contrast, those who seek truth in God will find eternal truth and liberation.

St. Thomas Aquinas, the great medieval scholar and "Angelic Doctor" of the Church, understood the natural world according to what is commonly called the "Great Chain of Being."[11] For Thomas, all of creation reflects a divinely created cosmic hierarchy. According to this cosmic hierarchy, humanity finds itself straddling the spiritual world and the natural world. In the spiritual world, humans are just lower than the angels—God is on top. In the natural world, though, humans are on top, followed by animals, plants, and less complex organisms—a hierarchy seemingly confirmed by the Genesis creation accounts. Within this Great Chain of Being, humans are never isolated from the natural world. There is, Thomas believes, an interdependence between human persons and the natural world. But this interdependence does not mean that everything in creation is equal—there are, Thomas argues, gradations of value. For example, humans have a higher value than wild animals, fish, and plant life. According to this view, non-human animals are "ordered to man's use," Thomas writes, along with everything else that is below humanity in the cosmic hierarchy.[12]

Christian Anthropocentrism and the Roots of the Ecological Crisis

In the early 1960s, a number of scientists and political activists were raising concerns about an impending "ecological crisis." The central problem in this ecological crisis was that technologies ostensibly being used to make human lives better were in fact having adverse side effects on the environment. The book that signalled the ecological crisis and, as a result, initiated the modern environmental movement was Rachel Carson's bestselling *Silent Spring*, published in 1962. Carson, a biologist who had worked with the U.S. Fish and Wildlife Services, brought to the public's attention the reality that chemical pesticides being used to treat crops were killing birds that had ingested seeds and worms laced with lethal chemicals, specifically the insecticide DDT.[13] This situation resulted in a type of utilitarian calculus: crop yields were increasing with the use of DDT, which created more food and more efficient farming, but at the expense of birds. Following a utilitarian approach to ethical decision-making, the question thus became whether human happiness trumps the pain—in this case, death—of non-human animals. Similar kinds of utilitarian arguments were made in subsequent environmental controversies involving the snail darter in Tennessee, the Northern Spotted Owl in the northwest United States, and other endangered species. Many environmentalists said nature needed protection because of its essential goodness—some made the claim that all animals, not just humans, have a right to life and that no cost-benefit calculus could ever justify an animal's extinction. Many others claimed, however, that the benefit gained by inflicting some harm on non-human life was without question ethically justifiable.

By the late 1960s, Carson was not the only publicly recognizable environmentalist. Activists such as Ralph Nader, Barry Commoner, and Gaylord Nelson, the U.S. Senator from Wisconsin credited with being the founder of the first Earth Day in 1970, had become public figures as they spoke out against pollution, workplace exposure to harmful chemicals, land erosion, water toxicity created by petroleum and fertilizer waste, and the hazards associated with automobiles.

Moreover, by the late 1960s it had become fashionable in some circles to blame Christianity for the environmental depredation. Many beatniks, political radicals, and alienated university students concluded that environmental activism had to include not just criticism but repudiation of Christianity. In search of more environmentally friendly worldviews, many turned to other religions, such as Zen Buddhism and Native spirituality. What these religions offered disgruntled Westerners was a worldview in which nature is sacred and enchanted by sacred spirits. Others turned to earth-centred worldviews—such as Aldo Leopold's "land ethic" and later Arne Naess's "deep ecology"—which tended to be suspicious of modern technology and human interventions in nature.[14]

Amidst the growing environmental movement and anti-establishment protests of the late 1960s, Lynn White Jr., a well-respected medieval historian, published a provocative article in 1967 entitled "The Historical Roots of Our Ecologic Crisis," in which he argued that Christianity's conception of nature is one of the chief causes of the crisis.[15] According to White, Christianity in its Western form "is the most anthropocentric religion the world has seen." Or to put it another way, Christianity is the most human-centred of all the world religions. In antiquity, White asserts, people believed that trees, rivers, and hills were enchanted; they had guardian spirits that protected each of them. To ensure a harmonious relationship, people had to placate those guardian spirits before cutting down a tree, damming a brook, or mining a mountain. "By destroying pagan animism," White writes, "Christianity made it possible to exploit nature in a mood of indifference to the feelings of natural objects." By the Middle Ages, Christianity had come to the firm conclusion that nature was inanimate, without spirit, and basically meaningless apart from humanity's instrumental use of nature. "To a Christian a tree can be no more than a physical fact," White said. "The whole concept of the sacred grove is alien to Christianity and to the ethos of the West. For nearly two millennia Christian missionaries have been chopping down sacred groves, which are idolatrous because they assume spirit in nature." Nature does indeed have a natural end (or *telos*), according to some Christian theologians, but it is an end that ultimately serves humans.

White contends that Christianity's disenchantment and exploitation of nature provided the foundations for modern science and technology. By the eighteenth century, the study of natural matter was no longer based on religious grounds, as was the case with Galileo and Isaac

Newton, for example. Rather, science and technology became pursuits that objectified the material world to understand and manipulate it. Science and technology eschewed the belief that nature had a natural end; or if natural things did have an end, it was an end related only to other things in nature and not some cosmological Great Chain of Being that linked God to the lowest forms of creation. The natural world had scientific and technological explanations—there was no need to overlay those explanations with mythic creation stories. Although White may appear to be trying to turn Christianity into some kind of "eco-devil," his aim was actually to get people to think beyond science and technology by introducing their historical foundations. White writes, "I personally doubt that disastrous ecologic backlash can be avoided simply by applying to our problems more science and more technology." In other words, he didn't believe there was a technological fix to the crisis. He also didn't believe that looking to other religions, like Zen Buddhism, was the answer. Instead, White believed that there had to be a cultural change from within. To initiate that change, White insists, we need to revisit our intellectual and religious traditions to draw out alternatives to the exploitative practices of science and technology. White concludes his provocative article by turning to the theology of St. Francis of Assisi (1182–1226), the legendary preacher and founder of the Franciscan order, who attempted to "depose man from his monarchy over creation and set up a democracy of all God's creatures." According to White, Francis repudiated the idea that nature was merely for humanity's exploitation or just a repository of symbols to be used in homilies. For Francis, animals, plants, water, and fire are brothers and sisters to "brother man." According to White, Francis's theology of the brother- and sisterhood of nature is an attempt to say that all creatures are created equal. If we understand nature within the worldview offered by Francis, what this means in terms of ethics is that creation makes moral claims on us—we can no longer dismiss the natural world as matter to be exploited. To the contrary, we have a moral duty to engage God's creatures and the natural world as equals, where they are to be nurtured, protected, and loved.

Catholic Social Teaching and the Environment

Critics of White's argument often point out that his analysis of creation in the Christian tradition is too simplistic. No doubt it is.

Nevertheless, it did prompt Christian theologians and environmentalists to reassess the Christian tradition in light of the general criticism that Christianity's anthropocentrism had fostered an exploitative view of nature. For Catholics in particular, the challenge presented by White's argument gives us an opportunity to reflect on the development of the Church's ethical teachings on the environment.

In the social teachings of the Church, we find that our relationship to and treatment of land and the natural world have been concerns since the earliest days of Catholic Social Teaching. In his groundbreaking encyclical *Rerum novarum* (On Capital and Labour, 1891), Pope Leo XIII wrote that God gave the earth to "mankind in general" so that human persons, regardless of wealth or status, could use and enjoy it. No matter how property is divided among private owners, the pope wrote, "the earth, even though apportioned among private owners, ceases not thereby to minister to the needs of all, inasmuch as there is not one who does not sustain life from what the land produces" (RN, no. 8). For Pope Leo, the goods of nature and the gifts of divine grace belong in common and without distinction to all humankind. He wrote: "As for riches and the other things which men call good and desirable, whether we have them in abundance, or are lacking in them—so far as eternal happiness is concerned—it makes no difference; the only important thing is to use them aright." Quoting Thomas Aquinas, Pope Leo continued, "But if the question be asked: How must one's possessions be used?—the Church replies without hesitation in the words of the same holy Doctor: 'Man should not consider his material possessions as his own, but as common to all, so as to share them without hesitation when others are in need'" (RN, no. 21). In *Rerum novarum*, then, we see the emergence of an ethical principle based on the teachings of Thomas Aquinas: we are free to use, enjoy, and own land, but we must always remember that the land and humanity have an interdependent relationship.

In 1931, Pope Pius XI reaffirmed Leo's conclusion that humanity has the right to the private ownership of land. For Pope Pius, private ownership provided the best means of ensuring that land will be useable for future generations. In his encyclical *Quadragesimo anno* (On the Reconstruction of the Social Order, 1931), Pope Pius wrote that the Church has consistently taught that "nature, rather the Creator Himself, has given man the right of private ownership not only that individuals may be able to provide for themselves and their families but also that the goods which the Creator destined for the entire family of mankind may through this institution truly serve this purpose. All this can be achieved in no wise except through the maintenance of a certain and definite order" (QA, no. 41). According to Pope Pius, this order to be maintained was one that rejected both radical individualism and radical collectivism. (As we will note in a few paragraphs, Pope John Paul II will call this order the "integrity of creation.")

Pope John XXIII, in his encyclical *Mater et magistra* (Christianity and Social Progress, 1961), continued the Catholic tradition of placing the natural world under the authority of humankind to preserve an interdependent relationship between nature and human beings. Of particular concern was the so-called population explosion, which was brought to the public eye in a *Time* magazine cover story in early 1960. Reviving fears first expressed by the British political economist and Anglican clergyman Robert Thomas Malthus (1766–1834), environmentalists and certain economists predicted that sharp spikes in population were eventually going to lead to scarce resources, famine, social stress, violence, and eventually widespread death. They argued that, to avoid environmental destruction, starvation, and needless human deaths, fertility rates needed to be controlled, particularly in those areas of the world experiencing population explosions: Africa, Asia, and Latin America. In many cases, the arguments for controlling fertility rates ran counter to the Church's teaching on birth control. In *Mater et magistra*, Pope John tried to reconcile the good of family life with the good of the natural world:

> Genesis relates how God gave two commandments to our first parents: to transmit human life—"increase and multiply"—and to bring nature into their service—"Fill the earth, and subdue it." These two commandments are complementary. Nothing is said in the second of these commandments about destroying nature. On the contrary, it must be brought into the service of human life. (MM, nos. 196–97)

The question was how?

For Pope John, the answer had to spring from an analysis of the social, political, and economic structures linked to our use of nature. We can sum up the pope's analysis by highlighting three interrelated points. First, Pope John concluded that concerns over food shortages were based on faulty evidence. In those few cases where there might be potential shortages, the pope said, technology could be used to enhance crop productions—but that technology likely wasn't going to be needed for some time. He believed there were other ways of addressing food scarcity, which leads to the next point. Second, Pope John maintained that the causes of food shortages and famine were not due to nature's lack of capacity to produce food; rather, these conditions were created by poverty, political mismanagement, and deficient socio-economic structures. As a moral matter, humankind should work toward creating just social, political, and economic structures that recognize the dignity of the human person. And third, to address concerns that arise when the interdependence of humanity and the natural environment break down, Pope John argued that nations must work together in ways they never have before, because scientific and technological programs have made nations dependent on one another. "As a rule," the pope concluded, "no single commonwealth has sufficient resources at its command to solve the more important scientific, technical, economic, social, political, and cultural problems which confront it at the present time. These problems are necessarily the concern of a whole group of nations, and possibly of the whole world" (MM, no. 201).[16] Undoubtedly in Pope John's mind as he wrote this was the Catholic principle of *the universal common good*, which he developed in his next encyclical, *Pacem in terris* (Peace on Earth, 1963, especially nos. 100, 132–35), just two years later.

We can see at this point in the development of Catholic thinking regarding the environment that Lynn White's charge that Christianity is anthropocentric has merit. The Catholic position is certainly that the natural world remains under the authority of humankind. But we can also see, contrary to White's conclusion, that the Catholic position is that the natural world must not be exploited or abused—the reason being that there is a divinely ordered interdependence between the natural world and humankind, and if we exploit or abuse nature, this can lead to social, political, and economic injustice. As Pope Paul VI put it in *Populorum Progressio* (On the Development of Peoples, 1967), "The

229

Bible, from the first page on, teaches us that the whole of creation is for humanity, that it is men and women's responsibility to develop it by intelligent effort and by means of their labour to perfect it, so to speak, for their use. If the world is made to furnish each individual with the means of livelihood and the instruments for growth and progress, all people have therefore the right to find in the world what is necessary for them" (PP, no. 22). If populations are unable to draw what they need from creation, they suffer injustice.

The idea that nature must be preserved for the benefit of humanity was reaffirmed in Pope Paul's 1971 apostolic letter to commemorate the 80th anniversary of *Rerum novarum*. He wrote:

> Man is suddenly becoming aware that by an ill-considered exploitation of nature he risks destroying it and becoming in his turn the victim of this degradation. Not only is the material environment becoming a permanent menace—pollution and refuse, new illness and absolute destructive capacity—but the human framework is no longer under man's control, thus creating an environment for tomorrow which may well be intolerable. This is a wide-ranging social problem which concerns the entire human family. (*Octogesima adveniens*, no. 21)

With echoes of Pope John's plea for global cooperation in his encyclicals *Mater et magistra* and *Pacem in terris*, Pope Paul encouraged Christians to "take on responsibility, together with the rest of men, for a destiny which from now on is shared by all" (OA, no. 21). Indeed, by the early 1970s, Catholic Social Teaching had firmly established that the ecological crisis had to be addressed as a matter of global ethical concern. Although now somewhat of a cliché, the Church realized that local actions were increasingly affecting populations around the globe.[17] Even though people were far removed from one another geographically, they were increasingly bound together in a relationship created by environmental practices enhanced by science and technology.

The Development of Critical Stewardship

In his 1990 World Day of Prayer for Peace address entitled "The Ecological Crisis: A Common Responsibility," Pope John Paul II brought to prominence the growing trend in Catholic Social Teaching to address the environment as a central element of justice and peace. In particularly blunt words, Pope John Paul said to Catholics: "I would like to address directly my brothers and sisters in the Catholic Church, in order to remind them of their serious obligation to care for all of creation. The commitment of believers to a healthy environment for everyone stems directly from their belief in God the Creator, from their recognition of the effects of original and personal sin, and from the certainty of having been redeemed by Christ. Respect for life and for the dignity of the human person extends also to the rest of creation, which is called to join man in praising God (cf. Psalm 148:96)."[18]

Pope John Paul's example for this view of creation was St. Francis of Assisi, whom he declared the patron saint of ecology in 1979. "As a friend of the poor who was loved by God's creatures, St. Francis invited all of creation—animals, plants, natural forces, even Brother Sun and Sister Moon—to give honour and praise to the Lord," the pope wrote. "The poor man of Assisi gives us striking witness that when we are at peace with God we are better able to devote ourselves to building up that peace with all creation which is inseparable from peace among all peoples."[19]

Theologically, Pope John Paul's argument for creation care re-emphasized the sometimes overlooked, if not suppressed, doctrine of a redeemed earth. According to the pope, the death and resurrection of Christ "accomplished the work of reconciling humanity to the Father, who 'was pleased ... through (Christ) to reconcile to himself *all things*, whether on earth or in heaven, making peace by the blood of his cross (Colossians 1:19-20). Creation was thus made new (cf. Revelation 21:5). Once subjected to the bondage of sin and decay (cf. Romans 8:21), it has now received new life while 'we wait for the new heavens and a new earth in which righteousness dwells' (2 Peter 3:13)".[20] For Pope John Paul II, then, if we deny the essential goodness of creation, not only do we disregard the interdependence inherent in creation, but we also do violence to the integrity of creation.

Pope John Paul insists that the ecological crisis is fundamentally a moral problem. First, the crisis reveals the indiscriminate application of science and technology. Although science and technology have resulted in "undeniable benefits to humanity," it is now clear, the pope said, that their application has "produced harmful long-term side effects" to nature, putting at risk the well-being of future generations.[21] Such is the case with the gradual depletion of the ozone layers caused by industrial waste, greenhouse gases, deforestation, increased energy needs, the burning of fossil fuels, and the use of certain types of herbicides, coolants, and propellants.

Second, the crisis reveals a "lack of respect for life," which for Pope John Paul means both human and non-human life. When it comes to human life, often "the interests of production prevail over concern for the dignity of workers," he said, "while economic interests take priority over the good of individuals and even entire peoples."[22] When it comes to non-human life, the reckless exploitation of natural resources upsets natural ecosystems, which in turn harms not only animal and plant life but also human life.

In search of a solution to the ecological crisis, Pope John Paul called for a "new solidarity." Consistent with the emphasis in Catholic Social Teaching to bring countries together to solve international problems, Pope John Paul's call for a new solidarity means that highly industrialized countries must forge strong relations with developing nations to share responsibility. The basis of this relationship must be one that recognizes both economic justice and ecological concerns. According to the pope, "newly industrialized states cannot, for example, be asked to apply restrictive environmental standards to their emerging industries unless the industrialized states first apply them within their own boundaries. At the same time, countries in the process of industrialization are not morally free to repeat the errors made in the past by others, and recklessly continue to damage the environment."[23] To achieve any success in meeting the challenges of the crisis, world leaders must be convinced of the "absolute need for this new solidarity."[24] Moreover, this new solidarity means that there must be a critical assessment of the "structural forms of poverty that exist through the world."[25] The pope noted that rural poverty and the unjust distribution of land have resulted in unsustainable farming practices, such as exhausting soil through lack of crop rotation. In some cases, poor farmers have found themselves clearing forests for farmland—and once there is no more land to farm, they find themselves looking for work in urban centres. The pope concludes that the single most important element in this new solidarity is the cessation of war and the promotion of peace. Wars, whether regional or local, destroy fields, ruin crops and vegetation, and upset social, political, and economic structures. This, in turn, often adversely affects the environment.

In response to Pope John Paul's 1990 World Day of Prayer for Peace message, the U.S. Conference of Catholic Bishops released a twenty-page pastoral statement in 1991 entitled "Renewing the Earth." In this statement, the bishops summarized for the first time the nine ethical principles at the core of the Church's teaching on the ecological crisis: a sacramental universe, respect for life, the planetary common good, the new solidarity, the universal purpose of created things, the option for the poor, authentic development, limiting consumption while protecting life, and the interconnectedness of life. The following year, the U.S. bishops published a lengthy pastoral letter entitled "Stewardship: A Disciple's Response" (1992) that named the Catholic Church's approach to the environment: stewardship.

Critical Stewardship and the Demand of Justice

While the *stewardship* approach remains anthropocentric, in that human persons are on earth as caretakers, Catholic Social Teaching since the 1970s has been careful to suppress any inclinations toward slipping into a *dominion* approach that considers humans to be masters over the natural world and understands the relationship between humanity and the material world in dichotomous terms. In fact, since Pope John Paul II's 1990 World Day of Prayer for Peace message, the Magisterium and many Catholic ethicists have moved more toward a *creation-centred* approach to the environment. A creation-centred approach understands humans as fully part of creation—we are interconnected with other life forms through a web of life. With this approach, creation has intrinsic value, which means that all species deserve protection and care. The U.S. bishops' statement "Global Climate Change: A Plea for Dialogue, Prudence, and the Common Good" (2001) is a good example of the creation-centred approach in Catholic teaching. The bishops write: "Our Creator has given us the gift of creation: the air we breathe, the water that sustains life, the fruits of the land that nourish us, and the entire web of life without which human life cannot flourish. All of this God created and found 'very good.' We believe our response to global climate change should be a sign of our respect for God's creation." Some ethicists see a contradiction between the anthropocentric stewardship approach and the creation-centred approach, especially if the stewardship approach emphasizes humanity's managerial capacity over nature. However, it is possible to understand the Catholic position in another way—that is, as a "critical stewardship."[26]

Critical Stewardship as an Approach to Environmental Ethics

Although it has its weaknesses, the steward is a fitting symbol for us as we engage in environmental ethics. First, the steward is a scriptural symbol. Scripture as a whole, combining both the Hebrew Bible and the New Testament, contains some 26 direct references to the steward and stewardship. In the Hebrew literature, the steward is a servant who has been given the responsibility for the oversight of something belonging to another (e.g., Genesis 43 and 44). The prime example for the steward-ship of creation in scripture is found in Genesis 2:15: "The Lord God took the man and put him in the garden of Eden to till it and keep it." In this instance, God has created the man to be a caretaker.

You might ask, though: "How do we reconcile stewardship with the divine command in Genesis 1:26, 28 that apparently gives the man and woman 'dominion' over creation?" Many Christians today understand this passage as reflecting the "goodness" that ancient cultures saw in beneficent royalty—that is, a ruler who rules well is one who cares for the land and the people who live on the land. Dominion, in this ancient context, therefore doesn't mean "tyrannical rule" but instead conveys the nature of the relationship that God's people have with their Creator who sustains them. As a metaphor expressing a beneficent, sustain-ing relationship, dominionship is limited in the Christian tradition. Christians recognize that in the presence of God, "dominion" is never an appropriate stance. Instead, we understand that any authority we have is borrowed, temporary, likely shared with others, and always qualified by God's sole dominion. Consequently, to extend the dominionship beyond its metaphorical limits and then somehow claim that humans *are* "rulers" or "masters" over creation is risking the sin of hubris com-mitted by the man and woman in the Garden who desired to be "like

God." Indeed, the sin of Adam and Eve serves as a reminder to us of the dangers associated with human arrogance toward both God and creation. As a result, many Christians see their proper role on earth as stewards who till it and keep it not only for God, but also for those currently depending on God's creation, future generations, and the good of God's creation itself.

Second, the symbol of the steward fits with the metaphor we commonly use to describe a host of relationships important to Christians, from our relationship to the natural environment, to everyone in that environment, to other Christians—that metaphor is the *household*. In Greek, the term for household is *oikos*. From *oikos*, we derive the term *ecology* (*oikos* + *logos*), which in environmental ethics refers to the relationship between things in a given environment. Also from this Greek term, we get the word *economics* (*oikos* + *nomos*), which literally means "the rules of the household." And from the closely related Greek word *oikein*, a verb meaning "to inhabit" a house, region, or earth, we get the Greek term *oikumene*, translated into English as "ecumenical"—a term Christians have used since the fourth century to mean the "whole church." Following this metaphor, the steward is integral to the functioning of the household. As a servant to the housemaster, the steward is responsible for planning and administering the affairs of the household. Although in a position of responsibility, the steward never works independently of the master, who has ultimate authority. This means that the steward has no *autonomy* (self-legislation) over the household, but only limited authority to ensure that the "order of the household" (the *oikonomos*, the economy) is being responsibly looked after. As a symbol to help us consider our approach to environmental ethics, the steward reminds us that our relationship with creation is integrally linked with the economy, which today often determines the value and rules that govern our relationship to the natural environment.

And third, the steward is an apt symbol for us because it emphasizes the active role we humans play in the environment. Unlike some approaches to the environment, which treat humans as more or less passive actors caught up in a web of life or merely as members subservient to the logic of a biotic community, the steward symbol preserves the notion that we both shape and are shaped by our *oikos*. Indeed, one of the major criticisms that Catholic ethicists have of radical *ecocentric* approaches to environmental ethics is that creation can easily become overly romanticized as a "good" that determines proper moral action. Or, to put it another way, ecocentric approaches too often derive a moral *ought* directly from a naturally occurring *is*. Known among philosophers as the "naturalistic fallacy," this relationship between the "is" and the "ought" is ethically problematic because what occurs in nature is mediated by human experience and interpretation. As we recall from our discussions of sexuality in chapter four, the Catholic natural law tradition has itself wrestled with the limits of basing ethical prescriptions on "natural" sexual orientation, gender relationships, and even sexual interaction among people of differing races. In the case of some ecocentric approaches, actions undertaken in the name of the inherent goodness of creation may deprive humans of basic rights, such as the right to clean water, adequate housing, and even life (in those instances where advocates support the implementation of population control measures).

The "critical" aspect of critical stewardship is derived from the social teachings of the Catholic Church. More specifically, the critical principle in the preferential option for the poor calls us to begin with *and* to return continually to the stories of those people on the margins of society who are, in most cases, the ones who experience most profoundly the effects of our individual and collective environmental actions. In chapter two, we introduced to you the idea that ethics consists of two general tasks: (1) the descriptive task of identifying integral elements associated with the moral problem we are addressing, and (2) the prescriptive task of determining what we ought to do. Following our approach, the descriptive and prescriptive tasks work together to create a critical feedback loop that allows us both to assess whether our ethical prescriptions adequately addressed the moral problem at hand *and* to ask what new problems may have been created as a result of our actions. In our way of doing ethics, the "is" is not "nature" or a naturally occurring phenomenon, but instead the stories of those raising concerns over our actions. In turn, our "ought" is not determined by "nature," but by our attempt to act in such a way that fosters human flourishing. In terms of the Catholic ethical tradition, as ethical beings we are seeking to "do good and avoid evil."

The "critical" aspect of our stewardship reminds us of the constant need to ask whether we are indeed doing good and avoiding evil.

The Demand for Justice

In his book *Ecologies of Grace*, Willis Jenkins makes an important observation: In comparison to other fields of ethics, and especially in comparison to fields of practical ethics (such as biomedical ethics, business ethics, and professional ethics for lawyers, doctors, or social workers), environmental ethics possesses no agreed-upon social practices or standards on which actors can assess their moral actions. As Jenkins puts it, "there is no discrete set of environmental practices analogous to caregiving and research for biomedical ethics, no tradition of established normative principles in the way that fairness and trust function for business ethics, not even a bounded terrain of inquiry, if even in the expansive sense of political ethics."[27] Taken as whole, Jenkins concludes, the literature of environmental ethics demonstrates that it apparently lacks the essential foundations required even to organize a meaningful debate.

While there remains a good deal of discussion among Catholic ethicists about how prescriptive we can be when it comes to specific environmental practices—for example, getting involved in discussions of what kind of seed farmers ought to plant or whether the Church should support efforts to extract oil from Canada's tar sands—we generally agree that our environmental practices must at some foundational level be rooted in social, political, and economic justice. In the language of virtue ethics, we need to consider how our actions reflect the type of individuals, institutions, communities, and societies we want to become. Here we need to turn to the victims of our environmental actions and their stories of injustice. We don't need to look long or far to find them.

Women, in particular, suffer disproportionately from destructive environmental practices. Around the world, "women's work" is often most closely associated with nature: carrying water, washing clothes in polluted streams (in India, one of the primary pollutants is DDT), managing small farms, or digging through a city's garbage heap for food or something valuable to be traded or sold. Climate change can have immediate consequences for many women. For instance, water scarcity, heavy rainfall, and frequent flooding lead to additional burdens for women reliant on natural water sources. To provide water for their households and subsistence agriculture, women often have to walk long distances with water barrels. In East Africa, women sometimes expend up to 27 percent of their caloric intake on collecting water. Moreover, women reliant on natural water sources are more susceptible to water-borne illnesses such as diarrhea, malaria, and hepatitis. According to the World Health Organization, 80 per cent of all illnesses in the world are attributable to unsafe water and sanitation.

Environmental refugees are another group that suffers from environmental injustice. According to the International Organization for Migration, "environmental migrants are persons or groups of persons who, for compelling reasons of sudden or progressive changes in the environment that adversely affect their lives or living conditions, are obliged to leave their habitual homes, or choose to do so, either temporarily or permanently, and who move either within their country or abroad."[28] In Bangladesh, for example, changing sea levels due to recent changes in the climate are threatening the living situation for nearly 75 million people who make their homes less than 12 metres above sea level. Environmental refugees typically try to make their way to urban centres in search of jobs. In Bangladesh, though, the capital city of Dhaka is already at capacity, there are few jobs, and sanitation is poor, which dramatically increases the spread of infectious diseases.[29] And perhaps most alarmingly, experts estimate that by 2050, there may be some 150 million environmental refugees around the world.[30] To put that figure in some perspective, it represents a population nearly five times that of Tokyo or almost 25 times that of the Greater Toronto Area.

Also, migrant workers are people who suffer from environmental injustice on a number of levels. On one level, migrant workers have traditionally laboured under unsafe agricultural practices, such as the spraying of pesticides from a plane ("crop dusting") on the fields as they work. Although Canada and the United States have laws that are supposed to protect migrant workers from these kinds of practices, some workers choose to remain silent when these laws are broken, out of fear they will lose their jobs or be forced to return to their home country. At this level, migrant workers suffering from environmental injustice also experience economic exploitation. And at another level, migrant workers may be in their position as a result of changes to their land and natural environment back home. Take the situation we used to open this chapter: the biofuel industry and the production of corn. In Mexico, small farmers and agricultural workers who have relied on corn and other grain farming for a living have been displaced from their land and jobs by exorbitantly high corn prices created by the biofuel industry. With few prospects in Mexico, many of these dispossessed farmers and agricultural workers look for work and economic opportunities in the United States, which has contributed to the increased rates of illegal immigration in recent years.

And finally, the hungry suffer injustice. Although it is difficult to establish how many people live in hunger around the world, many food security and hunger organizations estimate the figure at nearly a billion people.[31] Although it may sound ludicrous, hunger is not caused by a global food shortage; rather, hunger is the result of a variety of factors, including global economic decisions, political corruption, population shifts, and local weather conditions. Take the case of West Africa's Sahel region, where as of May 2012, more than 17 million people are facing possible starvation. According to a World Bank report, the crisis in Sahel is due to a combination of drought caused by poor rainfall in 2011, too little food, high grain prices, environmental damage, and a large number of internal refugees.[32] With world grain prices set to go higher at the end of 2012 because of drought in the U.S. Corn Belt, external factors contributing to the crisis in Sahel will likely only put more people at risk of starvation. Tragically, we note that the corn used to produce one car tank of ethanol fuel is enough to feed a person for a year. In sum, there is no reason, other than placing human desires for convenience and wealth over the human need for food, why anyone must suffer from starvation. The "fix" isn't more technology or science—it's an ethical commitment to justice.

Conclusion

In his encyclical *Caritas in veritate* (Charity in Truth, 2009), Pope Benedict XVI taught that every "economic decision has a moral consequence" (CV, no. 37). The same is true of every action that affects our environment—it has moral consequences. In economically developed societies, the so-called North, our environmental practices affect people around the globe, particularly those in developing and poor countries. The distance between us can make it difficult for us to realize any injustice stemming from our actions. To bridge the gap between the global North and South, we must pay attention to grassroots organizations and those who work in solidarity with the poor and the marginalized. While we are likely to participate in acts of injustice, especially given that we live in structures tainted by social sin, we remain called to do good and avoid evil.

One obvious question we face is "What do we do?" Another way of putting this question is "How shall I, or how shall we, live?" As noted at the outset of this book, ethical reflection can often leave us with more questions than answers. This is especially true of environmental ethics, since almost everything we do in this world affects our environment. In fact, each topic we covered in this book—sexuality, life and death, war and peace, and the economy—could be examined in light of its environmental impact and moral consequences. Oftentimes we feel as though we are called upon to provide *the* exact right answer in each and every instance. Of course, this isn't possible. So we ask another question: "What kind of person do we wish to become?" This is the question of ethical being, and it requires us to ask questions of our morality, values, and character. As we engage in ethical reflection, we would do well to listen to the prophet Micah, who reminds us that knowing what is good requires action: "He has told you, O mortal, what is good; and what does the Lord require of you but to do justice, and to love kindness, and to walk humbly with your God?"

Notes

Introduction

1   Alasdair MacIntyre, *After Virtue: A Study in Moral Theory*, 3rd ed. (South Bend, IN: University of Notre Dame Press, 2007 [1981]). In the first two editions, MacIntyre concludes that it is by returning to Aristotle that we begin to reconstruct the cohesive moral language he so desires. In the third edition's prologue (p. x), he confesses that he overlooked Thomas Aquinas and that he now realizes Thomas provides us with that language of ends.

2   Plato, *The Republic*, trans. G.M.A. Grube, rev. by C.D.C. Reeve (Indianapolis: Hackett, 1992), 338c.

3   Ibid., 338e.

4   Ibid., 344c.

5   Vatican II, *Gaudium et spes* (Pastoral Constitution on the Church in the Modern World, 1965), no. 4. Unless otherwise noted, the source for Vatican documents is the Vatican website: www.vatican.va. All subsequent references will appear in the text directly after the quote.

6   This approach to moral theology provided the basis for the moral manual tradition, which dominated the Catholic tradition from the sixteenth to the twentieth century, or just prior to Vatican II. We will briefly discuss these manuals in chapters one and two.

7   This phrase is our shorthand definition of ethics, which we develop in detail in chapter one.

Chapter One

1   James Bone, "The Humble Fruit Seller Whose Struggle for Justice Has Made History," *The Times* (U.K.) (December 28, 2011). Available online for a fee at www.thetimes. co.uk (accessed July 27, 2012). For more on the life of Mohamed Bouazizi, see the Aljazeera English report on him and his family at www.aljazeera.com/indepth/featur es/2011/01/201111684242518839.html/ (accessed July 27, 2012).

2   In German, the phrase is far more expressive: "*Erst kommt Fressen, dann kommt die Moral.*" *Fressen* refers to the way non-human animals eat, as opposed to the way humans eat (*Essen*). Compare Bertolt Brecht, *The Threepenny Opera*, lyrics by Eric Bentley (New York: Gove Weidenfeld, 1960 [1928]), Act. 2, Scene 3; p. 67.

3   United States Conference of Catholic Bishops, *Economic Justice for All* (1986), no. 86.

4   Walter Brueggemann, *Peace* (St. Louis: Chalice Press, 2001), 67.

5   Rev. Robert Schenck, *ABC News, Nightline* (December 8, 1998).

6   Malcolm Gladwell, *Blink: The Power of Thinking Without Thinking* (New York: Little, Brown and Company, 2005), 17.

7   A couple of important exceptions are those in a persistent vegetative state (PVS) or those who have undergone serious trauma leading to amnesia. In these cases, we could conclude that there are persons who are, in effect, amoral. Note, however, that we are

not saying that morality is required for personhood, an issue that becomes important in the debates over the right to life and euthanasia.

8   Daniel Ellsberg, *Secrets: A Memoir of Vietnam and the Pentagon Papers* (New York: Viking Press, 2002), 352.

9   Richard M. Nixon, "Remarks at a Reception for Returned Prisoners of War," (May 24, 1973), www.presidency.ucsb.edu/ws/index.php?pid=3856#axzz20JFlBfak (accessed July 8, 2012).

10 Note that in Judges 3, Ehud, a left-handed soldier, is sent by God to defend the Israelites. Ehud uses a concealed dagger to kill Eglon, the Moabite king and an enemy of the Israelites. In this instance, the use of the left hand was devious but divinely ordained.

11 Daniel D. Maguire, *Ethics: A Complete Method for Moral Choice* (New York: Doubleday, 1978), 5. Fortress Press published a completely revised version of this book in 2009, but it does not include this quote.

12 Lululemon Athletica Inc., "Workplace Code of Conduct" (June 2007): www.lululemon. com/about/lululemon_code_of_conduct.pdf (accessed July 8, 2012).

13 BBC News, "Bush and Putin: Best of Friends" (June 21, 2001): news.bbc.co.uk/2/hi/1392791.stm (accessed July 8, 2012).

14 See Thomas Aquinas, *Summa theologica* I.11.Obj. 1–2. The phrase in Latin is *quod est in se indivisum, ab aliis vero divisum*. All subsequent references to the *Summa* will appear in the text directly after the quote.

15 Charles Taylor, *The Malaise of Modernity* (Toronto: Anansi, 1991).

16 Ayn Rand, *The Virtue of Selfishness* (New York: Signet Books, 1961), 18.

17 Friedrich von Hayek, *The Road to Serfdom* (New York: Routledge, 2001 [1944]), 246.

18 Bernard J.F. Lonergan, *Method in Theology* (Toronto: University of Toronto Press, 1971), 79.

19 Anthony Giddens and Christopher Pierson, *Conversations with Anthony Giddens: Making Sense of Modernity* (Palo Alto: Stanford University Press, 1998), 77.

20 See Miroslav Volf, *A Public Faith: How Followers of Christ Should Serve the Common Good* (Grand Rapids: Brazos Press, 2011), chap. 1. Volf argues that Christians seek to transform the world because Christianity is a prophetic religion. My contention is that modernity enabled lay Christians to take responsibility, along with Church leadership, for bringing the prophetic vision of Christianity to the public sphere.

Chapter Two

1   OECD. *OECD Employment Outlook* (Paris, 2008), 358.

2   *God's Work in Women's Hands: Pay Equity and Just Compensation*. General Assembly, Presbyterian Church USA (Louisville: Presbyterian Church USA, 2008).

3   Jody Heymann and Alison Earle, *Raising the Global Floor: Dismantling the Myth that We Can't Afford Good Working Conditions for Everyone* (Stanford: Stanford University Press, 2010), 111.

4   Susan Neiman, *Moral Clarity: A Guide from Grown-Up Idealists*, rev. ed. (Princeton: Princeton University Press, 2000), 95.

5   National Religious Campaign against Torture, "Torture Is a Moral Issue," (2006). Available online at http://www.nrcat.org/index.php?option=com_wrapper&Itemid=140 (accessed May 27, 2012).

6   Karl Marx, *Critique of Hegel's 'Philosophy of Right,'* ed. Joseph O'Malley (Cambridge: Cambridge University Press, 1977), 127.

7   Immanuel Kant, "What Is Enlightenment?" (1794).

8   *Catechism of the Catholic Church* (1993), no. 357. All subsequent references to the Catechism will appear in the text directly after the quote.

9   Mang Juan, from *Asian Action Newsletter*, Asian Cultural Forum on Development, 1977; cited in Antonio J. Ledesma, *Landless Words and Rice Farmers: Peasant Subclasses Under Agrarian Reform in Two Philippine Villages* (Manila: International Rice Research Institute, 1982), 2.

10 Gregory Baum, *Amazing Church: A Catholic Theologian Remembers a Half-Century of Change* (Ottawa: Novalis, 2005), 9.

11 Peter Hoffman, *Stauffenberg: A Family History, 1904–1945*, 2nd ed. rev. (Montreal: McGill-Queen's University Press, 1995), 283.

12 See Hans-Georg Gadamer, *Truth and Method*, 2nd ed. rev. (New York: Contiuum Press, 2004 [1960]).

13 Alasdair MacIntyre, *After Virtue: A Study in Moral Theory* (South Bend, IN: Notre Dame Press, 1981), 201.

Chapter Three

1   U.S. Catholic Bishops, *The Christian in Action*, No. 11, 1948; reprinted in Hugh J. Nolan, ed., *Pastoral Letters of the American Hierarchy, 1792–1970* (Huntington, IN: Our Sunday Visitor, 1971).

2   John F. Kennedy, "Address of Senator John F. Kennedy to the Greater Houston Ministerial Association," September 12, 1960. Transcripts and video are available online at the John F. Kennedy Presidential Library, www.jfklibrary.org (accessed June 2, 2012).

3   These four sources of authority are derived from the Wesleyan formula called the "quadrilateral." Catholic ethicists, including Sr. Margaret Farley, in her book *Loving Justice: A Framework for Christian Sexual Ethics* (New York: Continuum, 2006), often use variations of the Wesleyan quadrilateral.

4   Kenneth R. Himes, "Scripture and Ethics: A Review Essay," *Biblical Theology* 15 (April 1985): 65–73. Quotations below are from this article.

5   As the Jesuit scholar of church governance Frances Sullivan has remarked, it is regrettable that the Latin words *authenticum* and *authentice* have been translated in these passages as "authentic" and "authentically," since in context the accurate translation would be "authoritative" and "authoritatively." The problem is that, in English, when we encounter the words "authentic" and "authentically," we tend to think in terms of "truth" or "accuracy." So if we were to designate the Magisterium as the body solely responsible for promoting "true" moral teaching and as the only body to act with "accuracy," we would be denying the possibility that theologians (and ethicists) are producing "authentic" work, that is, work faithful to the witness of the Church. But of course, this is not the case. Instead, the thrust of both Council statements is that the teachings of the

Magisterium have special authority, significance, and weight because they have been taught by the bishops, who in their official function as teachers are "endowed with the authority of Christ" and, for that reason, exercise their authority to teach "in the name of Jesus Christ." In other words, the Magisterium has the sole responsibility to represent the Church's teachings as "official" or "authoritative."

6   Gregory Baum, *Amazing Church: A Catholic Theologian Remembers a Half-Century of Change* (Ottawa: Novalis, 2005).

7   U.S. Conference of Catholic Bishops, *The Challenge for Peace* (1982), no. 15.

8   U.S. Conference of Catholic Bishops, *Economic Justice for All* (1986), no. 124.

9   Ibid., no. 87.

10 Pope John Paul II, "Holy Mass of Pentecost: Homily of John Paul II," Coventry, England (1982), no. 2.

11 Pope John Paul II, World Day of Prayer for Peace Message (1990), no. 15.

12 Immanuel Kant, *Groundwork for the Metaphysics of Morals* (1785), 4:421.

13 Ibid., 4:430.

14 John Stuart Mill, *Utilitarianism* (1863), chap. 2.

15 Martha C. Nussbaum, "Mill between Aristotle and Bentham," *Daedalus*, 133:2 (2004): 60–68.

16 Daniel J. Harrington and James F. Keenan, *Jesus and Virtue Ethics: Building Bridges Between New Testament Studies and Moral Theology* (Lanham, MD: Rowman & Littlefield, 2002).

17 Ibid., 40.

18 For example, see Michael G. Lawler and Todd A. Salzman, "Human Experience and Catholic Moral Theology," *Irish Theological Quarterly* 76 (2011): 35–56; Lisa Sowle Cahill, *Sex, Gender, and Christian Ethics* (Cambridge: Cambridge University Press, 1996); and John T. Noonan, *A Church that Can and Cannot Change: The Development of Catholic Moral Teaching* (Notre Dame, IN: University of Notre Dame Press, 2005).

19 Aristotle, *Nicomachean Ethics*, VI, viii, 5–6.

20 Canadian Conference of Catholic Bishops, *Ethical Reflections on the Economic Crisis* (1983).

21 Lawler and Salzman, "Human Experience and Catholic Moral Theology," 36–37.

22 Until 1890, in a small letter by Pope Leo XXII entitled "On Slavery in the Missions," the Church was not formally opposed to slavery. To the contrary, in 1866 the Holy Office, now the Congregation for the Doctrine of the Faith, said this in regard to slavery: "Slavery itself, considered as such in its essential nature, is not at all contrary to the natural and divine law, and there can be several just titles of slavery and these are referred to by approved theologians and commentators of the sacred canons. It is not contrary to the natural and divine law for a slave to be sold, bought, exchanged or given." Today, we (should) understand that this teaching was in error.

23 We should note that traditionalists such as Germain Grisez and John Finnis do allow for moral norms to change as a result of experience. However, it is solely the Magisterium that can make these changes. This means that, regardless of our experiences and the

reasonableness of a "new moral norm," only the Magisterium has the authority to recognize the moral legitimacy of the new norm. See, for example, Germain Grisez, *The Way of the Lord Jesus. Volume One: Christian Moral Principles* (Chicago: Franciscan Herald, 1983), 10–11.

24 For example, see Pope John Paul II, *Sollicitudo rei socialis*, no. 42.

Chapter Four

1 The judge was Leon M. Bazile, who later went on to become Chief Justice of the Virginia Supreme Court. See *Loving v. Virginia* (June 12, 1967), U.S. Supreme Court. Although Judge Bazile's reasoning may have been accepted by a number of Catholics, it contradicted the position of certain U.S. bishops regarding civil rights in the United States. By the 1950s, bishops such as Joseph Rummel of New Orleans were arguing that U.S. Catholics should support desegregation, especially in schools. Still, many Catholics, like many Americans, remained uncomfortable with interracial marriage.

2 Peter Brown, *The Body and Society: Men, Women, and Sexual Renunciation in Early Christianity*, Twentieth Anniversary Edition (New York: Columbia University Press, 1988; 2008), chap. 1.

3 Ibid., 34.

4 Jean Porter, *Natural and Divine Law: Reclaiming the Tradition for Christian Ethics* (Ottawa: Novalis, 1999), 188.

5 For instance, see Pope John Paul II, "Man's Awareness of Being a Person," *Theology of the Body* (24 October 1979).

6 Miguel de la Torre, *A Lily Among the Thorns: Imagining a New Christian Sexuality* (San Francisco: Jossey-Bass, 2007), 89–90.

7 *The Code of Canon Law* (1983), Canon 1061.

8 For a close examination of the social effects of clandestine marriage in sixteenth-century Europe, see Sarah McDougall, *Bigamy and Christian Identity in Late Medieval Champagne* (Philadelphia: University of Pennsylvania Press, 2012).

9 U.S. Conference of Catholic Bishops (National Conference of Bishops), *Marriage Preparation and Cohabitation* (Washington, D.C.: USCCB, 1999).

10 It is important to note that the Magisterium makes a distinction between fornication (unlawful sexual intercourse) and cohabitation. See the *Catechism of the Catholic Church*, nos. 2353, 2390–91.

11 For example, see Stephen L. Nock, "A Comparison of Marriages and Cohabiting Relationships," *Journal of Family Issues* 16 (1995): 53–76; and Linda J. Waite, "Cohabitation: A Communitarian Perspective," in *Marriage in America: A Communitarian Perspective*, ed. Martin K. Whyte (Lanham, MD: Rowman and Littlefield, 2000), 11–30.

12 Centers for Disease Control, *Marriage and Cohabitation in the United States*, Vital Health Statistics 28:3 (February 2010).

13 See Todd A. Salzman and Michael G. Lawler, *The Sexual Person: Toward a Renewed Catholic Anthropology* (Washington, D.C.: Georgetown University Press), esp. 211.

14 *The Code of Canon Law* (1917), Canon 1013, par. 1.

15 Augustine, *City of God*, XIV, 16–18.

16 For an excellent overview, see Lisa Sowle Cahill, "Marriage: Developments in Catholic Theology and Ethics," *Theological Studies* 64 (2003): 78–105.

17 The *Catechism of the Catholic Church* (1983) teaches: "The marriage covenant, by which a man and a woman form with each other an intimate communion of life and love, has been founded and endowed with its own special laws by the Creator. By its very nature it is ordered to the good of the couple, as well as to the generation and education of children" (no. 1660).

18 For example, see Raymond F. Collins, *Divorce in the New Testament* (Collegeville, MN: Liturgical Press, 1992), 144.

19 Canon law is the law of the Catholic Church. Although it has no binding authority today in secular societies, canon law continues to maintain functioning courts, legal experts, lawyers, and judges.

20 Foremost among this group is Michael G. Lawler, *Marriage and the Catholic Church: Disputed Questions* (Collegeville, MN: Liturgical Press, 2002). Also, see Cahill, "Marriage: Developments in Catholic Theology and Ethics," 78–105.

21 Also note, the term "contract" is used in the 1917 edition of *The Code of Canon Law* (Canon 1012), while the 1983 edition uses the term "covenant" (Canon 1055).

22 Clement, *Christ the Educator*, II:10:97–98. In this statement, Clement quotes the Greek philosopher Epicurus (341–270 BC).

23 The Catechism is quoting Pope John Paul II, *Familiaris consortio* (The Christian Family in the Modern World, 1981), no. 11.

24 Lisa Sowle Cahill, "On the Connection of Sex to Reproduction," in *Sexuality and Medicine*, volume 2, ed. Earl E. Shelp (Dordrecht: D. Reidel 1987), 39–50.

25 Porter, *Natural and Divine Law*, 197.

26 Gallup, "Americans, Including Catholics, Say Birth Control Is Morally Okay," (May 22, 2012): www.gallup.com (accessed January 22, 2013).

27 These statistics were compiled by the Guttmacher Institute, a pro–family planning research organization. When these numbers were made public, some members of the media inaccurately claimed, partly because of poor writing in the Guttmacher report, that 98 percent of Catholics of childbearing age were currently using artificial birth control. According to other research and polls, current usage is likely around 85 percent. In any case, the numbers are only slightly lower than the percentages in the general population. Also, there is little debate on the percent of people who have consciously used NFP—most studies have Catholics using NFP at around 2 to 5 percent.

28 Cristina L.H. Traina, "Papal Ideals, Marital Realities: One View from the Ground," in *Sexual Diversity and Catholicism: Toward the Development of Moral Theology*, ed. Patricia Beattie Jung, with Joseph Andrew Coray (Collegeville, MN: The Liturgical Press, 2001), 278.

29 Huffington Post, "Vatican Invites Experts to Talk Prevention" (May 27, 2011), www.huffingtonpost.com/2011/05/27/vatican-invites-aids-expe_n_867939.html (accessed June 21, 2012).

30 Agence France Presse, "Pope Says Condoms Acceptable 'In Certain Cases'" (November 21, 2010).

31 Congregation for the Doctrine of Faith, *Persona humana* (Declaration on Certain Questions Regarding Sexual Ethics, 1975), nos. 9–10.

32 The Magisterium addressed the specific issue of female masturbation in 1904 when The Sacred Penitentiary declared all masturbatory acts by women in the absence of their husbands to be gravely illicit. Cited in Anthony Kosnik, et al., *Human Sexuality* (New York: Paulist Press, 1977), 221.

33 The Kinsey Reports of 1948 and 1953 found that roughly 10 percent of the population is homosexual. While some studies have been close to replicating that number, many suggest a lower number. But when people are asked whether they've had same-sex encounters, the numbers generally climb to around 10 percent. It would seem that people are making a distinction between homosexual acts and *being* homosexual.

34 Salzman and Lawler, *The Sexual Person*, 167; citing *Persona humana*, no. 1.

35 Salzman and Lawler, *The Sexual Person*, 168.

36 Ibid., 259, 49.

37 USCCB Committee on Doctrine, "Inadequacies in the Theological Methodology and Conclusions of *The Sexual Person: Toward a Renewed Catholic Anthropology*" (Washington, D.C.: USCCB), 23.

38 Ibid., 8.

39 Ibid.

40 Ibid., 16; citing Salzman and Lawler, *The Sexual Person,* 8–9.

41 USCCB Committee on Doctrine, "Inadequacies," 18.

42 Ibid.

43 Ibid., 9.

44 Ibid., 11.

45 Ibid., 20.

Chapter Five

1 William Shakespeare, *Macbeth*, Act 5, Scene 5, ll. 19–28.

2 There are various definitions for assisted reproductive technologies (ART). In this chapter we will follow the one used by the Centers for Disease Control and Prevention. ART includes all fertility treatments in which both the sperm and egg are handled outside the body for reproductive purposes. Not covered under this definition are treatments to stimulate egg production (without retrieval) or intrauterine/artificial insemination. See the CDC website at www.cdc.gov/art/ (accessed June 25, 2012).

3 Centers for Disease Control and Prevention, "Is Infertility a Common Problem?" Available online at www.cdc.gov/reproductivehealth/infertility/#2 (accessed June 25, 2012).

4 American Society for Reproductive Medicine, "Is In Vitro Fertilization Expensive?" Available online at www.asrm.org/awards/index.aspx?id=3012 (accessed June 25, 2012).

5 For example, see Mark P. Connolly, Stijn Hoorens, and Georgina M. Chambers, "The Costs and Consequences of Assisted Reproductive Technology: An Economic

Perspective," *Human Reproduction Update* 16 (2010): 603–13. In this study, the average cost in the U.S. was roughly €35,000. I have converted the amount to dollars.

6 For example, see the NHS website at http://www.nhs.uk/Conditions/Infertility/Pages/ Treatment.aspx (accessed June 25, 2012).

7 Charles A. Sims, "A Private Sector Problem," *New York Times* (September 13, 2011): http://www.nytimes.com/roomfordebate/2011/09/13/making-laws-about-making-babies/the-fertility-industry-can-solve-donor-concerns (accessed June 25, 2012).

8 Adrienne Asch and Rebecca Marmor, "Assisted Reproduction," in *From Birth to Death and Bench to Clinic: The Hastings Center Bioethics Briefing Book for Journalists, Policymakers, and Campaigns*, ed. Mary Crowley (Garrison, NY: The Hastings Center, 2008), 5–10.

9 André Picard, "Canada's Fertility Law Needs a Reset," *The Globe and Mail* (April 16, 2012).

10 Congregation for the Doctrine of the Faith, *Donum vitae* (Instruction on the Respect for Human Life in Its Origin and on the Dignity of Procreation, 1987), introduction, 2.

11 Ibid., II, B, 6. Emphasis mine.

12 Ibid., II, A, 3.

13 Ibid., II, A, 3, b.

14 Ibid., I, 3.

15 Congregation for the Doctrine of the Faith, *Dignitas personae* (Instruction on Certain Biological Questions, 2008), 4.

16 Ibid., 5. Emphasis in original.

17 Ibid., 27. Emphasis in original.

18 Ibid., 18–19.

19 Ibid., 14.

20 U.S. Conference of Catholic Bishops, "Life-Giving Love in an Age of Technology," (November 2009), 2.

21 Richard McCormick, *The Critical Calling: Reflections on Moral Dilemmas Since Vatican II* (Washington, D.C.: Georgetown University Press, 1989), 347–49.

22 Foremost among this group of theologians is Todd A. Salzman and Michael G. Lawler, *The Sexual Person: Toward a Renewed Catholic Anthropology* (Washington, D.C.: Georgetown University Press, 2008).

23 Michael J. Sandel, "Embryo Research: The Moral Logic of Stem Cell Research," *The New England Journal of Medicine* (July 2004): 207–09.

24 For example, see the argument in Maura A. Ryan, *The Ethics and Economics of Assisted Reproduction: The Cost of Longing* (Washington, D.C.: Georgetown University Press, 2001).

25 For a brief analysis, see John L. Allen Jr., "Vatican Academy Mulls Over How Pro-Life Is Pro-Life Enough," *National Catholic Reporter* (May 30, 2010): ncronline.org/news/ vatican/vatican-academy-mulls-how-pro-life-pro-life-enough (accessed January 21, 2013).

26 Pope Benedict XVI, *Address to the Participants in the Symposium on the Topic: "Stem Cells: What Is the Future for Therapy?"* Pontifical Academy for Life (September 16, 2006). Also quoted in CDF, *Dignitas personae*, 32.

27 CDF, *Dignitas personae*, 4. The CDF made this same argument in *Donum vitae*, I. 1.

28 Mitchell Landsberg, "Vatican Signs Deal to Collaborate on Adult Stem Cell Research," *Los Angeles Times* (October 20, 2011): articles.latimes.com/2011/oct/20/business/la-fi-vatican-stem-cells-20111020 (accessed July 1, 2012).

29 Ted Peters, *For the Love of Children* (Louisville: Westminster/John Knox Press, 1996), 96–100.

30 Ted Peters and Karen Lebacqz, *Sacred Cells: Why Christians Should Support Stem Cell Research* (Lanham, MD: Rowman & Littlefield, 2010), 122–21.

31 See Elliot N. Dorff, "Stem Cell Research: A Jewish Perspective," in *The Human Embryonic Stem Cell Debate*, ed. Suzanne Holland, Karen Lebacqz, and Laurie Zoloth (Cambridge: MIT Press, 2001), 91.

32 Lisa Sowle Cahill, book review of *The Human Embryonic Stem Cell Debate*, ed. Holland, Lebacqz, and Zoloth (Cambridge: MIT Press, 2001), in *National Catholic Bioethics Quarterly* 2:3 (Autumn 2002): 562.

33 Augustine, *On Marriage and Concupiscence*, available online at www.newadvent.org/fathers/1507.htm (accessed June 30, 2012).

34 Augustine, *Enchiridion*, no. 85; also see the discussion following through no. 92, which has to do with the resurrection of the body. Available online at www.ccel.org/ccel/augustine/enchiridion.chapter23.html (accessed June 30, 2012).

35 Cited in John T. Noonan, *The Morality of Abortion: Legal and Historical Perspectives* (Cambridge: Harvard University Press, 1970), 20. Noonan notes that this perspective slipped in through a misquoted passage from Augustine.

36 For Thomas's understanding of ensoulment, see *Summa theologica* I.118. We might add that Thomas also believed that it was a mortal sin to engage in sexual intercourse with one's wife when she was pregnant, particularly if she was late in her pregnancy, because of the profound risk of causing an abortion.

37 CDF, *Declaration on Procured Abortions* (1974), no. 19

38 See Catholic World News, "Phoenix Catholic Hospital Defends Abortion that Took Place There," *CatholicCulture.org*, www.catholicculture.org/news/headlines/index.cfm?storyid=6341 (accessed July 4, 2012).

39 In the summer of 2010, Catholic Healthcare West obtained the services of the Catholic moral theologian M. Therese Lysaught. She summarized her findings this way: "The procedure performed at St. Joseph's Hospital and Medical Center on November 5, 2009, cannot properly be described as an abortion. The act, per its moral object, must accurately be described as saving the life of the mother. The death of the fetus was, at maximum, nondirect and *praeter intentionem*. More likely, the fetus was already dying due to the pathological situation prior to the intervention; as such, it is inaccurate to understand the death of the fetus as an accessory consequence to the intervention." Bishop Olmsted rejected her conclusion. Moreover, he revoked the hospital's Catholic status.

40 Public Religion Research Institute, "Committed to Availability, Conflicted About Morality: What the Millennial Generation Tells Us About the Culture Wars" (June

2011): publicreligion.org/research/2011/06/committed-to-availability-conflicted-about-morality-what-the-millennial-generation-tells-us-about-the-future-of-the-abortion-debate-and-the-culture-wars/ (accessed July 3, 2012).

41 For example, see Timothy Sawa and Annie Burns Pieper, "Fetal Gender Testing Offered at Private Clinics: Raises Fears that Gender Selection Happening in Canada," *CBC News*, www.cbc.ca/news/canada/story/2012/06/12/ultrasound-gender-testing.html (accessed July 3, 2012).

42 Steve Jobs, "Stanford Commencement Address," (June 15, 2005), news.stanford.edu/news/2005/june15/jobs-061505.html (accessed July 4, 2012).

43 See David S. Jones, Scott H. Podolsky, and Jeremy A. Greene, "The Burden of Disease and the Changing Task of Medicine," *The New England Journal of Medicine*, (June 21, 2012): 2333–38.

44 CDF, *Declaration on Euthanasia* (1980), sec. IV.

45 Pope John Paul II, "Life-Sustaining Treatments and Vegetative State" (March 20, 2004), no. 4. Italics in original (accessed July 4, 2012).

46 Richard A. McCormick, *Corrective Vision* (Kansas City, MO: Sheed & Ward, 1994), 232.

47 U.S. Conference of Catholic Bishops, *Ethical and Religious Directives for Catholic Health Care Services*, 5th ed. (2009), nos. 56–58.

48 Ibid., no. 59.

49 Ibid., no. 60.

50 USCCB, *Ethical and Religious Directive for Catholic Health Care Services*, no. 61.

51 The Oregon Health Authority has archived annual reports on a wide range of activities associated with the DWDA. public.health.oregon.gov/Pages/Home.aspx (accessed July 4, 2012).

52 See, for example, USCCB, *Ethical and Religious Directive for Catholic Health Care Services*, no. 61.

Chapter Six

1 The full text of this letter may be found at the Canadian Conference of Catholic Bishops website: http://www.cccb.ca/site/eng/media-room/official-texts/pastoral-letters/769-the-struggle-against-poverty-a-sign-of-hope-in-our-world (accessed May 24, 2012).

2 See Joe Gunn, "Muted and Maligned Voices: Public Justice and the Canadian Churches," *The Ecumenist* 47:4 (Winter 2010): 1–6. This anecdote is based on his recollection of events.

3 Adam Smith, *The Wealth of Nations* (New York: Penguin Classic, 1982 [1776]), Book II, Chapter 3.

4 William Blake, "Jerusalem," from his epic poem *Milton* (1802). Blake introduced this term to the English language, which became a shorthand description of life in nineteenth-century factories.

5 Friedrich Engels, *The Conditions of the Working Class in England in 1844* (1845).

6 Donal Dorr, *The Option for the Poor* (Maryknoll, NY: Orbis, 1996), 15.

7   Iqbal Masih's tragic story caught the attention of Craig Kielburger, a thirteen-year-old Catholic schoolboy from Thornhill, Ontario. Along with eleven of his friends in Grade 7, Kielburger established Free the Children to help combat child labour. Today, Free the Children is the world's largest network of children helping children through education, with more than one million youth involved in innovative education and development programs in 45 countries.

8   UNICEF, *State of the World's Children: Adolescence—An Age of Opportunity* (2011). Available for download at www.unicf.org/publications (accessed May 27, 2012).

9   For a written and video report, see http://espn.go.com/espn/otl/story/_/id/7435424/dallas-cowboys-dip-sports-apparel-business-comes-allegations-sweatshop-labor (accessed May 27, 2012).

10 Pope John Paul II, "Address to the Academy of Social Sciences," (April 27, 1997).

11 Pope John Paul II, "Homily of Pope John Paul II, Edmonton Airport," (September 17, 1984), no. 4.

12 Gregory Baum, *Amazing Church: A Catholic Theologian Remembers a Half-Century of Change* (Ottawa: Novalis, 2005), 56.

13 Second General Conference of Latin American Bishops, "Document on Justice," in Alfred T. Hennelly, ed. *Liberation Theology: A Document History* (Maryknoll, NY: Orbis, 1990), 97.

14 Second General Conference of Latin American Bishops, "Document on Peace," 8; in Hennelly, ed., *Liberation Theology*, 107.

15 Second General Conference of Latin American Bishops, "Document on Peace," 9e; in Hennelly, ed., *Liberation Theology*, 107.

16 Alfred Hennelly, "Introduction to the Second General Conference of Latin American Bishops," in Hennelly, ed., *Liberation Theology*, 89.

17 United States Conference of Catholic Bishops, *Economic Justice for All: Catholic Social Teaching and the U.S. Economy* (1986), no. 87.

18 Mitt Romney, "Let Detroit Go Bankrupt," *New York Times* (November 19, 2008), A35.

19 Pontifical Council on Justice and Peace, *Towards Reforming the International Financial and Monetary Systems in the Context of Global Public Authority* (October 24, 2011).

Chapter Seven

1   Roland H. Bainton, *Christian Attitudes Toward War and Peace* (New York: Abingdon Press, 1960), 66.

2   The one notable exception where Christians are praised for helping the Roman army is the case of the "Thundering Legion," during the reign of Marcus Aurelius. In 174, the Twelfth Army was in the Balkans fighting against German tribes and was suffering badly from dehydration caused by drought. Desperate, the Christians soldiers knelt down and prayed. Suddenly, a bolt of lightning struck the ground, sending the German forces into retreat and the rain down from the sky. Tertullian, one of the most ardent pacifists of early Christianity, recorded that Marcus Aurelius ascribed the event to the intervention of the Christian God. See Tertullian, *Apology*, 5.

3   Clement of Alexandria, *Protrepticus,* 10 and 11, 116.

4 Tertullian, *On Idolatry*, chap. 19.

5 Justin Martyr, *Dialogue with Trypho, a Jew*, 110.

6 Origen, *Against Celsus*, book 8, chap. 73.

7 See James Turner Johnson, *The Quest for Peace: Three Moral Traditions in Western Cultural History* (Princeton: Princeton University Press, 1987), 42–43.

8 In making this argument, Ambrose was refuting Tertullian, who not only believed that "Athens" had absolutely nothing to do with "Jerusalem," but also that the teachings of Jesus prohibited worldly violence. In practical terms, Ambrose had little option but to refute Tertullian and the earlier pacifist theologians because their conclusions only undermined Roman authority. To put matters bluntly, Ambrose's task was to construct an ethic for the Empire, while Tertullian and the early theologians were focused on developing a theology that anticipated the kingdom of God.

9 Ambrose, *On the Duties of Clergy*, 2.6–7.

10 Augustine, *Enarrationes in psalmos* 149.7, in *Saeculum: History and Society in the Theology of St. Augustine*, 2nd ed., trans. R.A. Markus (Cambridge: Cambridge University Press, 1989), 30. .

11 See Augustine, *City of God*, XIX.

12 See Pope Pius XI, *Paterna sane sollicitudo* (Apostolic Letter to the Bishops of Mexico, 1926) and *Iniquis afflictisque* (On the Persecution of the Church in Mexico, 1926). In 1940, Pope Pius XII reached an agreement with Mexican President Manuel Ávila Camacho, a Catholic, to have Catholic churches returned to the bishops.

13 See Ronald G. Musto, *The Catholic Peace Tradition* (Maryknoll, NY: Orbis, 1986); also Scott T. Kline and Megan Shore, "Catholic Peacemaking and Pax Christi," in *The Ashgate Research Companion to Religion and Conflict Resolution* (Farnham, Surrey: Ashgate, 2012), 353–368.

14 U.S. Conference of Catholic Bishops, *The Challenge of Peace*, 1983, nos. 71–79.

15 Francis Fukuyama, *The End of History and the Last Man* (New York: Penguin, 1992).

16 Samuel P. Huntington, *The Clash of Civilizations and the Remaking of the World Order* (New York: Simon & Schuster, 1996).

17 See J. Bryan Hehir, "Intervention: From Theories to Cases," *Ethics and International Affairs* 9 (1995): 1–15. The fundamental principle of state sovereignty is enshrined in the United Nations Charter, Article 2.7.

18 International Commission on Intervention and State Sovereignty, *The Responsibility to Protect* (Ottawa: IDRC, 2001).

19 Pope John Paul II, World Day of Prayer for Peace Message (1999), no. 11.

20 Pope John Paul II, World Day of Prayer for Peace Message (2000), nos. 9–12.

21 Ibid., no. 11.

22 Pope Benedict XVI, Meeting with the Members of the General Assembly of the United Nations Organization (2008).

23 U.N. Resolution 1970 (2011).

24 John Siebert, "Libya and the Responsibility to Protect," *The Ecumenist* (Winter 2011): 19.

25 Richard Falk, "Defining a Just War," *The Nation* (October 29, 2001).

26 George W. Bush, "Remarks by the President Upon Arrival" (September 16, 2001): georgewbush-whitehouse.archives.gov/news/releases/2001/09/20010916-2.html (accessed July 15, 2012).

27 George W. Bush, "Address to Joint Congress" (September 20, 2001): edition.cnn.com/2001/US/09/20/gen.bush.transcript (accessed July 15, 2012).

28 Pope John Paul II, "Address to the Diplomatic Corps," January 13, 2003.

29 Glen Stassen, *Just Peacemaking* (Louisville: Westminster/John Knox Press, 1992); and Glen Stassen, ed. *Just Peacemaking: The New Paradigm for the Ethics of Peace and War* (Cleveland: Pilgrim Press 2008).

Chapter Eight

1 Iowa is the leading corn producer in the United States, ahead of Illinois, Nebraska, and Minnesota. In 2011, Iowa produced 2.3 billion bushels of corn on 13.7 million acres of land, or roughly 18 percent of all corn produced in the U.S. The corn brought roughly $14.5 billion to the state in 2011. See Iowa Department of Agriculture, "Quickfacts," www.iowaagriculture.gov/quickfacts.asp (accessed July 14, 2012).

2 In the 2006 State of the Union Address, President George W. Bush began talking about America's "addiction" to foreign oil and the need for a new energy plan. See the transcript at C-SPAN, www.c-span.org/SOTU/ (accessed July 21, 2012). Also, the U.S. government has long subsidized corn and grain farmers. The point I make here is that Congress upped its annual subsidy to include ethanol producers.

3 The State of Nebraska, "Ethanol Facilities Capacities by State and Plant," www.neo.ne.gov/statshtml/122.htm (accessed July 15, 2012).

4 Unless cited otherwise, the statistics regarding Iowa corn and ethanol production used above are from the website Iowa Corn, sponsored by the Iowa Corn Promotion Board and the Iowa Corn Growers Association. www.iowacorn.org (accessed July 15, 2012).

5 Aditya Chakrabortty, "Secret Report: Biofuel Caused Food Crisis," *The Guardian* (July 3, 2008): www.guardian.co.uk/environment/2008/jul/03/biofuels.renewableenergy.

6 British Broadcasting Corporation, "Mexicans Stage Tortilla Protest," (February 1, 2007): http://news.bbc.co.uk/2/hi/6319093.stm (accessed July 15, 2012). Eventually, the Mexican government agreed to put a cap of 8.5 pesos per kilo—in early 2007 the price was 10 pesos per kilo. One way that Mexico keeps corn prices low domestically is by purchasing corn futures and importing corn from the U.S. for consumption, even though Mexico easily has the land capacity to grow its own corn.

7 *The Economist*, "Let Them Eat Baklava" (March 17, 2012): www.economist.com/node/21550328 (accessed July 15, 2012).

8 Augustine, *De Trinitate*, 8.3.4.

9 Augustine, *Confessions*, 3.8.

10 Ibid., 9.4.

11 The term "Great Chain of Being" has become shorthand for a worldview that holds to a cosmic hierarchy of creation. Plato, Aristotle, Augustine, and many medieval scholars promoted such a view.

12 Thomas Aquinas, *Summa contra gentiles*, 3.2.112.

13 Rachel Carson, *Silent Spring* (New York: Houghton Mifflin, 1962). Carson's book helped lead to a 1972 ban on the pesticide DDT in the United States.

14 See Aldo Leopold, *A Sand County Almanac* (Oxford: Oxford University Press, 1948). Also, the Norwegian philosopher Arne Naess coined the term and philosophy of "deep ecology" in the article entitled "The Shallow and the Deep, Long-Range Ecology Movement," *Inquiry* 16 (1973): 95–100.

15 Lynn White Jr., "The Historical Roots of Our Ecologic Crisis," *Science* 155 (March 10, 1967): 1203–1207. To reduce the number of notes, all of the following quotes attributed to White come from this article.

16 These three points summarize much of Pope John's argument in nos. 188–206.

17 The phrase "Think globally, act locally" has become an important slogan for environmentalists. Although there is an ongoing debate about its origin, it was in common usage by the late 1970s.

18 Pope John Paul II, "The Ecological Crisis: A Common Responsibility," 1990 World Day of Prayer for Peace (January 1, 1990), no. 16.

19 Ibid.

20 Ibid., no. 4.

21 Ibid., no. 6.

22 Ibid., no. 7.

23 Ibid., no.10.

24 Ibid.

25 Ibid., no. 11.

26 See Pope Benedict XVI, *Caritas in veritate* (Charity in Truth, 2009), no. 50.

27 Willis Jenkins, *Ecologies of Grace: Environmental Ethics and Christian Theology* (Oxford: Oxford University Press, 2008), 33.

28 International Organization for Migration (IOM), www.iom.int/jahia/Jahia/definitional-issues (accessed July 24, 2012).

29 See Sheila Murray, "Environmental Migrants and Canada's Refugee Policy," *Refuge* 27:1 (2011): 89–102.

30 Environmental Justice Foundation, *No Place Like Home: Where Next for Climate Refugees?* (London, 2009). www.ejfoundation.org (accessed July 24, 2012).

31 For instance, see Bread for the World, which uses the widely cited but also controversial estimate from the U.N. Food and Agricultural Organization: www.bread.org/hunger/global/facts.html (accessed July 26, 2012).

32 The World Bank, "Drought Worsens in the Sahel Region of Africa—Millions of People at Risk (May 31, 2012). www.worldbank.org (accessed July 26, 2012).

Index